NINA HAMNETT

Nina, 1917, by Roger Fry

Nina, c.1926, by Jacob Kramer

Denise Hooker

NINA HAMNETT

queen of bohemia

Constable · London

To Michael

First published in Great Britain 1986
by Constable and Company Limited
10 Orange Street London WC2H 7EG
Copyright © 1986 by Denise Hooker
Set in Monophoto Perpetua 12pt by
Servis Filmsetting Ltd Manchester
Printed in Great Britain by
BAS Printers Ltd Over Wallop

British Library CIP data
Hooker, Denise
Nina Hamnett : queen of bohemia
1. Hamnett, Nina   2. Painters – England –
Biography
I. Title
709'.2'4   ND497.H33

ISBN 0 09 466970 8

Contents

Illustrations

All works reproduced in the text by Nina Hamnett unless otherwise stated.

All measurements given below are in inches.

Acknowledgements

M Y greatest thanks to Michael Parkin, who first introduced me to Nina's
work and world and helped me in innumerable ways throughout the
writing of this book.

I am indebted to all those who kindly answered my requests for information
and allowed me to see work by Nina in their possession. Many of Nina's friends
and acquaintances generously shared their memories of her with me; meeting
them was one of the greatest pleasures of writing this book. My sincerest thanks
to the following for their help:

Annie and Charles Allchild, Martin Anderson, Dr Igor Anrep, Isabelle
Anscombe, Alan Arnold, Lady Ashton, the late Georges Auric, Barbara Bagenal,
Camilla Baggs, Jack Barker, Dr Wendy Baron, Harry Barr, Quentin Bell, Bruce
Bernard, Gaston Berlemont, John G. Bernasconi, Georges Bernier, the late
Oswald Blakeston, Elliot Bliss, Ian Board, Baronne de Bosmelet, Richard
Brewis, Hugh Brogan, Louisa Buck, Richard Buckle, Robert Buhler, John
Byrne, Arthur Calder-Marshall, Tom Clarke, Douglas Cleverdon, Roger Cole,
Judith Collins, Anna Cook, Raymond Coxon, Edward Craig, John Craxton, the
Hon. Clare Crossley, Sheila Cutforth, Adrian Daintrey, Bernard and Joan
Denvir, the late Pamela Diamond, Alan Dixon, Edgar Duchins, Peter Eaton, Bill
Ewer, the late James Fitton, Stephen Fothergill, Lucian Freud, Edna Ginesi,
Freddie Gore, Polly Gray, Maureen Harris, Rupert Hart-Davis, William
Hayter, John Heath-Stubbs, Nicholas Hely Hutchinson, George, James and
Margaret Hepburn, Zoë Hicks, Michael Holroyd, Felix Hope-Nicholson,
Nicholas Horsfield, the late Jean Hugo, Sally Hunter, Brian Desmond Hurst,
Sheelah Hynes, Flora and John Isserlis, Harry Jonas, Karin Jonzen, Alice Kadell,
Billy Kaye, Barbara Ker Seymour, the Rt. Hon. Lord Kilanin, Michael Law, John
Lehmann, Jeremy Lewison, Jack Lindsay, William Mason, Robert Medley,
Dora Meninsky, the Viscount Moore, Richard Morphet, Elinor Moynihan,

Rodrigo Moynihan, Anne Obermer, Joan Osiakovski, Pat Piper, Euan Phillips, Dorothy Phillips, the late Bob Pocock, Diana Porter, Tristram and Virginia Powell, Dr Precope, Brian D. Price, Hugh Pulley, Peter Quennell, Keidrych Rhys, Alan Ross, Sophie Royde-Smith, Godfrey Ruben, Adrian Ryan, Richard Sadler, Michael Savage-Watts, Maria Scott, Desmond Shawe-Taylor, Nora Shawe-Taylor, Nicolette Shephard, Richard Shone, John Singer, Francis Sitwell, Reresby Sitwell, Frances Spalding, Isobel Strachey, Simonette Strachey, John Symonds, the late Tambimuttu, Maggie Thornton, Bill Tilly, Fred Tomlinson, Felix Topolski, James Tower, Julian Trevelyan, Constance Tudor-Hart, Chloë Tyner, Leigh Underhill, Tony van den Bergh, Sheila Varley, Julian Vinogradoff, R. Vint, Alison Waley, Donald Walker, Sir John Waller, John and Vivien White, Anne and John Willet, Sarah Wilson, Denis Wirth-Miller, the late Edward Wolfe, Tamsyn Woollcombe, David Wright, and the late Gerald Yorke.

My research for this book drew on the resources and help of the staff of many libraries, museums, art galleries and public institutions too numerous to list. I am particularly grateful for the indispensable cooperation of the Parkin Gallery and would like to acknowledge my thanks for the assistance I received from the British Library; the London Library; the Victoria and Albert Museum Library; the Westminster Reference Library; the Witt Library; the Tate Gallery Archives; Kettle's Yard, Cambridge; King's College Library, Cambridge; the University of Essex Library; the Harry Ransom Humanities Research Center, the University of Texas at Austin (special thanks to Cathy Henderson); the Huntingdon Library, California; the Mugar Memorial Library, Boston; the Royal School, Bath; Cartwright Hall, Bradford; the Courtauld Institute Galleries; Leeds University Art Gallery; the Anthony d'Offay Gallery; Browse & Darby, the Fine Art Society; the Mayor Gallery; the New Grafton Gallery, the Redfern Gallery, Christies, Phillips and Sotheby's.

I am very grateful to all those who allowed me to reproduce works of art and photographs in public and private collections and to Hugh Kelly, who took many of the photographs in this book. My thanks to the following for their permission to quote from unpublished copyright material: Betty Taber and Annabel Cole for letters by Roger Fry; Henry Lessore for letters by W. S. Sickert; Dr Margaret Bennet for letters by Winifred Gill; Romilly John for a letter by Augustus John; Frank Magro for a letter by Sir Osbert Sitwell; Nigel Nicolson for a letter by Sir Harold Nicolson; Guy Savage for an extract from the autobiography of Henry Savage; F.C.C. Todd for extracts from the autobiography of Ruthven Todd; Mark Holloway for extracts from his *Memories of Sylvia Gough and Nina Hamnett*; the late Bob Pocock for extracts from *It's Long Past the Time*.

Special thanks to the late Julius Horwitz for his generous help and hospitality and for permission to read and publish letters housed in the Mugar Memorial Library, Boston University.

Works by Nina Hamnett are reproduced with the permission of Edward Booth-Clibborn.

Particular thanks to my publishers, especially Miles Huddleston who has helped in many ways, Ben Glazebrook and Prudence Fay.

Finally, I would like to express my gratitude to my parents for their unfailing support and encouragement.

Denise Hooker

1986

Permission has been granted by the Executor of Nina Hamnett's Estate for the use of quotations from her autobiography, *Laughing torso*.

Foreword

Until recently Nina's work has been little known, hidden away in the storerooms of public galleries, private collections and the pages of old periodicals. This difficulty of access has meant that her contribution to the English modern movement during the First World War years and early twenties has not been properly recognized. However, if until now she has been neglected as an artist, she has never been forgotten as a personality. By the late twenties she had already assumed her role as presiding Queen of the London Bohemia then burgeoning in Fitzrovia. Her familiarity with pre-war Montparnasse, birthplace of the great artistic innovations of the century; her intimacy with Modigliani and Gaudier-Brzeska, both ill-fated artists *maudits* in the grand tradition; her close friendships with Roger Fry, Sickert and Augustus John, all key figures in the London art world; as well as her central position in the hectic life of Paris in the twenties, made Nina a unique link with a glorious past. The last of the old-style bohemians, she was a well-known figure in the pubs, clubs and restaurants of Fitzrovia and Soho where she held court until the fifties. Books by her contemporaries abound in fleeting glimpses of her and she lives vividly in the memories of her surviving friends. Mention of her name evokes an instant nostalgic response, a profusion of anecdotes and imitations of her very idiosyncratic manner of speech and way of walking. This book is an attempt both to recreate the myth and to suggest the real talent for art and for life that lay behind it.

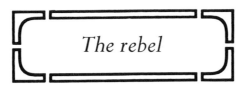

1

The rebel

NINA HAMNETT was a legend in her own lifetime. A star of Montparnasse and Fitzrovia, she was immortalized in the paintings, sculptures, novels, poems and memoirs of her contemporaries. From the first she was a self-conscious rebel and she inspired and perpetuated the myth of herself through her genuine artistic talent, the flamboyance of her lifestyle, and her love affairs and friendships with the artistic pantheon of her time.

Nina was born in her grandparents' house at 3 Lexden Terrace, Tenby, South Wales, on 14 February 1890, the eldest of two brothers and a sister. Nothing could have been more conventional than Nina's respectable background and upbringing. Her family had a long tradition of public service. Nina's father, George Edward Hamnett, the son of an Indian Civil Servant, was a twenty-six-year-old captain in the Army Service Corps. He had met Mary Elizabeth De Blois Archdeacon, who was the same age as himself, when he was serving with the Royal Artillery in Pembroke Dock and married her on 18 February 1889. She was the daughter of Captain William Edwin Archdeacon, a naval officer and fine draughtsman who had conducted the surveys of West Australia, Heligoland and much of western Wales, illustrating and drawing all the maps himself. On a visit to Canada with his ship he had married one of three beautiful sisters descended from the famous orator Joseph Howe, who federated the Canadian states. Nina always claimed that she had inherited her artistic talent from her grandfather, who died in 1893, and from her great-grandfather, who had won a certain fame with his drawings of ships at the beginning of the last century.

The early years of Nina's childhood were spent at a succession of army camps in Aldershot, Devonport, York, Chatham and Belfast. In the intervals when her father was serving abroad, Nina was sent to stay with her grandmother in Tenby. Her mother seems to have been a very modest and retiring woman who played little part in her upbringing. It was left to her father and grandmother, often in

Nina's birthplace – Lexden Terrace, Tenby

violent disagreement, and a series of nursemaids, to attempt to control Nina's boisterous high spirits.

It was not an easy task. Nina's parents had been dismayed that their first-born child was a girl, and as soon as she became conscious of the fact herself, Nina fully shared their sentiments, dismissing the members of her own sex as gutless half-wits. She detested the cumbersome and restrictive clothing she was obliged to wear and whenever she could she dressed up in her brother's sailor suits with long trousers. Nina was far from being the sweetly docile and obedient child beloved of Victorian story-books. She hated her father, whom she thought selfish and bad-tempered, and considered her grandmother stupid and sentimental. Nina's childhood was marked by a succession of head-on collisions with social convention and authority. Her father regularly tried to beat her into submission with a bamboo cane, until her legs were cut and bleeding. Nina vented her feelings of helplessness and frustration on a large doll she had been given in a vain attempt to instil into her some appropriate feminine feelings. Far from having the desired effect, Nina promptly placed the hapless doll over the nursery fender and soundly beat it with one of her father's canes so that its head was battered on the grate. Other appeals were made to her vanity and already well-developed instinct for self-display. When she was six she was allowed to choose her own party dress of purple satin and cream lace with large balloon sleeves, in the hope that it might inspire her to behave in a demure and ladylike fashion. But the first time she wore it she was so insufferably pleased with her appearance that another child set upon her and the party quickly developed into a free-for-all, with Nina being taken home by her nurse and thrashed.

In 1898 Nina's father, by then a major, was posted to Belfast. Nina and her brother were sent to the local Irish mixed school, an experience which only served to sharpen her taste for battle. She quickly learnt to give as good an insult as she got from the other children who taunted them as foreigners, and was very reluctant to leave at the end of the year when her father was stationed in Malta.

Nina went to live with her grandmother in Tenby. The family house stood in a terrace of six built high on a cliff with a communal garden overlooking the sea at

Nina and her brother in fancy dress, Tenby 1899

the rear. At that time the town was much favoured by retired naval and army officers, and the strictest rules of correct social conduct prevailed. In the summer Tenby was a fashionable resort for the upper middle classes, who came to play golf and lawn tennis, and to attend the regattas and balls that took place in the Royal Assembly Rooms. Apart from the picturesque harbour with its fishing fleet and tall, plain houses, the main attraction was the two-mile long golden beach. A brass band played while over-dressed children rode donkeys on the sands and the bathing-machines were hauled in and out of the sea by horses. The social high point of the day was the ritual evening promenade along the Esplanade, the Castle Hill or the Croft.

Nina resisted all her grandmother's efforts to make her behave like a lady and roamed among the sand-dunes, exploring the caves cut deep into the cliffs. Her favourite occupation was sitting alone at the end of the pier, fishing for pollock and sprats. She made friends with the bathing-machine boys, who taught her their extensive vocabulary of swear words. Nina could stand her own with any of the boys and did not hesitate to express her dislike of the local butcher-boy by kicking over his tray of meat and punching him in the stomach. She had equally violent arguments with her grandmother, who was quite unable to control her.

At their wits' end as to how to manage her, the family decided to send Nina to a private academy for young ladies at Westgate-on-Sea. The prospect filled her with gloom, but she was vastly consoled by the initialled writing-case and bag given to her by her grandmother and took delight in seeing her name in gold letters on her new leather-bound Bible. Once there, however, she cried every day for a week from rage and a feeling of imprisonment. She made a valiant attempt to escape one morning, but was caught by the headmistress as she sat on the roadside disconsolately munching raw turnips while she waited for a train to London. Faced with the inevitable, Nina accepted her fate and even won a prize for writing an essay about Shakespeare; but apart from this she showed little aptitude for her studies. Her moment of glory came when she was chosen to play the lead in the school performance of *Jack and the Beanstalk*. Nina was a natural extrovert and liked nothing better than dressing up as a boy and parading herself before an admiring audience. Wearing red tights, high-heeled shoes and a feathered cap, she climbed the beanstalk and gaily danced the hornpipe to delighted applause and cheering. She dreamed of a career on the stage, but her horrified family made it quite clear that this was not a suitable profession for a lady.

Nina's stay at Westgate proved short-lived as her parents decided that it was too expensive and that they would try and obtain votes for her to go to the Royal School for Daughters of the Officers of the Army in Bath. Since her father was away at the war in South Africa, Nina went back to Tenby to prepare for the strict entrance examination. Despite her grandmother, Nina was happy to see her old friends and was made an honorary member of a gang of little boys who did battle with their rivals every Sunday. She liked to accompany the milkman on his morning rounds, quickly hiding behind the big cans whenever she spotted one of her enemies. In such time as she could spare from the tribal warfare of Tenby, Nina attended a girls' class at her brother's school. She started to write stories but was so dissatisfied with the results that she consoled herself with drawing, which at that time she considered an inferior art.

Nina easily passed the entrance examination to the Royal School and she began there in 1902. There were 150 girls at Bath and Nina was delighted with it. She thrived in the more robust atmosphere of a girls' public school, so different from the hot-house exclusivity of Westgate. The school was a gaunt and imposing mock-Gothic building where the wind whistled through the corridors of the dormitories, which were made of Portland stone and named after military heroes. The prefects and the head-girl administered an austere regime. The girls were always hungry, cleanliness was definitely next to godliness, and silence and a rigid discipline were strictly imposed.

Nina started well by winning the foreign-language prize at the end of her first term, but this was only because she had had the verbs 'to be' and 'to have' drummed into her at Westgate, and the rest of her academic career was undistinguished. She excelled at drawing and dancing and drew a friend's maps for her in exchange for help with her arithmetic. By this time Nina had abandoned her earlier attempts at writing and was concentrating on art. She illustrated a magazine that she produced with a friend and painted the programmes for the school plays. For Nina, the high point of her years at the Royal School was playing the Mad Hatter in *Alice in Wonderland*, wearing an old top hat donated by the Archdeacon of Bath.

In 1903 she developed glandular fever and had to stay at home for a term. Her family was then at Portsmouth awaiting her father's return from the Boer War and Nina was sent to the Portsmouth School of Art. She soon became bored with making watercolour copies of pictures of Venice and would wander around the school, where she was fired with enthusiasm by the nude studies done by the other students. Nina thought the plaster casts in the Antique Room, with their strategically placed fig leaves, were silly and ugly. Her overwhelming desire to take a hammer to the offending additions was an early expression of her lifelong impatience with hypocrisy and sham conventions.

Back at Bath, Nina's artistic talent was becoming very evident and she passed the South Kensington Art Examinations first-class in freehand in 1904. But the warm, wet climate of Bath did not agree with her and by the end of the following year she became ill again and was forced reluctantly to leave. If the school had not succeeded in turning Nina into a lady, it certainly stamped her for life with an unmistakable county manner and voice, and deeply ingrained in her those traditional British virtues of confident self-reliance and stoicism in the face of all adversity – qualities she was amply to display in later years.

Nina joined her parents in Dublin and went for a short while to the Dublin School of Art. Although the other students called her 'the foreigner', they greatly admired her work and Nina found them friendly and easy-going. She studied hard and was very proud of a copy she made of the head of Michelangelo's *David*, lovingly labouring over every curl. In November her father, who had been appointed a lieutenant-colonel, was moved to the Curragh, where Nina had a fine time hunting with the Kildare on the army horses. But in less than a year the crash came. In October 1906 her father was court-martialled and cashiered for misconduct allegedly involving the taking of a bribe or the misuse of army funds. The family shamefacedly packed their belongings into a jaunting car and left under cover of night. It was a bitter blow. Nina's upright and authoritarian father was not the model of probity that he had seemed. The solidly respectable wall of convention and gentility that Nina had so rebelled against was shattered for ever. Now it was a question of keeping up appearances, constructing a façade.

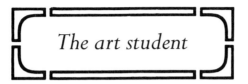

2

The art student

THE family installed themselves in Nina's grandmother's large flat in Chiswick while they tried to plan their future. Life was dramatically changed. Nina's father's fellow officers had clubbed together to buy him a cab so that he had some means of earning a living, but Nina now had to support herself. Much against her will, she was sent to the Regent Street Polytechnic to train to become a post office clerk. Nina, who had always been hopeless at figures, resigned herself to despair and drawing on the blotting paper. It was only at the end of the first term, when her teacher told her father that she would never succeed, that she was allowed to go to art school, a decision not unconnected with the discovery that five years' free education was to be had at the Royal Academy Schools.

Nina prepared for the entrance examination at the Pelham School of Art in South Kensington, which was run by an old Scotsman whose paintings of Highlanders and romantic dawn scenes meant very little to her. Dressed in a prim white blouse with a starched collar and tie, Nina was deadly serious and had no time for the other refined young lady students, who were merely filling their days in an agreeable manner before they found husbands. She drew diligently from the Antique and went to lectures in anatomy at the Royal Academy. George Clausen appeared from time to time to criticize the painting class, while Sir Arthur Cope tried hard to impress upon his students in the Life class the importance of line. He reduced most of the young ladies to tears, but in later years Nina always spoke of him with gratitude.

Nina was now sixteen and although she drew from the nude in the Life class, she had never seen herself naked. She had always obeyed her grandmother's strict Victorian code of morality and dressed and undressed under her nightgown. One day, feeling very daring, she flung off her clothes and gazed at herself in the mirror for the first time. She was proud and delighted with what she saw, finding herself far superior to the models in the Life room, and eagerly took up a pencil and began to draw.

At Christmas Nina won a silver medal with four watercolour landscapes that she had painted on a summer holiday with her family at Margate, but she was becoming increasingly disillusioned with the thoroughly academic training she was receiving. She was far more interested in painting life around her than the carefully composed, idealized version of it beloved by the Academy, which she now found dull and uninspiring. Camille Mauclair's book on the French Impressionists was a revelation to her and opened her eyes to completely different ways of painting. When she met the girl who had won the gold medal for portrait painting at the Royal Academy Schools, Nina was dismayed to find that she had never even heard of Manet. The crunch came when Nina went to an evening sketch class at the London School of Art in Earls Court, where the students drew from clothed models, workpeople and character models. Once she had discovered this window on the real world, Nina became convinced that the Royal Academy Schools were not for her. With great difficulty she persuaded her grandmother to pay the fees for her to go to the London School of Art, known simply as 'Brangwyn's' after the name of its most popular professor.

For Nina this was paradise at last. The school was run like a French *atelier*. A *massier* posed the models and arranged the still lifes, and the professors came round once a week to correct the students' work. Most of them hero-worshipped Frank Brangwyn, but Nina did not think he was a good teacher. His strong personality and vigorous painting style, with its broad sweeps of brilliant colour and exuberant detail, tended to overwhelm his students, who imitated him rather than developing their own vision. Nina preferred the animal painter John Swan, whose severe manner thoroughly intimidated the class. He was notoriously difficult to please and Nina was very encouraged when he praised her drawing from a Negro model. Later, William Nicholson and George Lambert were the professors. They were both excellent teachers. Nicholson, who always arrived on a bicycle, immaculately dressed in a white duck suit with matching spotted tie and socks, tried to instil a professionalism into the students' still lifes and did not hesitate to recommend that they use compasses to achieve the necessary roundness of a plate. Lambert was Nina's favourite teacher. Apart from being himself a very talented draughtsman, he went to great lengths to help anyone he thought promising and once spent a whole morning painting a leg for Nina.

At Brangwyn's, Nina found herself amidst a group of lively and intelligent young people, including the talented painter Gladys Hynes and the future art critics Jan Gordon and Wilenski, the latter resplendent in a large sombrero and cloak with a silver-topped cane. She became very friendly with Valentine

Savage, whose brother Henry knew Richard Middleton and was later to edit the arts magazine the *Gypsy*. Valentine had a room in Chelsea where she and Nina shared models and read poetry by John Davidson and A. E. Housman. Through her brother, Valentine knew a lot about literature and talked to Nina about people such as Frank Harris and Edward Thomas. Another friend was the beautiful half-Russian, half-Spanish Dolores Bastien, known as 'Moucha'. She was the daughter of the Spanish Consul in St Petersburg and had been born and brought up in Russia. Moucha was later to marry the American journalist and theosophist Ralph Courtney, who introduced his friend Arthur Ransome, the exuberant young author of *Bohemia in London,* to the crowd at Brangwyn's. He called Nina 'Ham' or *'Mademoiselle de Jambon'*[1] and she liked him immediately. Tall and thin, with a red bushy moustache, dressed in a corduroy jacket and knickerbockers, Ransome was a countryman at heart and entertained the company with tunes on his penny whistle.

After a hard day at Brangwyn's the students often went roller-skating. In the summer they joined the throng at the Artists' Revels, a large fancy-dress dance held in the Botanical Gardens in Regent's Park. One year Nina went in sandalled feet, flimsily dressed as Ariadne. It was always a boisterous rout, but at least for Nina and her friends the Revels were remarkably innocent. Indeed, such occasions were often even more harmless than they appeared. Henry Savage gave a comic account of a party at which he found himself secluded alone with Nina in an alcove: 'although we both knew what was expected of us, we were too shy to begin the preliminaries even. Finally, Nina, who probably knew her Shaw, took the initiative. With a desperate effort she convulsively encircled my neck with her arms and with firmly-closed lips pressed them tightly against mine. It so seemed that I was kissing a cold codfish as to inhibit me altogether. By tacit mutual consent we returned to the party and by smiles indicated that all had gone as it should have gone.'[2]

Before long, Nina fell in love with a fellow student known to everyone as 'The Genius', who specialized in painting souls in torment. Nina visited him at his studio in Chelsea and posed for him lying on a sofa with her hand outstretched in a suitably spiritual manner to represent one of the phases of the soul. They read d'Annunzio together and went to see Sarah Bernhardt in a play at the Coliseum, imagining that their passion was greater than that of all the lovers in history. Nina's father protested loudly about virtue when she got home late at night. But he need not have worried. Theirs was a love of the purest and most exalted kind. One day 'The Genius' was bold enough to kiss her, but the most daring thing they did was drink crème de menthe and feel wicked.

Nina found temporary relief from what she was pleased to consider her fatal and hopeless passion when a friend at Brangwyn's called simply by her surname

Gellibrand, who was the daughter of a Russian mother and an English father who shipped timber for pit-props from the northern forests, invited her to spend the summer of 1909 with her family in Russia. It seemed like a great adventure to Nina and she readily accepted, taking the last ten pounds out of her savings bank. When the boat left the Millwall Dock she felt an exhilarating sense of freedom at escaping from home and the two friends spent every evening of the journey drinking port and singing songs with some students who had guitars. As the boat passed Kronstadt, Nina had her first glimpse of the golden domes and spires of St Petersburg rising above the water. The girls were met at the quayside and driven in a droshky over the cobblestones to the Gellibrands' grand and spacious apartment in St Petersburg. The next day they went to the Finland Station, where the booking office was adorned with ikons and candles, and took the train to Terioki on the Finnish border.

The family's wooden dacha was near the coast among forests of pine trees. At first Nina found the white nights of the almost Arctic summer very disorientating. The nightingales sang all night and she would wake at one thinking it was five in the morning. The Gellibrands were an intellectual family and her friend's mother was never without a book. Students and young officers came to visit and they spent the evenings arguing about the merits of Dostoevsky and Shakespeare. Nina avidly read the life of Marie Bashkirtseff during her stay. Born in 1860, Marie Bashkirtseff was a rich Russian emigrée to France who dedicated her short life to her painting, which was strongly influenced by her mentor and admirer Bastien Lepage. In her frank and revealing diary, published to wide acclaim three years after her death in 1887, she poured out all her impatience with the conventional pieties of the day and expressed her ardent longing for life, love and fame. She was a romantic idealist who yearned to live on an operatic scale and had a burning ambition to achieve something of lasting worth. Nina greatly admired her character and determination to succeed as an artist, an aspiration which was already fully formed in Nina's own mind.

During her two months in Russia, Nina learnt a little of the language and went to the cinema for the first time, seeing silent Italian comic films. She drank Swedish punch at the *Kursaal* and danced the mazurka with Russians and Finns at the local fêtes. Before she left she spent a week visiting the sights of St Petersburg, where the Russian Ballet impressed her most. She was thrilled to see the great ballerinas Pavlova and Karsavina dancing in *The Sleeping Beauty* and had an early foretaste of the delights which were to enrapture London a few years later.

Nina was very sorry to leave Russia and felt all the more confined and restricted at her grandmother's after her taste of independence. Her family refused to pay the fees at Brangwyn's any longer, but the manager allowed her to continue studying there in exchange for acting as the *massière* to the still-life class. Nina still saw her friend 'The Genius' and worked in his studio, although the differences between them were becoming more pronounced as he continued to paint agonized souls while she preferred to draw small children and charwomen. Nina longed for the wider world and worshipped her artistic heroes from a distance, following Augustus John down the King's Road and standing outside Epstein's house in Cheyne Walk in the hope of catching a glimpse of him. Desperate to find out something about life and to relieve her boredom, she read everything she could lay her hands on, eagerly devouring Kant, Schopenhauer and Baudelaire.

When the art-school year ended, Nina miserably went to live with her parents at 23 Avenue Gardens, Acton. She had no money for paints or canvas and her father poured scorn on her serious reading and reproductions of Whistler etchings, gleefully predicting that the lunatic asylum would be her next refuge. Instead, her state of general frustration led to her becoming paralysed and losing the use of her hands. The doctor diagnosed spinal adhesion and made her lie down for hours every day, which only made her worse. Nina knew that her malady could be more accurately termed virginal hysteria and boredom.

A more obliging doctor told her family that she needed work to occupy her mind. They had evidently given up all hope of Nina's behaving like a lady and did not object when she wrote to a second cousin who was Thomas Beecham's manager and asked him if he could get her a walk-on part in a play. He duly found her a job in the chorus of a Scottish play written by Hemmerde called *Proud Maisie* at the Aldwych Theatre. She was to earn a pound a week – a fortune to Nina – for singing a drinking-song with eleven other girls dressed in eighteenth-century costumes and powdered wigs. But the glamour of acting on a London stage and realizing her childhood ambition lasted an even shorter time than the run of the play, which closed after only two weeks. Nina spent the next three weeks sitting in the crowded waiting room of Mr Blackmore, a theatrical agent in Garrick Street, until finally one morning there came a request for a 'little bit of fluff'.[3] Thoroughly disillusioned, Nina realized that however long she sat there she would never be the desired 'little bit of fluff' and returned home to work at her painting, convinced she had been right to choose art rather than acting.

She went to Life classes in the evening at the polytechnic at Turnham Green and a young neighbour sat for her. Nina was immensely encouraged when the Walker Art Gallery in Liverpool accepted a watercolour study of a child for its Autumn Exhibition of Modern Art in 1911 – her first work in a public exhibition. It was a start, however modest. She had achieved something through her own efforts and felt that she was truly launched on an artistic career.

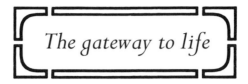

3

The gateway to life

Nina's personal rebellion and struggle for independence echoed the wider social, economic and political climate of late Edwardian England. There was an upsurge of vigorous forces challenging the old order: the woman's suffrage movement, the great series of workers' strikes, and the attack on the centuries-old privileges of the House of Lords. Socialism was becoming an important factor and the problem of Ireland came to dominate the political stage. All these various rebellions found simultaneous violent expression in the years 1910–14 and reached a fever-pitch of intensity as determination for change grew. Liberal England was suffering its death throes. The historian George Dangerfield characterized the general mood of the period as

> an unconscious turning from respectability[1] . . . For the assaults upon Parliament of the Tories, the women, and the workers have something profoundly in common. In each case, a certain conscious security was in question . . . The workers did not want to be safe any more; they wanted to live, to take chances, to throw caution to the winds: they had been repressed too long.[2]

Similarly strong forces were welling up to sweep aside the traditional provincialism and insularity of the English art world. Publicly accepted canons of good taste were still dictated by the backward-looking, solidly conventional Royal Academy. The virtual exclusion from its walls of younger French-trained or -influenced painters had led to the formation of the New English Art Club in 1886. This provided a much-needed alternative exhibiting society, but by the first decade of the twentieth century it had become almost as tame and conservative as the Academy itself. Reaction to the French dealer Durand Ruel's exhibition of Impressionism in London in 1905 showed that as far as the British public was concerned, Impressionism was still considered daringly modern and controversial, even though it had long been accepted in Paris and New York. Official opinion was no more enlightened. The National Gallery had turned down the gift of a Degas in 1904, and in 1907 refused to show Sir Hugh Lane's collection which included works by many Impressionists.

Certainly the general public was quite unprepared for the revelation of the new French art sprung upon it by Roger Fry's exhibition *Manet and the Post-Impressionists*, which opened at the Grafton Galleries in November 1910. Younger painters and those who had never travelled abroad had their first startling taste of the liberation of colour and form taking place on the Continent. Fry's approach had been characteristically thorough and didactic in aim. Apart from eight canvases by Manet to demonstrate the link with the earlier Impressionists, he included numerous works by Cézanne, Van Gogh and Gauguin, many of them painted at least twenty years previously. The younger generation was well represented by Matisse, Picasso, Derain, Friesz, Redon, Rouault, Signac, Seurat and Vlaminck. Here was a departure from realistic representation far more radical than Impressionism. Fry explained to the hundreds of shocked visitors who daily flocked to the gallery that these canvases ablaze with colour and distorted shapes did 'not seek to imitate form, but to create form'.[3] They were conceived as equivalents for the artist's subjective experience in front of nature rather than attempts to depict appearances objectively.

The public's reaction was one of astonished disbelief, outrage and laughter. A torrent of abuse and mockery descended on Fry, hitherto a highly respected and influential connoisseur, writer, critic and lecturer on art. Nothing had so disturbed the equilibrium and complacency of the English art establishment since the celebrated *Whistler v. Ruskin* trial in 1877 when Whistler successfully sued Ruskin for libel over his comment that he charged 200 guineas for 'flinging a pot of paint in the public's face'. There was a widespread feeling that the Post-Impressionist exhibition was either a bad joke at the public's expense or a confidence trick. It was considered an insult, a dangerous threat to English art and life, undermining the whole moral fabric of society and heralding imminent anarchy. The paintings themselves were seen as childish scrawls or the work of madmen. One disgruntled viewer, the poet and diplomat Wilfred Blunt, characterized the exhibits as

nothing but the gross puerility which scrawls indecencies on the walls of a privy. The drawing is on the level of an untaught child of seven or eight years old, the sense of colour that of a tea-tray painter, the method that of a schoolboy who wipes his fingers on a slate after spitting on them. They are the works of idleness and impotent stupidity, a pornographic show.[4]

There were some voices of sanity to temper the prevailing emotional excesses. The novelist Arnold Bennett, writing in the *New Age*,[5] saw the absurdity of the spectacle of London fighting over art whose reputation had been firmly established in Paris some twenty years earlier. Walter Sickert, an early exponent of English Impressionism, wrote an influential article in the *Fortnightly Review*.[6] He had long known the work of the artists in question and although his dedication to traditional methods and draughtsmanship prevented him giving it his unqualified approval, he recognized the importance and necessity of the exhibition. For the first time England was brought into contact with the mainstream of modern art and forced to recognize that vital developments were taking place on the Continent. Like Fry, Sickert knew that all modern painting was founded on the French school.

Once the first breach had been made in the wall of English cultural isolation, the way was open to all manner of artistic invaders. Late Edwardian England undoubtedly witnessed a new receptivity to foreign influences. In particular all things Russian enjoyed a spectacular vogue. But more than anything else, the barbaric splendour of Diaghilev's Russian Ballet took London by storm in the years 1911–13. Intensely modern, it dazzled with its music by Stravinsky and Debussy; dancing by Karsavina and Nijinsky; brilliantly coloured, fantastical costumes and décor by Bakst. The public was enraptured by *Le Spectre de la Rose*, *L'Après-Midi d'un Faune* and *Le Sacre du Printemps*. Nina joined the eager crowds which flocked to the first season at Covent Garden. She recorded her excitement in quick pencil and watercolour sketches of Adolf Bohm, Cecchetti, and Nijinsky dancing with Karsavina in *Carnival*. Edward Marsh, Winston Churchill's private secretary and an important patron of young artists, enthused about the Russian Ballet: 'It's a Post-Impressionist picture put in motion . . . it has almost brought me round to Matisse's pictures!'[7] Like Post-Impressionism, the Russian Ballet swept aside past conventions and had the same power to disturb profoundly and question old assumptions. Suddenly art was exciting, powerful, dangerous: a herald of new aesthetic and moral freedoms. The modern age had arrived. Here was liberation from English restraint and gentility. Decorum was dead. Long live imagination and instinct!

Nina came of age at the same time as England could be said to have gained her artistic majority and finally woken up to the potent reality of Europe. Marooned at home until now, straining against the leash of parental restriction, she suddenly found herself free. A sympathetic uncle by marriage took pity on her plight and arranged for her to receive £50 in advance from some money left by her paternal grandfather, to be distributed eventually among his grandchildren. In addition, two kindly aunts decided to give her an allowance of two shillings and sixpence a week each to enable her to pursue her chosen career. She

Nina Hamnett, Self Portrait, 1913

supplemented this by giving painting lessons as a form of therapy to the suicidal aunt of a fellow student at Brangwyn's. With her new-found financial independence Nina rented a room at 41 Grafton Street, off Fitzroy Square, for seven shillings and sixpence a week, chasing the bugs away with a can of petrol. She now had a place she could call her own, where she could work and live as she chose. Even so, she scarcely had any money left over for food, and after a day spent painting in her room she often went home to sleep and have a good meal.

But it was a beginning. Life beckoned. She was soon introduced into that charmed circle of artists who had been surrounded with such an aura of glamour in her student days. She was taken to one of Sickert's Saturday afternoon 'At Homes' just round the corner at 19 Fitzroy Street. He took an immediate liking to her and she became a regular visitor, meeting there many of the most interesting artists in London. Before Fry shot to public notice as the champion of the avant-garde, Sickert was the acknowledged leader of the English modern movement. An enthusiastic, if idiosyncratic, teacher and writer of vigorous, witty articles on art, he was much respected by the younger generation.

Sickert's immensely popular 'At Homes' started in 1907 when he returned to England after a long absence abroad. He felt that the only way to accustom people to looking at his own and other new work was to exhibit it himself, so he banded together with Spencer Gore, Harold Gilman, William and Albert Rothenstein, Walter Bayes, Nan Hudson and Ethel Sands to form the Fitzroy Street Group. They jointly rented a first-floor studio and store-room where they showed their modestly priced pictures, which were piled in stacks against the walls, to interested visitors every Saturday afternoon. By 1910, Fitzroy Street had established itself as the forum for all that was newest in English art and its membership soon swelled to encompass almost every progressive artist in London. There was always a large crowd of painters, young students, critics, collectors and potential patrons. Friendship and professional interest brought together a host of overlapping artistic strands. Even Roger Fry and his Bloomsbury friends made occasional appearances at Fitzroy Street. Sickert's attitude to Bloomsbury was one of benevolent cynicism. Despite their publicly aired differences, there was a long-standing mutual respect and esteem between Sickert and Fry, who had at one time been a pupil of Sickert's.

The furore caused by the Post-Impressionist show led to an almost hysterical hostility on the part of the art establishment towards any new art with a foreign flavour. The old guard of the New English Art Club, which had reluctantly begun to admit paintings by members of the Fitzroy Street Group, now abruptly closed ranks against them. They reacted by forming the men-only Camden Town Group, whose central core consisted of Sickert, Gore, Gilman, Charles Ginner, Robert Bevan and Lucien Pissarro. Their typically small-scale work, painted in a basically Impressionist-inspired style, depicted the often sordid, humble reality of everyday urban life: shabby Camden Town interiors, nudes on a bed or at their *toilette*, street scenes, the back views of houses and gardens, and informal portraits of friends and favourite models. All this seemed very tame in comparison with the work of the Post-Impressionists and even at the time of the Camden Town Group's first exhibition in 1911, many of its most important members had already begun to assimilate the new techniques. The Camden Town Group broke up after only three shows at the Carfax Gallery (two in 1911, the third in 1912) and was for the most part absorbed into the more amorphous London Group, formed in October 1913.

Nevertheless, even if the artistic tide was turning against Sickert, he remained a magnet for the young. They were captivated by his knowledge, quick wit and repartee, his chameleon-like changes of mood and character, and his adoption of a whole range of disguises. An actor in his early days, he had a great talent for self-dramatization. Sometimes he would appear fastidiously dressed as a dandy in morning coat, striped trousers, top hat and cane. At other times he was the artist in smock and slippers; the farmer in a Norfolk jacket and leggings; or one of the more sinister characters from his own paintings with a red and white handkerchief tied round his neck. One day he would be cropped like a convict, the next he would be sporting a full, square beard. The variations were endless and reflected his ability to be as equally at home in high society as with the humble folk of Camden Town. He had a keen sense of humour and liked nothing better than to provoke a reaction.

Sickert greatly enjoyed being surrounded by young people and was stimulated and flattered by their attention. He was a very popular teacher and always had a large band of female followers. Fifty-one years old in 1911, Sickert knew he was good-looking and attractive to women, and liked to boast that he was 'the Lewis Waller of the Arts schools'[8] (Waller being a matinée idol of the day). One of his students, Enid Bagnold, wrote: 'We were all enslaved, enchanted. The day glittered because of him.'[9] His women pupils hero-worshipped him and willingly undertook to do his chores and perform the routine tasks of preparing his copperplates and squaring up his canvases before he began work on them. Wendela Boreel recalled how she became his '*petit nègre*, to do all and to be at his beck and call'.[10] In return he certainly knew how to charm, and another devotee, the young painter Marjorie Lilly, described how he kept her and her friend Christina Cutter laughing 'literally for hours on end, with his quips, his extravagances, his imitations of our friends, sharpened by the stately and mock-pompous English with which they were presented'.[11]

Nina was no exception to the feminine rule and she declared Sickert one of the kindest, most intelligent and most charming men she had ever met. For his part,

The Fairground, 1912

he was greatly attracted to her and enjoyed her company. He took a genuine interest in what she was doing and Nina was immensely flattered that he came to look at her work in Grafton Street and seemed to like it. Although she was never formally one of his pupils, Sickert gave her much advice and encouragement.

At the same time as Nina was taking her first steps in the wider artistic world, she was also introduced to the hidden world of occultism and magic, which flourished in the late Victorian and Edwardian period in reaction to the prevailing materialism. Early in 1912 she met the small bird-like poet Victor Neuberg – called Vickeybird – and his girlfriend Jeanne Hayse, who was known by her professional name, Ione de Forrest. A little younger than Nina, Ione was startlingly beautiful, with a pale oval face, golden eyes and long black hair down to her waist. She had made a certain reputation by acting in Maeterlinck's *The Blue Bird*, but after a very brief marriage she was now living alone in Rossetti Studios, Chelsea, and studying art. Although her husband had instigated divorce proceedings he still made her a very generous allowance and she frequently took Nina out to the theatre and other entertainments, paying for both of them. This was the great age of musical comedy and the music-halls were still at the height of their popularity. Nina and Ione often went to the Chelsea Palace, where many of

Zadkine, 1914

The Landlady, 1917

the great stars such as George Robey, Harry Lauder, Marie Lloyd and Little Tich performed. One night they saw Charlie Chaplin, who made the whole house roar with laughter simply by walking up and down the stage.

Neuberg and Ione were both ardent devotees of the poet, mountaineer and master magician Aleister Crowley, and talked a lot about him to Nina. Crowley – otherwise variously known as The Beast 666, Lord Boleskine, Frater Perdurabo, Prince Chioa Khan or The Master Therion – was a megalomaniac with a talent for self-dramatization and a pathological need for extreme experiences. He announced the formation of his Order of the Silver Star in the first issue of his magazine the *Equinox*, published in March 1909. The Silver Star was a rival offshoot of the Rosicrucian Order of the Golden Dawn and used the same rituals, teachings and magical weapons. Neuberg had come powerfully under Crowley's influence whilst still a student at Cambridge and when he graduated in 1909 he joined him as his assistant on the *Equinox*. His volume of poetry, *The Triumph of Pan*, published to wide reviews in 1910, shows to what extent he was thoroughly imbued with Crowley's philosophy.

Crowley first came to general notice in the autumn of 1910 when he staged a series of public displays of the magic rituals of his Order of the Silver Star at Caxton Hall. Entitled *The Rites of Eleusis*, Crowley devised a rite for each of the planets, exalting Pan, the ancient Greek god of lust. The performances took place in a darkened, incense-filled room on seven successive Wednesdays in October and November. The audience, many in evening dress, sat on rows of low stools to watch Crowley, wearing long robes, recite the lyrics while his mistress – or 'Scarlet Woman' – Leila Waddel played the violin and Neuberg performed an allegorical dance. As Mars, he sought to comprehend the riddle of the universe, making appeals to Saturn, Jupiter, the Sun, Venus, Mercury and the Moon. None of them could provide the solution and in the end they all turned to Pan, who did so. The published aim of the series was to inspire a state of religious ecstasy in the audience but as Crowley's biographer John Symonds wrote, 'the point of Crowley's rites, in line with Crowley's philosophy, is that there is no God, and that one can therefore do what one wills. The characters who, during the performance, hammer on the doors of heaven, are informed that God is dead. (But Pan, apparently, is still alive.) The aim of man, therefore, is pleasure among the living.'[12] Public reaction to Crowley's antics differed widely. The *Daily Sketch* dismissed them as harmless eccentricity, while *John Bull* pilloried Crowley 'for his bestial posturings and his disgusting blasphemies', decrying him as 'the inventor of a new religion, with its pseudo-teaching supposed to be derived from the medieval alchemists, and its licentious cult in which dark rooms, impressionable women and poems recited to throbbing music played their part'.

Ione made her first appearance in Crowley's circle when she played the role of the Moon in *The Rites of Eleusis*, dressed in a flowing white robe with a fillet of silver leaves around her head. Neuberg fell violently in love with her ethereal beauty and wrote many poems to her. But things did not go smoothly. Ione was highly strung and hysterical, subject to fits of deep melancholy when she would talk of suicide. Neuberg was torn between his love of Ione, his dedication to the magical path, and his sense of loyalty to Crowley, who had a strong emotional hold over him and deeply resented their mutual absorption. In December 1911 Ione suddenly married an old friend of Neuberg, a wealthy engraver called William Merton, and after the ceremony they all three went to Paris, apparently on the best of terms. But Ione soon bitterly regretted her rash act and left her husband after only six months, when she went back to Neuberg.

Nina was naturally very curious to meet the notorious Crowley about whom she had heard so much. Neuberg and Ione took her along to his headquarters at his flat at 124 Victoria Street, which was decorated with red cushions and curtains, several Buddhas and a stuffed crocodile. It was with some trepidation that Nina confronted the penetrating gaze of the so-called wickedest man in the world and heard his habitual greeting, 'Do what thou wilt shall be the whole of the law', to which her companions intoned the ritual reply, 'Love is the law, love under will.' The arch-magician, reputed drug fiend and sex maniac was a middle-aged, conventionally dressed portly figure whose head was completely shaven except for a single lock of hair which symbolized the Sun's viceregent, or the phallus. Nina was struck more by Crowley's intelligence than his wickedness, and accepted his offer to decorate his studio with four panels representing the elements of fire, earth, air and water. But things were not quite as harmless as they appeared. While she was painting the panel of fire, it seems that the fire element escaped and three fires mysteriously started in the studio that same day.

Worse was to follow. In August 1912 Ione wired to Nina to visit her that evening. During the visit, she announced that she was pregnant and asked Nina to come round again the next morning at eleven so that she could give her some clothes as she was going on a long journey. Nina assumed that Ione meant to go away until the baby was born, but her fears were awakened the following day when she found pinned to Ione's door an envelope addressed to her and containing the keys. After a moment's hesitation, Nina went in and drew aside a heavy red curtain to reveal Ione lying dead, fully dressed for walking, among the cushions on a divan in a corner of the studio, a mother-of-pearl revolver beside her on the floor. She had placed the gun inside her dress and shot herself through the heart. Deeply shocked and horrified, Nina ran to call the caretaker and waited for the police.

Nina gave evidence at the Chelsea Coroner's Court, which passed the verdict of suicide during temporary insanity. Notwithstanding this judgment, Ione had evidently planned her action with great care and deliberation. She had purchased the gun some weeks beforehand, written a last note to her husband in which she said simply 'You have killed me,' and even thoughtfully provided a statement for the coroner to be read at the inquest in which she declared that 'although of sound mind I intend committing suicide to-night, because of the unbearable position my extremely rash and unfortunate marriage has placed me in.'[13] Nina had known that her friend was often severely depressed and spoke of killing herself, but like everyone else never thought she would really do so. Neuberg always blamed Crowley for Ione's suicide, believing that he had magically willed it.

The whole affair upset Nina considerably for some time, but she continued her association with Crowley. She appears on the list of members of the Order of the Silver Star for 1913. That same year she painted a portrait of the poet and novelist Ethel Archer, who was a contributor to the *Equinox*. Nina depicted her dressed in black, looking pale and thin, and holding a yellow tulip. Crowley called the picture the *Dead Soul* and later referred to Nina as one of his students, so she may have taken part in some of the Silver Star's ritual ceremonies. But fortunately for her, she was not rich or influential enough for Crowley ever to take a serious interest in her and he never offered to give her any drugs. For her part, Nina was far too irreverent and carefree to dedicate herself to Crowley; besides, her real interests lay in quite a different direction. But she never underestimated him, always retaining a certain wariness of him throughout her life. Beneath his theatrical posturings Crowley undeniably did possesss a sinister power, even if it was nothing more than a talent for manipulating people and subordinating them to his will. Nina's brush with Crowley was part of her personal rebellion. It was dangerous, faintly illicit – and it made a change from home.

According to Frank Harris, the notoriously smooth-talking, high-living womanizer, writer and editor of a string of publications including the *Fortnightly Review* and the *Saturday Review*, sex was the gateway to life. Or so he told the aspiring young writer Enid Bagnold before helping her across the threshold in an upstairs room at the Café Royal. Nina had quite independently reached the same conclusion and coolly decided that at twenty-two the time had come for her to consider the question of sex. All the indications suggest that Allan Odle, a talented graphic artist of the same age as Nina, was the man chosen for the honour of relieving her of her unwanted virginity. Tall and emaciated, with long dark hair, a pale face, and luminous eyes, Odle was a rather dandified nineties figure with Aubrey Beardsleyesque elongation of features and fingers. His fantastically detailed, highly sensual pen and ink drawings displayed a fascination with the macabre and the grotesque. Nina thought him 'too beautiful for words',[14] his long hands reminding her of Filippo Lippi's *Angel* in the National Gallery. Odle took two rooms at 35 Howland Street, off Fitzroy Square, and Nina arranged to meet him there at ten-thirty one evening, admitting that when the moment came she was more terrified than a soldier going over the top. The deed done, she commented in her characteristically matter-of-fact way that she did not think much of it. Nevertheless, the following morning she confessed to feeling a 'sense of spiritual freedom and that something important had been accomplished'.[15]

Nina was even more pleased when she discovered that her so-called initiation into life had taken place in the same house where the French poets Verlaine and Rimbaud had stayed when they first arrived in London. Knowing how much Sickert would appreciate this quirky coincidence, she hurried round to his studio to tell him her news. He listened while he carried on painting, at the same time using the other end of his brush to stir some scrambled eggs. Very amused, he commented drily that in a hundred years time they would put up a blue commemorative plaque for Nina on the front of the house and another for the two poets – appropriately – on the back.

In the autumn of 1912 Nina went to Paris for five days with her beautiful admirer. But his attention soon wandered and Nina saw very little of him. Instead she met up with Epstein, who was in Paris to put the finishing touches to his huge, carved stone tomb of Oscar Wilde in the Père Lachaise cemetery. Archaically primitive in style, the tomb took the form of a flying demon angel, like a winged Greek sphinx, powerfully thrusting forward into eternity. Fame with her symbolic trumpet was carved on the forehead, while above were figures representing Intellectual Pride and Luxury. The tomb's unmistakable male attributes had led the outraged French authorities to ban it as indecent and it was now permanently covered with a tarpaulin and guarded by a gendarme. Nina went every day with Epstein and a few of his friends, including the Romanian sculptor Brancusi, to uncover it so that Epstein could carry on his work. It was a hopeless battle. No sooner was the tarpaulin removed than the police replaced it. The issue caused an outcry and Epstein was publicly supported by eminent artists and writers on both sides of the Channel; but to no avail. Eventually Robert Ross, Wilde's literary executor, who had commissioned the monument, had a bronze plaque or fig-leaf placed over the offending part. However, when word of this scandalous sacrilege to art got round, a band of artists and poets raided the cemetery and removed it. One evening Crowley appeared in the Café Royal immaculately attired in full evening dress with a daringly original accessory. Round his neck the plaque dangled on a significantly long string.

Thoroughly enjoying the sensation he was causing, he solemnly presented it to Epstein. It was not until the outbreak of the First World War that the tarpaulin was finally removed without comment or affront to public morality, which was then preoccupied with more serious matters.

Nina's first taste of Paris had whetted her appetite. She loved Montparnasse, the artists' quarter where everyone worked hard during the day and stayed up all night in the cafés. She made up her mind to return as soon as she had enough money. When she got back to London she cried for a few days over her lost love, who had so quickly tired of her. But she soon dried her tears. Consolation was at hand in the shape of a tall, fair poet who provided a suitable passing distraction.

Her confidence restored, Nina decided to celebrate her independence in a defiant gesture of liberation. She cut her hair short – and felt a new sense of freedom. Turning to face herself in the mirror, she painted a clear-eyed self-portrait. Wearing a wide-brimmed hat and an artist's smock, with one hand on her hip, the other extended to her easel, she gazed straight out at the viewer. She unashamedly delighted in the rather romanticized image of herself as a Bohemian artist. She was consciously adopting the time-honoured pose for a self-portrait of the artist, jauntily confronting the male tradition head-on with no concessions to her femininity and no attempt to charm. The picture (see page 29) is powerfully self-assertive. It is a declaration of faith; a wager with herself and the world.

4

The Café Royal

WITH her tall, boyish figure and attractive, laughing face, Nina easily made up in charm and exuberant good humour what she lacked in conventional beauty. Conspicuously dressed in a clergyman's hat, checked coat and skirt with red facings, Nina enjoyed the stares her white stockings and men's dancing pumps received in the Tottenham Court Road. She was well known among the band of artists, models, writers and composers who gathered together at the Café Royal, and was always surrounded by a large crowd of friends.

The Café Royal, at the Piccadilly end of Regent Street, played a unique part in the artistic and literary life of London. Founded in 1865 by the enterprising Daniel Nicolas Thévenon, alias Daniel Nicols, a bankrupt in exile from his native France, it first achieved fame and notoriety in the nineties when it was the favourite haunt of artists and writers such as Whistler, Oscar Wilde, Max Beerbohm, Arthur Symons, Aubrey Beardsley, Charles Conder, James Pryde, William Nicholson, G. B. Shaw and A. E. Housman. Strictly speaking, the Café Royal comprised three distinct areas: the Restaurant, the Grill Room and the Brasserie or Domino Room. Hidden from general view were numerous private and banqueting rooms, and a Masonic temple. But for the motley collection of artists, nostalgic expatriate Frenchmen, plotting foreign anarchists, raucous bookmakers, shady-looking crooks, con-men, pimps, blackmailers and less respectable members of the aristocracy, all of whom used the place as a second home, the Café Royal undoubtedly meant the Domino Room.

It was the nearest thing in London to a French café, with its marble-topped tables, red plush banquettes, and sawdust-strewn floor. The gilded ostentation of the Domino Room held a powerful fascination for its habitués and many writers and artists celebrated its overblown splendour, by now somewhat faded and tarnished. Famous paintings of the Domino Room by William Orpen, Charles Ginner, and Adrian Allinson show the walls lined with long, gilt

The Café Royal, 1915–16, by Adrian Allinson
Allan Odle and Nancy Cunard are seated in the left foreground. Behind them, from left to right, are Horace de Vere Cole, Iris Tree, Evan Morgan, David Sampson (standing), P. G. Konody, Dorelia John, Augustus John and Adrian Allinson (seated to the right of the pillar)

mirrors, flanked on both sides by plaster caryatids, and lit by heavy glass chandeliers. Blue pillars entwined with golden vine leaves supported the elaborately festooned, ornate turquoise ceiling across which nymphs and cupids disported themselves, hidden from a too-prurient gaze by the perpetual fug of tobacco smoke.

Nina, going to the Café Royal for the first time in 1912, must have felt something of the same awed excitement as Max Beerbohm when he was introduced to this 'legendary haunt of intellect and daring' in the nineties:

There . . . in that exuberant vista of gilding and crimson velvet set amongst all those opposing mirrors and upholding caryatids, with fumes of tobacco ever rising to the painted and pagan ceiling, and with the hum of presumably cynical conversation broken into sharply now and again by the clatter of dominoes shuffled on marble tables, I drew a deep breath and 'This indeed', I said to myself, 'is life?'[1]

For the price of a drink one could sit all day talking to friends, playing dominoes and planning the next artistic coup. Crème de menthe frappée – a sweet, sticky, green concoction sipped through a straw – had replaced the absinthe of the nineties as the favourite Café Royal drink. For those too poor to afford this there were tall glasses of mazagram, a coffee and milk mixture, or beer. As in its Continental counterparts, foreign and English newspapers and writing materials were provided. There was a constant bustle of activity as the waiters hurried by in their long white aprons and voices were raised in greeting and animated discussion.

Some of the original habitués such as Frank Harris, T. W. H. Crosland, George Moore and Lord Alfred Douglas were still frequent visitors. But in these pre-war days the acknowledged master of the Café Royal was Augustus John, the Bohemian artist *par excellence*. A tall, flamboyant figure with a flaming red beard and unruly hair, he affected a buccaneering gypsy style with his black cloak, wide-brimmed hat, bright neckerchief and gold earrings. Such was his reputation that the students from the Slade would stand up in silent homage when he entered 'like a pirate king getting onto his quarterdeck'.[2] He would frequently be accompanied by his latest exotically dressed model and by artist friends such as Epstein and the landscape painter James Dickson Innes, who was himself an arresting sight with his cadaverous features set off by a Quaker hat, silk scarf, long black overcoat and gold-topped ebony cane. John was adored by his models and lionized by smart Society ladies, who according to Nina used to buy and frame the tablecloths he drew on. He was twelve years older than Nina and they became firm friends for life when they discovered that they had both been born in Tenby and shared the same dancing- and German-teacher. If not drinking his favourite hock and seltzer, John was known to demolish a bottle of brandy with little apparent effect and it was said that he had the drinks while his friends had the headaches. More affluent than most because of his early success, he invariably paid the bill and was very generous to younger artists. Belonging to no particular group, he had a foot in all camps and would sometimes join Sickert when he was holding court to his Fitzroy Street associates. With his habitual talent for witty *bons mots*, Sickert described art schools as 'places which serve as a kind of day-nursery, with prospects of promotion to the Café Royal'.[3]

George Moore and Lord Alfred Douglas in the Café Royal, 1915

Certainly the Café Royal acted as a powerful magnet to younger painters eager to rub shoulders with the artistic great of the day. Bloomsbury was always well represented there and Roger Fry was often to be found expounding his latest theories. The fact that his second Post-Impressionist exhibition, held at the Grafton Galleries from October to December 1912, contained work by English artists as well as Russian and French was ample testimony to the influence of the earlier show.* Yet ironically, by the time of this second exhibition, Post-Impressionism was already somewhat *vieux jeu*. In March 1912 there had been a · show of Italian Futurists at the Sackville Gallery and younger artists were eagerly discovering Cubism and Futurism. The fiery, combative Wyndham Lewis jealously guarded his position as leader of those young Slade-trained painters moving towards abstraction, such as the flame-haired and bearded David Bomberg; William Roberts; the volatile C. R. W. Nevinson, nicknamed 'Bucknigger' because of his bulging forehead, flat nose and crinkly hair; and Edward Wadsworth, who cut a dash with his large bow ties, waisted coats, and matching peacock-blue handkerchiefs and socks.

The theorists and exponents of the avant-garde were to be found grouped around the table of A. R. Orage, the tough-looking, plain-speaking Yorkshire editor of the Socialist *New Age*. One of the liveliest intellectual weeklies in London, it printed articles on Picasso, reproduced Cubist works, and published the full text of Marinetti's *Futurist Manifesto*. Regular contributors included Richard Aldington, Ezra Pound, Katherine Mansfield, Beatrice Hastings and the influential poet, mathematician and philosopher T. E. Hulme.

One of the Café's most notorious characters was the loudly whooping, fiery Anglo-Irish practical joker Horace de Vere Cole. He was a good-looking, wealthy old Etonian of aristocratic bearing whose appearance was distinguished by his mane of abundant hair and upswept moustaches. Excessively vain and self-assured himself, he claimed that his elaborately plotted practical jokes were designed to puncture pomposity. In inimitable style he dared all, operating on a grand scale with great panache. Luck always seemed to be on his side and, however outrageous his exploits, he got away with them. One of his best-known jokes at the expense of the Admiralty took place in 1910, when he and a group of supporters, which somewhat improbably included Duncan Grant, Adrian Stephen and his sister Virginia (later Woolf), impersonated the Emperor of Abyssinia and his entourage. Sending a faked telegram from the Foreign Office to announce their supposedly official visit, they were royally entertained and

* Apart from works by Fry himself, the English section included paintings by Vanessa Bell, Duncan Grant, Frederick and Jessie Etchells, Bernard Adeney, Wyndham Lewis, Spencer Gore, Stanley Spencer and Henry Lamb, as well as sculpture by Eric Gill.

shown over the warship *HMS Dreadnought* at Weymouth. This widely publicized prank was greeted by public hilarity and official fury, and led to embarrassed questions about naval security being raised in Parliament. On another occasion, Cole displayed his fine taste for the absurd by inviting a number of people whose name ended in 'bottom' — Ramsbottom, Winterbottom, and so on — to a banquet, where they were loudly and solemnly announced by a major domo before being served with the inevitable rump steak. Not surprisingly, Cole was far from universally liked and admired, and some considered him a tiresome old bore. Indeed, there was an unpleasant side to his character and he was a dangerous person to offend. If his vanity was wounded he could be malicious and belligerent, lashing out with fists and tongue.

The Café Royal still had its share of exquisites and aesthetes who carried on the tradition of the nineties. Foremost amongst these was the wealthy young writer Ronald Firbank, soon to become known as the author of stylishly inconsequential novels such as *Valmouth* and *Caprice*. Tall and thin with a fine face and aquiline features, he was the self-nominated 'ballerina' of literature. Very shy and nervous, he usually sat alone, his long, pale hands constantly fluttering to adjust his tie or smooth his hair. An alleged affliction of the throat prevented him eating more than the bare minimum, although he was capable of consuming prodigious quantities of champagne. On one occasion, at a dinner given in his honour, he distinguished himself by eating nothing but a single green pea. He was so highly strung that the intolerable effort required by speech shook his whole delicate frame and he rarely finished a sentence, often being convulsed by fits of high-pitched giggles which he was powerless to control. Wyndham Lewis characterized his manner as that of 'a talking gazelle afflicted with some nervous disorder'.[4] When not alone Firbank was usually accompanied by the young aristocrat Evan Morgan, who dabbled in painting, poetry and music. The son and heir of Lord Tredegar, Morgan would entertain friends at his family seat in Wales with displays of boxing against his pet kangaroo. When Firbank first met Morgan he whispered to him that his name was Rameses and insisted on taking him to the British Museum to show him his likeness. They subsequently became what Morgan euphemistically termed 'fairly close acquaintances',[5] adding that he considered Firbank 'as one might some rare bird to be cherished for its exquisite exotic qualities, rather than as a human being'.[6]

The equally arresting Allan Odle, with his half-inch long fingernails with which he was said to draw, would sit for hours discussing literature with the young Armenian writer Dikram Kouyoumdjian, who as Michael Arlen became one of the most famous and fashionable novelists of the twenties. They were often joined by the painter Adrian Allinson, a lively and high-spirited young man of private means who liked to dress the part of an early Victorian Bohemian artist, complete with side whiskers, a black jacket, checked trousers, frilled shirt and stock. Rather incongruously he rode everywhere on a motor cycle. He had been at the Slade with Mark Gertler, who was already making a name for himself with his pictures of Jewish immigrant life in the crowded East End slums. Small and slight, with thick curly hair and delicately chiselled features, Gertler had a surprisingly robust good humour and was an amusing raconteur and mimic. He invited Nina to tea and she was one of the first people to make the pilgrimage to Bishopsgate, where Gertler lived with his parents. It seemed like a foreign country to Nina, teeming with Russian, Polish and central European Jews, very few of whom spoke English. Although Gertler was sensitive to his humble origins, this element of otherness, of belonging to a richly alien culture, only added to his considerable attractiveness. He was madly and unhappily in love with Carrington, one of the most talented of the Slade girls. Self-possessed, with a thick thatch of short fair hair cropped to frame her face, wearing one red shoe and one blue, Carrington drew attention to herself wherever she went. She was often to be seen at the Café Royal with friends from the Slade such as the Hon. Dorothy Brett, Barbara Hiles and Faith Bagenal.

The women who frequented the Café Royal were just as strongly individual as the men. Nina became friends with the tall and striking poet Anna Wickham, who was large and free in manner and appearance. Six years older than Nina, Anna's bitter personal conflict between the demands of domesticity and her compulsive need to write found expression in her passionate, witty, feminist-inspired poetry. When Nina had 'flu in 1913 Anna, with her generous motherly instincts, looked after her in her beautiful house in Downshire Hill, Hampstead. D. H. Lawrence, his wife Frieda and Katherine Mansfield were frequent visitors there and Lawrence spent hours talking and singing hymns with Anna in the drawing-room. But Nina, who was confined to bed with a high temperature, never met Lawrence, only catching a glimpse of him as he walked in the garden deep in discussion with Anna.

Although unaccompanied women were not allowed in the Café Royal, there was always a large floating population of artists' models who used the place as a labour exchange. These might include a diminutive girl who stood only four feet four inches, known as 'The Bug' or 'The Pocket Edition'; another called 'The Limpet', who fell in love with a different man every week; and the blonde ballet dancer Jessica Valda. There was sure to be a good sprinkling of John models, of whom the most beautiful was the passionate and impetuous Euphemia Lamb, with a pale oval face and heavy blonde hair. Bobby Channing was a famous Chelsea model of a more Mediterranean type whose quick temper earned her the nickname 'Puma'. For Philip Heseltine (the composer Peter Warlock) who regularly frequented the Café Royal and was inordinately devoted to cats, she was the perfect embodiment of feline beauty and he later married her.

Betty May, called the 'Tiger Woman' on account of her wild-cat temperament, was one of the Café's best-known models and personalities, immortalized in a fine sculpture by Epstein. Very small, with tiny hands and feet, a broad face, generous mouth and widely spaced green eyes, her sweet child-like appearance hid a toughly independent nature. She was completely unreliable, her spontaneous high spirits easily turning into a savage ferocity. She had been introduced to the Café at a very young age and in her own words, 'No duck ever took to water, no man to drink, as I to the Café Royal.'[7] Dressed in multi-coloured gypsy-style clothes to match her flamboyant character, she was never less than herself. Betty did just what she liked and delighted in shocking the proper sentiments of her more conventional admirers. On one notable occasion an elderly gentleman who was trying to educate her taste gave her extra-dry champagne. She took one sip and spat it out in disgust, ordering the astonished waiter to bring some sugar, which she then liberally mixed with her drink before downing it with relish. Many of the Café's habitués flirted with drugs out of curiosity or affectation, but it was more than a fashionable indulgence for Betty. She became seriously addicted for a time and her numerous admirers and friends, such as David Garnett and Duncan Grant, would be coerced into providing her with the cocaine which only exacerbated her naturally volatile temperament.

Lillian Shelley, another favourite Epstein model and singer with a dead-white face and black hair, was one of the leading female lights of the Café. Amid shouts of approval and roars of laughter she would leap on to one of the marble-topped tables and give a brazenly provocative rendering of the popular song 'Popsy Wopsy'. Taking off her large hat so that her hair tumbled around her neck, she accompanied her song with suggestive gestures and upward jerks of her hatpin, to the delight of the assembled crowd.

Just before the outbreak of the First World War, the young Nancy Cunard, strikingly tall, thin and elegant with short dark hair and piercing blue eyes, took to going to the Café Royal with the small, fair Iris Tree. In open rebellion from smart Society, their lavish use of cosmetics was daring at a time when the only painted ladies were prostitutes. They were a startling sight with their faces powdered chalk white, lips rouged scarlet, and dark, kohl-rimmed eyes. Iris, the youngest daughter of the famous actor-manager Sir Herbert Beerbohm Tree, was studying painting at the Slade; while Nancy had serious literary ambitions and wrote poetry. They rented a chaotic studio together in Fitzroy Place at the top of Charlotte Street, where they could escape to meet their friends, work and do as they pleased. They were often joined by the dazzlingly beautiful Lady Diana Manners (later Duff Cooper), third daughter of the Duke of Rutland, who was always surrounded by a crowd of admirers. She also studied painting at the Slade, arousing the curiosity of her fellow students by appearing late to class one morning wearing a *décolleté* red velvet evening dress, which gave rise to speculations that she had been out all night and had not gone home to bed.

Far from being mutually exclusive, all these different groups of people overlapped and intermingled. Everyone knew everyone else and there was a continual coming and going from table to table. The Café Royal, affectionately referred to as 'the hot-air cupboard' and the 'home of lost causeries',[8] was the most famous artistic club in London, a democracy of talent and sartorial extravagance. There was even a Café Royal drinking-song, rendered to the tune of 'Greensleaves':

Jove be with us as we sit
On the crimson soft settees;
Drinking beer and liking it,
Most peculiarly at ease.[9]

For those unwilling to go home to bed, the fun might continue all night at the Cabaret Club, known as the Cave of the Golden Calf, which was just round the corner in a basement beneath a cloth merchant's in Heddon Street, off Regent Street. It was opened in June 1912 by the Austrian Mme Frida Strindberg, the redoubtable second wife of the Swedish dramatist. According to the rhetorical wording of its brochure, the Cabaret Club was dedicated to 'gaiety, to a gaiety stimulating thought rather than crushing it . . . a gaiety that does not have to count with midnight'.[10] With an unerring instinct for talent, Mme Strindberg had commissioned Wyndham Lewis, Charles Ginner, Spencer Gore, Epstein and Eric Gill to decorate the club, which was the first of its kind in London offering a late-night venue for good food and drink, a cabaret and dancing. Mme Strindberg wanted something daringly modern, a place where conventional inhibitions and restraints could be cast aside. With this aim in mind, the décor, which was supervised by Gore, evoked the primitive and the savage. The low-ceilinged central room was supported by two massive totemic iron pillars of a barbaric intensity. Epstein had surrounded them with painted plaster sculptures lurid with scarlet details, incorporating human figures and heads of hawks, cats and camels. Lewis's design for the drop curtain, Ginner's three murals *Tiger-Hunting*, *Birds and Indians* and *Chasing Monkeys*, and Gore's *Deerhunting* combined primitive nude figures and wild animals in scenes of hunting and worship set in exotic tropical or jungle locations. The ritualistic aspect was emphasized by the free-standing gilded calf sculpted by Eric Gill which stood in the centre of the room, while a further painted relief of the golden calf was placed near the entrance to the club. Lewis's designs for the poster and programmes depicted aggressively abstracted figures dancing in positions of provocative sexual abandonment suggestive of the delights in store for members.

The club provided the setting for the most unlikely encounters. Its clientele was a mixture of impoverished artists, writers, actors and musicians, wealthy socialites, guardsmen and stockbrokers. Mme Strindberg encouraged impecunious artists by waiving the annual membership subscription of five guineas for those she liked personally, and a number of well-known artistic and theatrical luminaries such as Augustus John were made honorary members. Swathed in furs, with her chalk-white face and foreign accent, Mme Strindberg was always present to greet her clients – or not to greet them. Ezra Pound was delighted to witness her 'wave a customer away from her table saying as she did so that sleep with him she would, but talk to him, never; "One must draw the line *somewhere*." '[11]

Nina adored the Cave of the Golden Calf, finding it agreeably gay and cheerful. She went there one evening with the talented and wealthy young Slade student Alvaro Guevara. He was known as 'Chili' after his country of origin, and Nina was attracted by his athletic build and Latin good looks. Seated under the painted rafters on bentwood chairs at round tables covered with white cloths, the audience ate and drank while they watched a cosmopolitan cabaret which was billed to include 'the picturesque dances of the South, its fervid melodies, Parisian wit, English humour'.[12] The entertainments ranged from traditional folk songs and dances to the latest avant-garde experiments. In a single evening the programme might encompass 'Veil dances, Jester Songs, Breton Wakes, "Playing with Fire", Margaret Morris with her Greek Children Dancers, shadow-plays written and performed by Ford Madox Ford, "Exultations" and Russian stories recounted "in a very melodramatic fashion" by Frank Harris'.[13] The Italian Marinetti, all gold chains, diamond rings and gleaming white teeth, was the star attraction of November 1913 when he declaimed his Futurist concoctions with great force, vigorously accompanied by drums and loud noises from his band of 'cacophonists' and 'gluglutineurs'. Betty May regularly danced and sang songs such as 'The Raggle-Taggle Gipsies', 'Sigh No More Ladies' and 'Bonnie Earl O'Murray'; while Lillian Shelley performed her ever-popular versions of 'Popsy Wopsy' and 'You Made Me Love You'. Every evening at ten-thirty it was her special task to feed Mme Strindberg's pet monkeys, which were kept in her suite at the Savoy Hotel.

As the hour grew later, the tempo quickened and the atmosphere became more frenetic. An impassioned gypsy orchestra led by a frenzied Hungarian fiddler provided the music. Clients danced the Turkey Trot and the Bunny Hug into the early hours. Many years later, Osbert Sitwell vividly remembered how 'This low-ceilinged night-club, appropriately sunk below the pavement . . .

and hideously but relevantly frescoed . . . appeared in the small hours to be a super-heated Vorticist garden of gesticulating figures, dancing and talking, while the rhythm of the primitive forms of ragtime throbbed through the wide room.'[14]

The club's novelty and the excellence of its cuisine ensured that it was an instant success, and the artists were soon completely outnumbered by more worldly revellers. But the fun proved all too short-lived. In 1913 the club was raided by the police for breaking the law by asking non-members to pay for their food and drink. This was effectively its death-blow. Mme Strindberg was no business-woman and was heavily in debt; the liquidation sale took place in February 1914.

An alternative late-night meeting-place was provided by the Crabtree Club, which Augustus John helped to found in April 1914 with William Orpen, William Marchant of the Goupil Gallery and Lord Howard de Walden. To cater primarily for the purses of poor artists, poets and musicians, drink and cigarettes were cheap and a tax of one shilling was levied on those visitors ostentatious enough to appear in evening dress. The several bare rooms above a shop in Greek Street were sparsely furnished with deal tables and chairs. Apart from dinner, bread and cheese and beer could be had at any time. There were no waiters, everybody helped themselves, often just leaving their money at the counter if there was no one there to take it. The members were a mixture of artists and their models, actresses and dancers from the West End theatres, quantities of students from the Slade and South Kensington, Fleet Street journalists and seedy aristocrats. People sat and talked or danced and the members organized performances of modern music and poetry on the small stage. Lillian Shelley and Betty May were always very much in demand, dancing and singing to Carlo Norway's guitar.

As the night grew wilder there was a tendency for things to degenerate. Betty May, dressed in calico trousers and a red sash like a performing monkey, would swarm up a pole which reached to the ceiling to escape from some pursuer on whom she had played a prank. Fighting was often not confined to boxing matches, and disputes on artistic matters were frequently settled with the fist rather than native wit. But the combatants would quickly find themselves ushered to the stair head, where they were speedily propelled down the four steep flights of narrow wooden stairs to the landing below. The Crabtree never enjoyed the same popularity as the Cave of the Golden Calf. Nina claimed to have been there only once and Gertler deemed it 'just an inferior cabaret'.[15] Paul Nash was even more scathing in his criticism, describing it as 'A most disgusting place . . . where only the very lowest city Jews and the most pinched harlots attend. A place of utter coarseness and dull unrelieved monotony. John alone, a great pathetic muzzy god, a sort of Silenus – but alas no nymphs, satyrs and leopards to complete the picture.'[16]

Nina was a vivid figure, often seen in these haunts of artists and amateurs, on terms of friendship and easy badinage with her fellow painters and their models. But she was not content to be just an agreeable addition to the company. She wanted to be an artist among artists, accepted as a comrade in arms. To that end she was working hard in the solitude of her studio to assimilate the new ideas, to define her artistic aims and to discover her own personal style.

5

La Fillette

NINA showed her work for the first time in London in July 1913 at the annual exhibition of the Allied Artists' Association held at the Royal Albert Hall. The AAA, which was modelled on the Paris Salon des Indépendents, had been founded in 1908 by the critic Frank Rutter with the enthusiastic support of Sickert, and gave many young artists their first opportunity to exhibit. There was no jury, every subscriber being entitled to show three works. The allotment of wall space and the order of catalogue entries were decided by ballot and all members were eligible to serve on the hanging committee. Inevitably, the unwieldy size and arrangement of the exhibitions meant that good work tended to be swamped in a sea of mediocrity and it was difficult to discern any coherent artistic tendencies, but when one of the founder members had proposed that the best pictures by the better-known artists should be prominently displayed, Sickert retorted, 'In this society there are no good works or bad works: there are only works by shareholders.'[1]

Nina's three pictures were hung together in a group upstairs. She showed portraits of Crowley's 'Dead Soul' Ethel Archer; of John Alford; and of Dilys, a young girl whom Nina had noticed sitting opposite her on the tube one day. Her round, innocent face had reminded Nina of a painting by Ghirlandaio in the National Gallery and she persuaded the girl to pose for her. The resulting portrait had a rather studied seriousness in its rigidity of composition and sombreness of tone. The solidity of the girl's figure and the details of her clothing – the lace cuffs and demure brooch at the neck – emphasized her respectability. Dilys is the dutiful daughter that Nina refused to be. The painting was shown again later that year with the New English Art Club.

Another young artist exhibiting for the first time was the twenty-one-year-old Frenchman Henri Gaudier-Brzeska, who showed a group of five sculptures. Nina had already seen his line drawings in Middleton Murry's magazine *Rhythm*

Torso of Nina, 1913, by Henri Gaudier-Brzeska

and often studied his work on her frequent visits to the Albert Hall. She particularly liked a compact modelled figure of a wrestler which exuded a primitive force and strength. Gaudier could not help noticing that every time he went to the show Nina would be there, gazing at his wrestler, and he and his 'sister' Sophie called her 'La Fillette'. Nina was too shy to introduce herself or to tell Gaudier how much she admired his work, but she was delighted when she saw him looking at her paintings and determined to find a way of meeting him.

An opportunity presented itself when an elderly lady asked Nina if she could recommend a sculptor to give her lessons for half-a-crown an hour. Nina knew that Gaudier sometimes left work for sale at Dan Rider's bookshop in the Charing Cross Road, which was a favourite meeting-place for artists and writers, and she made enquiries about him there. Rider told her that Gaudier would welcome the chance to make some extra money, and Nina wrote to him proposing the lessons.

They met at the bookshop and talked and talked. Nina was completely captivated by Gaudier's playful gaiety and quick, darting intelligence. He was small and slight, with dark, wispy hair, a beard, and intense piercing eyes. Desperately poor, always dirty and dressed in tattered clothes, he was the archetypal Bohemian artist and had a contemptuous disdain for money and the *sales bourgeois*. His close friend, the Australian painter Horace Brodzky, described Gaudier as 'a faun, a clown and a demon for work'.[2] He had been living in England for the past two and a half years and was employed as a foreign correspondence clerk with a shipping firm in the City, rising early in the morning and working until late at night on his sculpture. His meagre wage barely paid for food and rent, let alone providing materials for sculpture, and he was dependent on Sophie's savings for survival. He was experimenting with a variety of styles ranging from the Rodinesque to the ancient and primitive, and he spent a great deal of time studying and drawing in the British Museum. After a lonely and difficult first year in London, he was beginning to find his feet. Friends and supporters included the collector Edward Marsh as well as writers and artists such as Haldane Macfall, Lovat Fraser, Frank Harris, Enid Bagnold, John Cournos, Alfred Wolmark, Epstein and Gertler. But Gaudier was not an easy person to help. Ruthlessly dedicated to his work, he was proud and highly strung. He could be charmingly gentle and whimsical, but at other times he was overweeningly cocksure, ungratefully pouring scorn and abuse on those closest to him.

Gaudier found Nina attractive, lively, amusing and intelligent. She laughingly admitted at their first meeting that she had no pretensions to being what she called 'a pure woman'[3] and Gaudier admired her direct, open manner. The attraction between them was instant and mutual and they saw each other

Gaudier-Brzeska, 1915,
by Roald Kristian (Edgar
de Bergen)

frequently. Gaudier often went to Nina's rooms in Grafton Street, where they talked and cooked spaghetti together, and she visited him once or twice a week in his cold and dirty studio in the Fulham Road. Bare and comfortless, it was full of stone dust and sparsely furnished with two work-benches, a table, some kitchen chairs and a canvas deckchair in which he sometimes slept. Nina's visits caused violent arguments betweeen Gaudier and Sophie, because he would ask Sophie for money to buy cakes for tea or food for supper, which she angrily refused.

Gaudier had not been as frank with Nina as she had with him and had not told her that Sophie was not his sister, as they pretended. He had met the Polish Sophie Brzeska in 1910 at the Ste Geneviève Library in Paris where he was studying anatomy and she languages. Sophie was just as convinced of her own artistic greatness as Gaudier was of his, and was engaged in writing a three-volume autobiographical novel. Twenty years older than him, she was small and gaunt and always dressed in curiously old-fashioned clothes. After a life of hardship and disillusion, she was broken down, ill and nervous. Poverty and loneliness drew them together and however outwardly incongruous their friendship might seem, the bond between them ran deep. The adoption of each other's name symbolized their union, but Sophie always insisted that Gaudier was her 'son' and refused to become his mistress. The harshness of their life together, their intolerably noisy rooms and biting poverty, added an extra strain to their relationship, which was fraught with violent conflict and arguments, and just as passionate reconciliations. Sophie was Gaudier's constant moral and financial support, and sacrificed her own work to look after him, adopting the uncongenial and thankless role of careful housekeeper and husbander of their meagre resources.

There was undoubtedly an alarming quality about Sophie which anticipated her later madness. As highly strung, volcanic and fiery in temperament as Gaudier, she was hypersensitive, suspicious and resentful, with a talent for offending and irritating people. In company Sophie easily became too intense and excited, overwhelming her listener with her sudden outbursts of enthusiasm. Starved of affection, she would pour out her heart in response to the least kindness, only to be bitterly disappointed when her proffered intimacy was rebuffed. Many people who admired Gaudier, such as Katherine Mansfield and Middleton Murry, could not tolerate her. Yet Gaudier was fiercely loyal and would rather abandon a friendship than accept any slight to Sophie, however much he may have publicly humiliated her himself.

Ferociously jealous and possessive, Sophie watched the developing friendship between Gaudier and Nina with mounting disquiet. Trying desperately not to reveal her fears to Gaudier, she gave free rein to them in her diary. When Gaudier told her how different Nina was from the other English people they knew and despised, that she was not at all prudish or hypocritical and had agreed to pose for him, she remarked with feigned indifference:

'Perhaps she wants to seduce you?', to which he replied brutally, 'Well, why not? I intend to make love with her! You're useless, you make me wait too long.'
'Very well, I give you my blessing . . . if that's what you want.'
'You can hide behind a screen to watch us.'
'I could ask for nothing more, that would amuse me.'
'Won't you be jealous?'
'I've told you a hundred times that since I can't give you what you want I am not so selfish as to try and stop you finding it elsewhere.'
'You will always be my favourite. She will only be a concubine.'[4]

Such taunting words were hardly consoling to Sophie, and her unease grew as Gaudier talked more and more about 'My Nina' and how much he liked her, even telling her that he thought Nina was in love with him. The arguments between them became increasingly bitter and Gaudier took to leaving their rooms early in the morning and not returning until late at night.

Sophie's fears were no doubt well founded. Although Nina had demurred when Gaudier asked her to pose for him, saying that she might look awful with nothing on, she knew that the opposite was the case and used the opportunity to show herself off to full advantage, slowly turning round while he made many drawings. Gaudier duly admired her and there is no reason to suppose that he resisted her flattering attentions. As much as anything, he was attracted by the fact that Nina was herself a talented and independent artist, and he did not treat her just as a model. When he had finished drawing, he took off his own clothes, struck a pose, and said, 'Now it is your turn to work.'[5] Nina did three sketches before they had tea.

Sketch of Gaudier-Brzeska, 1913

Gaudier's appreciation of Nina's physical beauty found tangible expression in two exquisite marble torsos. He also modelled another in clay from which two plaster casts were taken, one with a damaged left breast; both were later cast in bronze. The naturalism of these works differs radically from the style of his other sculptures of this time and he claimed that he had done them to show his accomplishment as a sculptor. Whatever he may have said, they are more than academic exercises in the Greek style and have a peculiarly intimate quality. They are not simply idealized female torsos but subtle, highly sensuous transformations of flesh into marble with a great delicacy and purity of form. When Gaudier showed Brodzky one of the marble torsos he was astonished by its uncharacteristic sweetness and suavity: 'The sight of such work from such an uncouth savage forced me to cry, ''What the devil did you do *that* for?'' His smiling reply was that he had been to the Museum and seen similar work, and that he could not but help doing what he had shown me.'[6] Nina also posed for a figure of a nude dancer with her arms raised above her head. Slightly elongated in style, it has a Rodinesque quality in its modelling and admirably captures a sense of rhythmic movement.

Nina not only posed for Gaudier but also helped him find the stone he needed to carve. In October 1913 he moved to a new studio under the railway arches in Putney. Although cheaper, it was even more uncomfortable and colder than his Fulham Road studio. Trains ran overhead at frequent intervals and with its bare, concrete floor it was difficult to heat. Here Gaudier often slept on a folding iron bed, proof of his conviction that artists should be indifferent to physical discomfort. His neighbour, a genial academic sculptor called Fabrucci who made his living carving monuments and doing ornamental work, generously gave Gaudier small pieces of stone, and he scavenged wherever he could for materials. He and Nina often wandered around stonemason's yards where tombstones were displayed, in the hope of finding odd bits of stone within easy reach of the railings. On one such occasion they discovered a promising piece of marble and arranged to meet at ten-thirty that night. Nina stood guard while Gaudier stole the marble from which he carved the first torso of her, now in the Tate Gallery.

Gaudier said little about his life with Sophie and Nina did not question him closely. Sophie, however, was very curious to meet Nina and Gaudier took her home unexpectedly one evening. He could not have chosen a worse moment. Sophie had barely recovered from 'flu and was sitting facing the wall so as not to see the squalor of the room. Having heard so much about Nina she was predictably scathing in her comments, deeming her ungainly and common-looking and declaring incredulously, 'Is *this* the young girl who is supposed to be so brilliant and perfect in every way?'[7] Nevertheless, she was eager to find out more about her and invited her to Sunday lunch the following day.

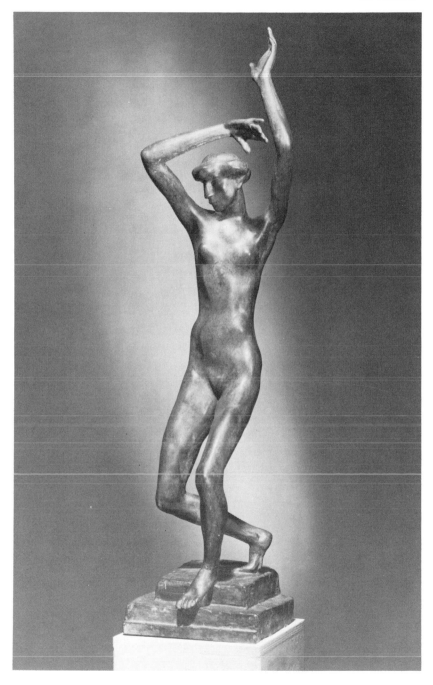

The Dancer, 1913, by Henri Gaudier-Brzeska

Sophie was no more charitable on Nina's next visit and took evident pleasure in reporting that, 'She wore a torn and dirty silk blouse. Her hands were filthy and she continuously ran her fingers through her unwashed short hair as if she were searching for fleas.'[8] She made no attempt to put Nina at her ease and she and Gaudier quarrelled violently throughout the meal. Sophie warned Nina not to get the mistaken idea from their behaviour that they hated each other: 'You see – he is a brute and I am not at all submissive or meek.'[9] Nina did her best to humour Sophie and sat down beside her to discuss books; Sophie grudgingly admitted that she was very well read. Gaudier soon got bored with the literary turn of the conversation and impatiently demanded that Nina should go with him to the British Museum, but Nina diplomatically refused, saying that she preferred to stay and talk with Sophie until it was time for her to go to tea with her aunt. When Gaudier scoffed at her for being bourgeois, Nina admitted that she hated these visits to her aunt, who was rich and lectured all the family, but she had to endure them because she gave her half-a-crown a week. 'What else can I do?' she shrugged. 'I don't earn enough. One has got to eat.'[10]

Despite all her jibes against Nina, Sophie was desperately seeking a kindred spirit and after Gaudier left she tried hard to make Nina like her, talking intently about herself and her ideas. When the conversation turned to the subject of women, Nina declared that she thought women were just as intelligent and more interesting than men, and that she would not exchange any of her close women friends for a man. She went on to mention a friend who was a very talented musician, and was astonished and rather alarmed at the excessive reaction this provoked in Sophie, who suddenly burst into rapturous ecstasies, proclaiming her readiness to kneel and kiss the hands of someone who could play so well and touch the chords of her soul. Sophie accompanied Nina to the bus stop and they parted with cordial smiles and handshakes, but Sophie regretted having opened her heart to Nina, whom she dismissed as typically English, cold and superficial, and suspected of disguising her real feelings in order to ensnare Gaudier. She concluded, no doubt rightly, that she was sure Nina was sorry she had not left with Gaudier.

Their return visit to Nina was even less successful. Nina had plainly invited them from a sense of social obligation rather than in any anticipation of pleasure, and Sophie was determined to find fault. The visit started badly. It was a rainy day and they were soaking wet when they arrived after tea with Gertler. Sophie showed little enthusiasm for Nina's paintings, disliking their dark tones – 'as if black was the cheapest colour you could buy'[11] – and managed to annoy both Nina and Gaudier by tactlessly remarking that one of her drawings was in Gaudier's style. When Nina hotly denied having imitated him, declaring that she had done the drawing a year ago from an idea she had had in the British Museum,

Sophie made things worse by suggesting that Gaudier must have been influenced by Nina.

Unknown to Nina, who usually went home to dinner or ate out, Sophie assumed that they were asked for a meal, and made a considerable grievance out of the ensuing misunderstanding. As they sat and talked by the fire, Nina kept going to the window to see if the rain had stopped. But it continued to pour and she asked them what they wanted to do and whether they were hungry, saying that she had intended to take them out to dinner. Sophie, who had a bad cold, said that she wanted to wait until her shoes were dry and that she was ravenous, rapidly devouring the bag of biscuits which Nina proffered. Since Sophie insisted on staying, Nina was forced reluctantly to offer them the meagre contents of her cupboard: spaghetti, some old cheese and tomatoes, and a bit of bread. She went out to buy some butter, leaving Gaudier to cook the spaghetti and exchange angry words with Sophie, who was bursting with indignation at Nina's supposed lack of hospitality. Sophie chronicled with self-righteous disgust how Nina placed the bread on the dirty table on which models posed without first spreading a cloth, served them half-cooked spaghetti on half-washed plates, and gave her a fork which still bore traces of the previous meal. Even if Sophie did have to swallow her food with her eyes shut, she derived a certain perverse pleasure from the visit. On the way home she had the satisfaction of delivering a moralizing sermon to Gaudier on the subject of physical dirt going hand in hand with moral dirt.

Gaudier was evidently not so concerned about Nina's moral shortcomings and they continued to see each other regularly, spending every Sunday afternoon together. They would go for walks and buy chestnuts to roast back in his studio, where he made drawings of her. Gaudier encouraged Nina to work and they sometimes went to an evening sketch class in Chelsea. The ease and fluidity of Nina's line drawing, its pared-down simplification of form, clearly owes much to Gaudier and he had a lasting beneficial influence on her style. He also introduced her to new ideas. Politically, Gaudier sympathized with anarchists, and took Nina to one of their meetings in Soho, which were held in a different language each week. This time it was in German and Gaudier translated for her. Although Nina knew almost nothing about anarchy – or politics of any sort – she was a natural rebel and fired with enthusiasm by what she heard. To Nina, revolt against anything seemed good. Revolt was all.

Meeting Nina had done nothing to relieve Sophie's jealous fears, and she tried to disguise her insecurity and sense of inferiority with an overdeveloped moral superiority. Whenever Nina came to visit them at their rooms in Putney she would listen with clenched teeth as Nina chattered exuberantly about art and mutual acquaintances. Sophie detested Nina's confident, very British manner and habit of exclaiming, 'Oh I say – this is ripping,' or 'That's rather nice,'[12] in admiration of Gaudier's work. One day, when Nina sold six of Gaudier's drawings to a friend for a pound each, he told her to tell Sophie that only five had been bought so that they could enjoy themselves with the rest of the money. During the meal of overdone steak and burnt potatoes – prepared by Gaudier as Sophie refused to cook for Nina – there was the usual violent row and Sophie angrily told Gaudier that he bored her and should take Nina out for a drink. They went to the Swiss pub in Soho and after a few beers Gaudier finally confessed that Sophie was not really his sister. Nina choked back her tears and came to the pragmatic conclusion that it made no difference, as Sophie did not seem to mind her seeing Gaudier but in fact rather encouraged it.

Nina, 1913–14, by Henri Gaudier-Brzeska

6

The Omega Workshops

I<small>T</small> was through Nina that Gaudier met Roger Fry. To supplement the allowance that her aunts gave her, Nina earned thirty shillings a week doing decorative work at the Omega Workshops in Fitzroy Street. When Fry opened the Omega in June 1913 he had had two aims: to provide employment and a living wage for young artists, and to apply Post-Impressionist principles to interior design. He wanted to sweep away the solid respectability and grave decorum which prevailed in Bird's Custard Island, as Fry called Britain. He told a journalist that, 'It is time . . . that the spirit of fun was introduced into furniture and into fabrics. We have suffered too long from the dull and the stupidly serious.'[1]

Duncan Grant and Vanessa Bell joined Fry as the other artist-directors of the Omega. Nina only started working there in the autumn after the much publicized departure of Wyndham Lewis, Cuthbert Hamilton, Edward Wadsworth and Frederick Etchells over an argument about a commission to decorate a room for the Ideal Home Exhibition. The affair caused much public mud-slinging and Lewis circulated a round robin in which he challenged Fry's position as leader of the avant-garde, scathingly dismissing the Omega as reactionary: 'The Idol is still Prettiness, with its mid-Victorian languish of the neck, and its skin of "greenery yallery", despite the Post-What-Not fashionableness of its draperies.'[2]

Recruitment to the Omega was haphazard. Nina described how, feeling brave one morning, she went along to Fitzroy Street and asked to see Fry. He said she could start work the following day, when she was taught how to do batiks. David Bomberg, William Roberts, Mark Gertler and Paul Nash were all associated with the Omega for varying periods and there was a floating population of young female helpers such as Barbara Hiles, Gladys Hynes and Winifred Gill, christened 'Cropheads' by Virginia Woolf. The artists, who worked upstairs in a studio above the showrooms, were only supposed to be at the Omega for three half-days a week so as not to interfere with their own work.

The Omega accepted commissions for complete interiors, mural paintings and mosaics, but when there was no particular order to fulfil the artists were encouraged to produce decorative designs with no special function in mind. All the work was done anonymously, the drawings being placed in a portfolio for the customer to choose from. The selected design would then be applied to whatever was required – rugs, furniture, screens, textiles, dress materials, fans, pottery, candlesticks, boxes, lampshades. The skilled jobs such as furniture-making, marquetry and textile-weaving were done by expert craftsmen. Even so there were constant complaints, particularly in the early stages, about the poor quality of Omega goods. Lewis commented justly that

> with no preliminary workshop training it was idle to suppose that half a dozen artists could cope with all – or indeed any – of the problems of waxing, lacquering, polishing and varnishing of furniture . . . or the hand-painting of textiles which the plan involved. Naturally the chairs we sold stuck to the seats of people's trousers; when they took up an Omega candlestick they could not put it down again, they held it in an involuntary vice-like grip. It was glued to them and they to it.[3]

Fry considered this lack of professional finish a positive recommendation and the very thing which differentiated Omega products from dull, machine-made goods. He stated in his preface to the Omega catalogue that the Workshops consisted of

> a group of artists who are working with the object of allowing free play to the delight in creation in the making of objects for common life. They refuse to spoil the expressive quality of their work by sand-papering it down to shop finish, in the belief that the public has at last seen through the humbug of the machine-made imitation of works of art.[4]

It is not without significance that Fry added that, 'The artist is the man who creates not only for need but for joy',[5] for his philosophy seems only to have applied to the male artists in his employ. Apart from Vanessa Bell, who as a director played an important part at the Omega, the women were engaged only in a secondary capacity, to translate the designs executed by the male artists on to fabrics, furniture, lampshades, and so on. Their main qualification for employment, in addition to their manual dexterity, seems to have been that Fry liked them and felt that he could influence them. Winifred Gill, Fry's chief help and mainstay of the Omega, commented, 'I seem to remember spending a long time painting the legs of tables . . . Trays, too, we painted . . . and endless

Nina (left) and Winifred Gill modelling clothes at the Omega Workshops

candlesticks, for electric lights. When I remember Nina Hamnett at work it is always a candlestick she has in her hand.'[6] Although skilled and painstaking, the women's work could hardly be described as creative.

But it was not all menial drudgery. A photograph shows Nina and Winifred Gill modelling Omega-designed clothes for a press preview. Nina stands with her back to the camera in a cheerfully flamboyant pose, blithely indifferent to the somewhat comic effect produced by wearing a delicate, oyster-coloured satin evening cloak painted by Doucet in greens and browns over her heavy walking shoes.

Nina never took any great pleasure in decorative work and felt that she had little talent for it. But she enjoyed the company, needed the money, and liked being at the centre of a new and daring enterprise. Apart from Fry's Bloomsbury friends such as Virginia Woolf, Maynard Keynes, and Lytton Strachey, there was a constant stream of literary and artistic visitors to the Omega, including G. B. Shaw, W. B. Yeats, H. G. Wells, Arnold Bennett, Sickert – who characteristically ordered an Omega chamberpot – and Augustus John. Such was John's reputation as a womanizer that the young girl assistants were warned to ring for the caretaker's wife as soon as he appeared. Smart Society also responded well to the novelty of the Omega, and distinguished patrons included the German Ambassadress, Princess Lichnowsky; Lady Cunard; and Lady Ottoline Morrell.

Nina's high spirits and boisterous irreverence must have added greatly to the gaiety and liveliness of the Omega and gone some way to banishing any element of self-conscious preciousness. Winifred Gill was very fond of Nina and wrote later how much she

> admired her good nature and her transparent honesty. She was the most spontaneous person I ever came across. And she was a hard worker. She had a very simple nature and seemed to direct her life by a series of original maxims. Once when I bent down to examine a curious little beetle, Nina wiped it out with her foot. 'Always stamp on anything that crawls', she remarked; 'Wash yourself all over and you won't smell', was another.[7]

Nina took delight in shocking the more conventional Winifred, who had been brought up a strict Quaker, and never let the truth spoil the dramatic effect of her comments. One morning, after Winifred had finished serving a customer in the showroom and wondered aloud why all Nancy Cunard's set spoke in a snoring kind of voice, Nina offered the simple explanation that they were 'Drunk . . . dead drunk'[8] – even though it was only ten o'clock. Winifred was equally disconcerted when she asked her what was threatening the eyesight of a mutual acquaintance and Nina replied sinisterly – and groundlessly – 'Gonorrhea'.[9] A complete realist, Nina had already acquired a certain worldly-wise cynicism. On another occasion, Winifred rang up a client to say that a card-table she had ordered six days before was ready and a man replied in shocked tones that the lady in question had just died. Nina knew all about it and commented in her characteristically forthright manner, 'Well you did put your foot in it . . . That would have been her landlord, at least that is what he was called. She shot herself, the silly fool, any of her men would have lent her a couple of hundred pounds.'[10]

Not long after Nina joined the Omega, she introduced Gaudier to Fry.

Gaudier never actually worked at the Omega but left drawings and small sculptures to be sold on commission, appearing regularly to see if anything had been bought or to bring new things. He did various works for the Omega, including a design of wrestlers for a marquetry tray, an earthenware cat cast from a mould, and a vase in the form of a water-carrier. Gaudier was working on a commission for two large stone vases for Lady Hamilton's entrance hall when he left to fight in France. Two plaster maquettes remain, both variations on the theme of a caryatid supporting a bowl.

Despite the fact that he accepted this last commission, Gaudier's increasingly abstract tendencies led him away from the Omega to a closer identification with Lewis and his Vorticist followers, who established the Rebel Art Centre in March 1914 in direct opposition to Fry. Gaudier was one of the signatories of the new movement's vigorous mouthpiece *Blast*, which was first published in June 1914. Although Nina must have been instinctively attracted by this new clarion call to rebellion, she had nothing in common with the abstraction of Vorticism. She remained far closer to the Francophile Bloomsbury group, even though she never aspired to a Post-Impressionist liberation of colour in her own work.

Nina's artistic affiliations were made clear early in 1914 when she exhibited at the Alpine Gallery with the Friday Club and the Grafton Group. Vanessa Bell had founded the Friday Club in 1905 to allow young artists to meet and exchange ideas as well as show their work. But by 1913 it had become purely an exhibiting society and, as it was open to all, traditional painting was shown side by side with more adventurous work by artists such as John Nash, Wadsworth, Nevinson and Gertler. Dissatisfied with this lack of any dominant aesthetic, Fry, Vanessa Bell, Grant, Lewis and Etchells left to form the Grafton Group, which held its first exhibition in March 1913. Fry, however, still encouraged younger painters associated with the Omega to show with the Friday Club and Nina exhibited a *Girl's Head* and a *Portrait* in February 1914.

By the time of the second Grafton Group show in January 1914, Lewis and Etchells had parted company with the Omega and the Grafton Group closely reflected Fry's own aesthetic interests. Apart from Fry, Vanessa Bell and Duncan Grant, the other Omega exhibitors included Nina – who showed a *Head of a Girl* – Gaudier, Winifred Gill and William Roberts. There were also examples of applied art and design, as well as works by Picasso and Derain belonging to Fry, and by a group of French painters associated with Charles Vildrac's gallery in Paris: Chabaud, Doucet, Friesz, Marchand, Lhote and Vilette. Critics were quick to point out the extent to which the show represented Fry's taste. T. E. Hulme, writing in the *New Age*, commented that it had a 'typical Cambridge sort of atmosphere' and echoed Lewis's earlier remarks about the Omega when he dismissed the work as 'all amusing enough in its way, a sort of aesthetic playing about. It can even be described in fact as a new disguise for aestheticism.'[11] Nevertheless, sales were encouraging and Nina, who was secretary to the exhibition, was delighted to sell Gaudier's sculpture of a fawn for £15, excitedly jumping up from her table at the Café Royal to announce the news to him as he entered. After his initial pleasure Gaudier was irritated that Nina should make such a fuss in public – as if a few pounds mattered to him!

Nina's charms were evidently strong enough to attract even the most unlikely admirers. Lytton Strachey described how on his visit to the exhibition he hardly looked at the pictures on the wall because he found himself alone with Nina and 'became a prey to the desire to pass my hand lightly over her mane of black hair. I knew that if I did she'd strike me in the face – but that, on reflection, only sharpened my desire, and eventually I was just on the point of taking the plunge when Fanny Stanley came in and put an end to the tête-à-tête.'[12]

Fry was particularly pleased with the exhibition and felt that it marked a great step forward for English painting. He wrote to Charles Vildrac:

> It strikes me for the first time that the French pictures do not stand out from our own. That is to say that I believe our mutual understanding has been so greatly to our advantage that now we are beginning to construct real pictures. I am very proud of it. But we must always be strengthening the bonds between us to allow the true aesthetic to emerge here where they really only like the romantic and the sentimental.[13]

Nina had been determined to go back to Paris ever since her brief visit in 1912. All the talk about French art at the Omega and her friendship with Gaudier made her even more eager to return. When a wealthy woman friend offered to give her £30 so that she could go, Nina did not hesitate. Adventure beckoned.

7

Montparnasse

PAINTERS flocked to Paris from all over the world, attracted by the brilliance of its artistic life, its academies and museums, and the special atmosphere of freedom and tolerance. Just to be in Paris, to sit at its café terraces and breathe the same air as the acknowledged masters of modern art, held an inestimable glamour for young painters. It acted as a powerful magnet to English artists for whom, in Wyndham Lewis's words, 'Paris was expansive and civilised, temperate in climate, beautiful and free.'[1]

Montparnasse had replaced Montmartre as the artists' quarter of Paris. As the picturesque slopes of Montmartre became increasingly invaded by cultural sightseers eager to catch a glimpse of the legendary *vie de bohème*, more and more painters migrated to the tranquil anonymity of Montparnasse, which had long sheltered its own more modest population of students and artists. The newcomers were first drawn to the quarter by the Tuesday evening gatherings at the Closerie des Lilas, presided over by Paul Fort, the 'Prince of Poets' and co-founder with André Salmon of the literary review *Vers et Prose*. In its heyday around 1910 as many as 200 writers, poets, painters, musicians, critics and journalists would meet at the café on the Boulevard Montparnasse. This weekly invasion from Montmartre gradually became permanent as a growing number of artists took studios in the neighbourhood. They were joined by a huge influx of foreigners. Some, particularly Jewish artists from Russia and Eastern Europe in flight from racial persecution, stayed for good and formed the École de Paris. Others came just to study and drink at the fountain of art before returning to their own countries.

Nina arrived in Paris in February 1914 and took a small, evil-smelling room overlooking a courtyard at the Hôtel de la Haute Loire, opposite the Café du Dôme. Before the war there were so many English and American artists living and working in Montparnasse that it was known as the *quartier anglais*. But although Nina knew hardly anybody and had only a schoolgirl knowledge of French, she had no intention of mixing just with her fellow countrymen. On her first evening she made her way to a small restaurant, little more than a hole in the wall in the Rue Campagne Première, run by the warm-hearted Italian, Rosalie Tobia. She had been Bougereau's favourite model in her younger days and extended a generous welcome to all the impoverished artists of the quarter, who came to enjoy her cheap and homely cooking. The restaurant was dark and smoky, its walls covered with paintings and drawings which Rosalie had obligingly accepted in exchange for meals from regular customers such as Modigliani, Utrillo, Picasso and Kisling, even though their work was little to her taste. In its modest way Rosalie's was one of the central pillars of the artistic community, a veritable Montparnasse institution, and it was not long before Nina met one of its legendary figures.

Rosalie's was a second home for Modigliani. She had a motherly affection for her handsome compatriot and allowed him endless credit. To pay for his meals he would often help her in the kitchen by peeling potatoes and preparing vegetables, enjoying her chiding. They had frequent volcanic arguments in full-blooded Italian when she decided that he was taking advantage of her good nature, and she did not scruple to throw him out when he became too drunk or abusive. Nina was seated at one of the marble-topped tables when the door opened and an immensely good-looking man of about thirty, with proud Latin features, dark wavy hair and brown eyes, came in, dressed in a corduroy suit and black hat. Without hesitation he presented himself to Nina as Modigliani, Jew; and immediately proceeded to unwrap the roll of newspaper he carried under his arm to display a number of quick portrait sketches in pencil and chalk, which he offered to her for five francs. Nina had heard a lot about Modigliani from Epstein, who had recommended her to Rosalie's, and she looked with professional interest at the oval faces with their pupil-less eyes and swan-like necks. She found them curiously beautiful and readily bought one of the pencil heads. Nina was just as fascinated by Modigliani himself who, the transaction completed, sat down beside her to talk. Communication was difficult as she understood little of his voluble outpourings, but she managed to convey to him that they had a mutual friend in Epstein and they got on very well.

Nina was eager to learn as much as she could in Paris. She paid her money into an English bank which sent her a fortnightly cheque, and rented a studio in a courtyard in the Boulevard Edgar Quinet for fifty francs a month, then about £2. She had an introduction to the Russian painter Marie Wassilieff and went to see her at her large studio in the Avenue de Maine where she ran a painting academy with Fernand Léger as the professor. There were Russian, German and Scandinavian students there, but no English or American, and Nina decided that it would be a good place for her to work. She drew and painted from the model in the morning and spent the afternoons visiting museums before going back to Wassilieff's for the afternoon sketch class. Between five and seven there were short poses lasting from five minutes to half an hour, with two models posing together on Fridays.

Nina became great friends with Wassilieff, who was a strong and vivid personality, fiercely independent and open-hearted. Almost dwarf-like in stature, with a clown's mop of hair, she always wore high boots and enjoyed giving energetic displays of Russian folk dances. Despite being an anarchist, Wassilieff liked to boast that she had first come to Paris in 1905 on a scholarship from the Tsar. She was only a little less proud of the fact that the Douanier Rousseau had proposed to her shortly after her arrival, and claimed that she turned him down because of his bad breath. Although she had studied with Matisse, the work which she exhibited in the Salon des Indépendents was a highly personal combination of Cubism and brightly coloured Slavic imagery. Wassilieff knew no English but Nina quickly learnt to speak a fluent, if idiosyncratic, French, characterized by its bad grammar and strong English accent. She often ate at Rosalie's with Wassilieff, Modigliani (whom everyone called Modi), the American sculptor Hunt Diederich, and his Russian wife Mariska, who designed and executed exquisite embroidery. They would then spend the rest of the evening at the Rotonde, which had rapidly eclipsed the Closerie des Lilas as the unofficial headquarters of the neighbourhood.

The Rotonde was situated at the very heart of Montparnasse, at the vital Carrefour Vavin where the Boulevard Raspail cut across the Boulevard Montparnasse and several other small streets converged. The Rotonde was the artists' main venue for seeing friends, exchanging ideas and gossip, doing business, borrowing money, cadging a meal or a drink, finding a room to sleep, or simply whiling away an hour or two. Its success can be attributed largely to the personality of its astute proprietor Libion. He specialized in buying up failing businesses and making them a going concern before reselling them at a profit. In 1911 he had bought a shoe shop on the corner of the two boulevards and, after selling off the stock, transformed it into a small bar. It was almost entirely taken up by the counter, and painters and poets rubbed shoulders with local masons, butcher boys and cab drivers. 1911 was the year when the construction of the Boulevard Raspail was finally completed and the transformation of the quarter began in earnest. Libion was quick to see the way things were going and to grasp the potential of his site. A short while later he bought the adjoining shop and converted it into a second room, reserved for regulars. Artists squeezed through the swing doors and crammed into the small, smoke-filled room where they gathered in noisy groups around the ten or twelve tables.

The Rotonde had several advantages over the Dôme on the opposite side of the street, which pre-dated it by some fifteen years. The Dôme had been colonized by two groups of Germans and Scandinavians who spent their time in endless disputes and games of billiards. When the Rotonde opened the other artists were delighted to be able to escape from their rowdy Nordic companions and stake their own claim across the road. The Rotonde also benefited from a south-facing terrace which caught the sun in the afternoon whilst the Dôme remained in shade. Even more important was Libion's personal sympathy for the artists who came to be his main clientele. Fat and genial, usually in shirt-sleeves and waistcoat, with the butt of a cigarette drooping from his lips, Libion, like Rosalie, gave extended credit to his regulars, accepted pictures in exchange for long-unpaid bills, and helped them out with advice and a few francs when times were really bad. Artists could sit all day over a *café crème*, and frequently did, without being obliged to reorder, and Libion always gave them the benefit of the doubt when it was a matter of declaring the number of croissants or cups of coffee consumed. His waiters had strict instructions never to wake anyone and when the café closed at two in the morning it was not unusual for him to overlook a needy soul without a bed for the night and wake him at six with *café au lait* and croissants on the house. Libion's generosity had its practical side, for he knew that impoverished though his clients usually were, when they did have money they spent lavishly, and that in the long run their presence would attract people to his café. As he quite rightly said, 'They get themselves noticed, and they'll finish by making my café celebrated.'[2]

Libion's regulars were a varied and colourful crowd. At one time or another all the artists of note, regardless of their aesthetic differences, were sure to be seen on the terrace of the Rotonde. The models of the quarter were always well represented and there was a sizeable contingent of Russian intellectuals and revolutionaries such as Ilya Ehrenburg, Lunacharsky, Trotsky, even reputedly Lenin, who spent their time in earnest discussion, reading Russian newspapers and playing chess. Nina was in her element at the Rotonde and quickly met everyone. She did not go unnoticed and attracted a lot of attention in her Omega-designed clothes, which were quite new to Paris. She often wore a square-necked blouse with a bold abstract design in blue, orange and black, and was so well known for her collection of brightly coloured and patterned stockings that they were even mentioned in the *Paris Daily Mail*. The Rotonde was far less self-consciously Bohemian than the Café Royal. The *style rapin* – loosely tied bows, broad-brimmed hats and flowing capes – had definitely been left behind in Montmartre and for the most part the artists looked like the local bourgeois or workpeople of the quarter. Derain, Vlaminck, Matisse and Van Dongen would appear wearing bowler hats; while Kisling always dressed in a blue boiler suit and was described by André Salmon as looking like an Eskimo plumber. Picasso sported both a workman's cap and a gold watch chain.

Certain figures did, however, stand out because of their dress and behaviour. Perhaps most striking was the diminutive Japanese artist Foujita with his round, owl-like, horn-rimmed spectacles, hair cut in a fringe, small moustache, earrings and beads. He and his compatriot Kavashima were followers of Raymond Duncan, who advocated a return to the Ancient Greek way of life, and wore togas woven by themselves, hand-made sandals and headbands. They were immortalized in a Cubist portrait by the enormous Mexican artist Diego Rivera. The Chilean Ortiz de Zarate was another conspicuous South American artist experimenting with Cubism. Tall and well built, he took pride in proclaiming his descent from the conquistadores and strode around in sandalled feet with a tiny bowler hat precariously perched on top of his head.

Nina was particularly attracted to the Russian sculptor Ossip Zadkine, who was the same age as her and spoke good English as he had studied in London before coming to Paris in 1909. Dressed in a Russian smock, with his hair cut straight across in peasant style, Zadkine closely resembled one of his own carvings. When Nina's hair needed cutting he borrowed a pair of scissors from his concierge and transformed her into a Russian peasant too.

Nina saw a great deal of Modigliani and whenever she had the money she bought one of his drawings, which he hawked around the Rotonde every morning before starting work. At this time he was producing a series of elongated, oval stone heads whose highly simplified, stylized features owed something to archaic sculpture, primitive masks and Brancusi. His drawings meant little to him and when times were really hard he would lower his price to a mere three francs and give them away freely to friends and creditors in exchange for a drink or meal.

Modigliani was a complex character made increasingly bitter and tormented by the non-recognition of his talent. Proud of his family, his Jewishness and his beloved Italy, he liked to trace his ancestors back to Spinoza and had a deep love of philosophy and poetry, often theatrically declaiming stanzas of Dante. He was never without a copy of Lautréamont's fantastical masterpiece *Les chants de Maldoror* and could recite verses by Villon, Leopardi, Rimbaud and Baudelaire. His paintings are full of a warm sensuousness and display an infinite delicacy and yearning wistfulness. Any money he earned or received from his family disappeared instantly in grandiose gestures of generosity to his friends, and on the drink and drugs indispensable to his work. Long years of poverty and hardship had seriously weakened his constitution, which was already undermined by tuberculosis. In his poor physical state he easily became blindingly drunk on very little alcohol and would engage in violent brawls and slanging matches which alienated even his friends and admirers. Modigliani was well known by the police in Montparnasse and many people regarded him simply as a nuisance.

Every evening Modigliani sat beside Nina at the Rotonde, drawing all the time until he became too drunk to continue. Then he would lean his head on her shoulder and go to sleep, while Nina self-consciously remained bolt upright, embarrassed yet flattered to be so singled out. Modigliani liked to be extravagantly gallant to Nina. He and Zadkine presented her with a giant bunch of roses and he always made a great show of chasing her up the Boulevard Raspail when the Rotonde closed, unfailingly recognizing her by her bright stockings. Nina entered into the spirit of the game and one night when he nearly caught her she swarmed up a lamp post to escape him. She was rather proud of the fact that Modigliani wanted to sleep with her, but she told Gaudier that she had refused him because he was always drunk and penniless. Although Nina liked Modigliani, admired his work and appreciated his beauty, she was as much afraid of him as she was attracted by his enormous physical magnetism and excess. She said later that she was careful to go only once to his studio because she was rather frightened of what she called his 'eccentricities of behaviour'.[3] However, had Modigliani really wanted her, it does not seem likely that Nina would have refused him. More probably he only made passes at her in jest or drink, late at night when she just happened to be the person beside him. Nina was not truly his type. He liked to dominate his women, expecting them to stay at home and look after him. He had any number of the pretty girls of the quarter at his beck and call: models, seamstresses and laundresses, who would fleetingly attract him by their smile or a certain way of walking. Nina was an interesting and amusing companion whom he could talk to as an equal. She was down-to-earth, straightforward, high-spirited and fun, but she held no mystery or challenge for him.

Beatrice Hastings was different. When Nina introduced Modigliani to the South African poet who had been Orage's mistress and effective literary editor of the *New Age*, she was on the face of it of the same breed of new woman as Nina. Sharply intellectual, she nevertheless had a strong streak of whimsy and liked to go to the Rotonde dressed in a Kate Greenaway-style costume, carrying an osier basket containing a live duck. Beatrice had a violence, passion and talent for self-dramatization that matched Modigliani's own, and their affair was to be stormy, tempestuous and mutually destructive.

Nina greatly admired the work of Cézanne, the Douanier Rousseau, Derain and Picasso, but apart from Modigliani the Parisian avant-garde made little obvious impact on her own style. Modigliani's fine, fluent line and purity of form had a lasting effect on Nina's drawing and confirmed her in the direction she was already taking under Gaudier's influence. She had two lessons at Wassilieff's with Léger and painted a life-size nude study of the two Friday models, which owed something to Cubism; but Nina was too rooted in tangible reality, too deeply involved in the immediate to be attracted to abstraction. She painted what she saw and felt about the people and scenes around her. The portrait she did of Zadkine* seated in his studio beside one of his sculptured heads is amongst her most accomplished work and says a lot for her essential seriousness of purpose and commitment to her art at this time. Thickly painted in sombre tones, Zadkine's features are solidly modelled with a multitude of subtly differentiated brush strokes. But it is far more than just a good physical likeness. Nina uses the contrast between Zadkine's lively intelligent face and the tense, anguished features of the sculpture to great psychological effect. The portrait manages to convey Zadkine's gaiety and love of life, his intensity and intellectual energy as well as his underlying melancholy.

Nina sent the picture to the Allied Artists' Association exhibition held at Holland Park Hall in June 1914. She also submitted her painting of the two nude models done at Wassilieff's and a portrait of Madame Bing, the wife of Henry Bing who worked for the German humorous paper *Simplicissimus*. It was a very striking work, Madame Bing's long black cloak and hat providing a dramatic contrast to her white face and short blonde hair. Gaudier was the chairman of the AAA hanging committee for 1914 and wrote to tell Nina how much he liked the paintings she had sent. He singled her out for praise in an article about the exhibition for the *Egoist*:

Miss Hamnett cares much about representation. It is very interesting to see a portrait of Zadkine, the wood-carver. In this work there are great technical qualities of paste and drawing – more amplified in the other portrait – where carefully chosen blacks and violets create a very distinguished effect. I see from the qualities of the 'women composition' that the affinities of this artist are coming nearer to a preference for abstract design.[4]

Nina continued to go regularly to Wassilieff's academy. As many as forty or fifty students attended the afternoon sketch class, including Modigliani who would often stumble drunkenly up the long stairway leading to the studio and cause a great disturbance before settling himself on the floor to draw. One day the other students, tired of the lifeless poses of the professional models, suggested that as Nina had a good figure she should take off her clothes and dance for them while they drew her. Posing for Gaudier had made Nina very proud of her body and she quickly overcame any residual feelings of modesty, improvising a dance to Debussy's 'Golliwog's Cakewalk'. The class was delighted with her exuberant vitality and persuaded her to dance for them two or three times a week. Zadkine

* facing page 32

and Modigliani often drew her and a German woman asked her to pose for a wood carving.

Dancing for the students at Wassilieff's appealed to Nina's vanity and gave her a taste for abandoned self-display. Her performances came to be in such demand at parties that Gaudier's sculpture of her dancing naked could well stand as her personal emblem for these Paris months. The Dutch Fauvist painter Van Dongen was one of the quarter's most celebrated hosts and his extravagant fancy dress parties raised even Montparnasse eyebrows. Nina often went to his riotous Thursday afternoons when he kept open house for friends and art critics. There was boxing and dancing, and one day Nina performed wearing nothing but a black veil. Such vestiges of respectability were quickly dispensed with at a party given by Hunt Diederich, where Russian musicians sang and played balalaikas. Nina began dancing in a veil but soon took it off and gaily pranced around naked, basking in the appreciative applause. She was a great success and Hunt Diederich painted a frieze around a lampshade of Nina dancing in different poses. She claimed that a French millionaire who wanted her to perform in cabaret bought it to console himself when she refused.

There was nothing sexual about Nina's dancing. Tall and angular, with small breasts, she was described by Wassilieff as 'Gothic'.[5] But Nina's performances were more than just good fun and an expression of her naturally high spirits. For her they were the ultimate liberation from her conventional upbringing and a declaration of her personal liberty. She was young, she was an artist in Paris, she could do whatever she liked, and she intended to. Inevitably it meant far more to Nina than to the assembled company who were used to public nakedness. At the more extravagant artists' dances such as the Bal des Quatz'Arts it was quite usual for the girls to dance naked as the night grew wilder, and models would go to the Rotonde with nothing on under their coats. Such self-display was not reserved for women, and both Modigliani and Ortiz de Zarate were notorious for stripping at the least opportunity. Modigliani's friends learnt to detect the signs of his imminent disrobing and when his hands went to the long red sash he wore round his waist they would good-humouredly band together to restrain him and tie him up with his scarf to prevent him making a nuisance of himself. Modigliani would always appear whenever he heard that Nina was dancing anywhere, evidently appreciating their mutual streak of exhibitionism. In her own way Nina was as big a showman as Modigliani.

As much as Nina enjoyed dancing naked, she also liked dressing up in elaborate fancy dress. For the annual 14 July celebrations she disguised herself as a typical Parisian Apache. With her hair pushed up into a cap, she swaggered in workman's peg-topped trousers and a blue jersey and corduroy coat belonging to Modigliani, brandishing a fierce-looking butcher's knife made of cardboard and

A fancy dress dance in the Avenue de Maine, 1914
Nina is seated in the middle foreground wearing an Omega designed blouse. Modigliani is standing second from the right in the
back row; Frederick Etchells is fourth from the right

silver paper. The whole quarter was festooned with flags and Chinese lanterns.
There was music and dancing in the streets and a fair outside the Closerie des
Lilas. Nina and her friends danced all night and nobody went to bed for three
days.

Nina's Apache costume was a great success. She often wore it to the three-
franc fancy dress dances which took place every few weeks at a large café on the
Avenue de Maine, and to the endless mad parties held all through that hectic
summer of 1914. Nina accompanied Hunt Diederich and Modigliani to
Wassilieff's annual studio party. Hunt Diederich dressed as an Arab and
Modigliani carried a huge copper kettle full of beer. Modigliani liked to play the
buffoon and was frequently the good-humoured butt of his friends' practical
jokes. He often went with Nina and a large group to the Gaieté Montparnasse,
where they paid fifty centimes and squashed together on a hard bench in the
gallery to listen to a variety of bedroom sketches, music-hall songs and bawdy

jokes, which were uproariously received by the audience of mainly local workpeople. One evening, when Modigliani was sitting at the end of the bench he pushed so hard that the others all joined forces to send him crashing to the floor, from where he retired in disgust to the bar. On such occasions Modigliani was just one of a laughing crowd, very far from the proudly tragic figure of legend, starving and crazed by alcohol and drugs.

Drink was not such an indispensable ingredient in the gaiety of Montparnasse life as it was to become later. As often as not Nina drank *café crème* at the Rotonde. She was so excited by just being in Paris that she had no need of alcohol to raise her spirits. Sometimes after the Rotonde closed at two, Nina and her friends would go on to the Café du Panthéon in the Boulevard St Michel, which was full of students, prostitutes and businessmen, and had quite a different atmosphere from the Rotonde. Occasional forays were made to other cafés such as the Closerie des Lilas, where Paul Fort, looking conspicuously the poet with his long hair and large black hat, still held court. On Friday evenings Nina went with Madame Bing and some of her German friends to the Restaurant Lavenue opposite the Gare Montparnasse. A German violinist played Beethoven and the restaurant was very popular with the older people of the quarter, who went there for a quiet game of dominoes away from the increasing hubbub of the Carrefour Vavin.

Apart from the new people Nina was meeting, there was a constant stream of English visitors to Paris. She saw Aleister Crowley from time to time and waited at a respectful distance while he said his midday prayer to the sun in the middle of the Boulevard Montparnasse. English eccentrics were nothing new to Paris. Sooner or later they all found their way across the Channel. The most recent was the flamboyant and pugnacious Wyndham Lewis, whom Nina had always liked and admired. He was in Paris to arrange for the publication of *Blast* and Nina was flattered to walk down the Boulevard Montparnasse on his arm while he expounded his theories in a dauntingly difficult French.

Nina's old friend Arthur Ransome was a regular visitor to Paris. His translations of French short stories and ill-fated book on Oscar Wilde, which led to his being sued for libel by Lord Alfred Douglas, had brought him into contact with many French literary figures and he was an accepted member of the group at the Closerie des Lilas. Ransome introduced Nina to his friend Ivar Campbell, who was the grandson of the eighth Duke of Argyll and had recently returned from a spell as honorary cultural attaché to the British Embassy in Washington. Like Ransome, he enjoyed tramping the open roads, and was the author of some rather idealistic youthful sonnets. Lively and talkative, Campbell made light of his aristocratic background and dressed the part of the poet in old clothes, dirty shoes and the obligatory black hat. The same age as Nina, dark and well built, with Rupert Brooke-style good looks, he was a well-known figure in Montparnasse and very popular with women. Campbell was extremely attracted to Nina and went to see her every day. But she was still influenced by Gaudier's anarchism and rather disapproved of him for being an aristocrat, thinking him conceited and spoiled. To make matters worse, he had behaved badly to a friend of hers, whom he had pursued for six months and begged to marry him; when she finally agreed he promptly ran off with a Frenchwoman. Campbell, however, genuinely cared about Nina and was to prove a very good friend to her, doing all he could to help her. When her money had nearly run out and she thought she would have to go back to London, he came to her rescue by buying two watercolours, one a rather tentative early work of a fair at Corfe Castle* done when she was staying with friends in Dorset in 1912. Campbell was very persistent and Nina was not completely impervious to his charms, confessing that she very nearly did fall in love with him. But when he proposed, she refused.

The truth is that Nina was in love with an unknown, mysterious stranger whom she admired from a distance at the Rotonde. She had been struck by a portrait at the Salon d'Automne of a young man with his coat collar turned up to frame his long pale face and slanted eyes. His sad and hungry look haunted her and she was astonished to recognize him later that same evening at the Rotonde. Nina was fascinated by him. He sat apart on his own and seemed to know no one. For weeks she stared at the stranger who so disturbed her thoughts, becoming daily more infatuated with him without ever exchanging a word. One evening when she was sitting with Modigliani and Beatrice Hastings she confessed how much she would like to meet him and Beatrice immediately rushed over and brought him to their table. The young man, who introduced himself as Edgar, was as taken aback as Nina and said little. But when later they went on to Zadkine's studio, they sat talking together on the roof amidst the chimney-pots until morning.

Nina discovered that the twenty-one-year-old Edgar was Norwegian, spoke perfect French and German, and was in Paris to study art, but he would not reveal his surname. Nina was more intrigued than ever and found him a very romantic figure. Even as she got to know him better he remained something of a mystery. On his marriage certificate he declared that he was a dramatist and his father an 'artiste', which suggests a theatrical background. But he told Nina very little about himself or his life and never asked her to visit his studio, although he often mentioned the fine books and furniture he had there. Nina was never quite sure what Edgar felt about her, and no doubt this element of uncertainty only added to his attraction, making him more of a challenge; she was soon desperately in love with him.

* see page 32

The development of their friendship into an affair was marked by the disappearance of the black cat which used to sit on Nina's skylight every night. Discovering that Nina was no longer alone, the cat never returned. Edgar divided his time between Nina's studio and his own, but their idyll was short-lived. On about 25 July Nina was sitting alone in a small restaurant near Wassilieff's when she was suddenly gripped by a sick feeling of icy horror and fear. She stared at the bare wall opposite, convinced that something awful was about to happen to punish her for having such a good time. Nina knew little about politics or the international situation, but her premonition was all too right – only the punishment was not for her alone, and the feeling of unrest and agitation was general.

A few days later all the Germans suddenly vanished from the quarter. On Saturday 1 August war was declared on Germany and the first mobilization orders were posted in public places. That weekend Paris went mad and took to the streets in massed processions, all shouting 'To Berlin!' and singing the 'Marseillaise' and other patriotic songs. As panic set in, paper money was refused everywhere, long queues formed for food, and the mob stormed the branches of the German-owned Laiterie Maggi, looting and killing any Germans they found. There was pandemonium amongst the expatriate community as everyone scurried to obtain the necessary papers and to register themselves. Nina and Edgar moved together into a studio hurriedly abandoned by a friend, and Nina managed to earn enough money for them to live on by posing for an American sculptress.

Nina acquired some identity papers from the British Consul so that she could return to England if necessary, but Edgar steadfastly refused to do the same. The only identification he had was his birth certificate, which declared him Edgar de Bergen, a dangerously German-sounding surname which Nina had not heard before. At the end of the two weeks allowed for the registration of foreigners two policemen appeared and took them both to the police station. Nina was locked up for the afternoon and questioned about Edgar, who was suspected of being a German spy on account of his surname and the many German friends he, like everyone else, was known to have had in the quarter. Nina was allowed to go but Edgar was detained in the Prefecture for an indefinite period.

The future seemed bleak. It was impossible to tell how long Edgar would be kept in prison or what would happen to him when he was released. Nina stayed with the American sculptress and her husband for a short while, but faced with so many imponderables she reluctantly decided that she had little alternative but to return to England and her family, a prospect which filled her with gloom and despondency. In the event, when she arrived at her parents' house, dirty and penniless after a three-day wait for a boat at Dieppe, they were no more pleased to see her than she was to be home.

Nina was, however, happy to see Gaudier again even though they were both very downcast. They went for a walk in Richmond Park, where Gaudier often drew the deer, and sat quietly on the grass eating plums. Gaudier had already returned to France once to volunteer for the French army, but had been turned down and imprisoned as a deserter for having evaded his military service. He managed to escape from his cell on that occasion, but he knew that he had to do his duty and fight, and was convinced that he would not come back alive. In her heart of hearts Nina felt the same and they walked back in silence to his studio under the arches in Putney where they had a very subdued tea. It was the last time Nina saw Gaudier before he was killed in the trenches in June 1915.

From time to time Edgar sent Nina postcards from prison. She complained that he never spoke plainly but always wrote in parables. Nina decided that one of his messages meant that he loved her and when she heard that he had been released from jail and was allowed to remain in Paris for the rest of the war she was determined to join him. Everybody told her she was mad to leave the comparative safety of England for France but nothing would deter her. Ivar Campbell, who had stoically resigned himself to Nina's infatuation with Edgar, generously gave her £5 so she could return.

After a long and difficult journey back to Paris, Nina booked into the Hôtel de la Haute Loire and met Edgar at the Rotonde. Many familiar faces had already left for the Front, but a surprising number of foreign neutrals and those unfit for military service still remained. A noticeably more subdued mood reigned on the terraces of the Rotonde and the Dôme. The war had brought curfews and rationing. There were no newspapers and Paris was blacked out every night. Cafés closed at eight in the evening, liquor was banned, and many bars were shut down – although what this meant in practice was that alcohol was served in coffee cups and secret drinking-clubs opened when the cafés closed. There were daily air raids at about six o'clock, the shout of *Garde à vous!* by the police and air-raid wardens becoming a new addition to the usual Paris street cries. The French merely shrugged and treated the bombing as an exciting spectacle. Nina and Edgar caught the general insouciance and would eagerly lean out of her hotel window to watch the raids. But they were soon forced to realize just how dangerous the situation was when a bullet narrowly missed Nina's head and entered the hotel window below.

As Nina had only a hundred francs in five-franc pieces tied up in a stocking, Edgar suggested that she should live with him in his studio at La Ruche, the famous artists' colony in the Rue Dantzig. With its entrance picturesquely flanked by two caryatids taken from the Indonesian pavilion at the 1900

Exposition Universelle, La Ruche was set amidst gardens and greenery. The octagonal building was divided into two floors, each having twelve triangular-shaped studios which were so narrow that the artists called them coffins. They were utterly comfortless, with no gas, electricity or running water, but the rent was minimal. Although some French painters and poets such as Léger, Apollinaire, Max Jacob and Blaise Cendrars had lived there, La Ruche was mainly inhabited by Russian and Polish artists who arrived in Paris with no money, possessions or knowledge of French. It was a veritable ghetto of poverty and genius, the birthplace of the École de Paris. At one time or another Chagall, Zadkine, Archipenko, Lipschitz, Kikoine, Kremegne and Soutine all had studios there. The war scattered many of the residents of La Ruche so that it had something of the aspect of a ghost town until 1915 when it was requisitioned to house refugees from the North.

Edgar lived in one of the separate studios in the garden originally intended to house artists with families, and it had an upper gallery reached by a rickety ladder. A Russian admiral's daughter was also staying there. She seemed to do nothing but drink wine all day and methylated spirits all night at Nina's expense, and, to make matters worse, stole her only calico nightdress which had belonged to her grandmother. Every morning Edgar made drawings of a spider that he had found in the garden, while Nina posed again for the American sculptress to support them. They all lived on stew which the Russian girl was sent to buy every day from a nearby soup-kitchen.

In the afternoon Nina and Edgar often went to visit Brancusi at his studio in the Rue de Montparnasse, which was something of a place of pilgrimage for artists, students and connoisseurs. Brancusi, who was then thirty-eight, looked like a large and burly peasant with his dark beard, protective skullcap, blue overalls and wooden clogs. He was of a mystical, philosophical turn of mind and lived with the purity and simplicity of a saint amidst the pared-down forms of his sculptures. He talked to Nina and Edgar about life and cheered them up by playing the guitar and singing songs from his native Romania. All the artists left in Montparnasse and those back on leave met up in the evening at the canteen Wassilieff had set up in her studio, where for fifty centimes they could have soup, a main course, a glass of wine and a cigarette. Wassilieff's friends had brought the tables and chairs and the cooking was done by three artists, including Foujita, who prepared Oriental dishes. Everybody came to drink, sing, dance, recite poetry, talk and forget the war. Picasso might play toreador while Modigliani, drunk as often as not, would invariably get involved in some heated discussion or argument until even the generous Wassilieff had enough of him and threw him out.

Despite the gaiety of these evenings, there was a growing unease as the

Germans drew ever closer to Paris. Nina and Edgar prolonged their romantic reverie as long they could and often sought refuge under the trees in the shade and quiet of the Cimetière Montparnasse, drinking wine and enjoying the late summer. But outside the haven of the cemetery where time stood still, life in Paris was becoming increasingly difficult and those who could left for the South. Edgar asked Nina how much it cost to get married in England, and when he discovered that it was only seven shillings and sixpence, proposed to her. Ever matter-of-fact, Nina replied that she didn't mind if she did.

Once again the long-suffering Ivar Campbell, who was back in France as an ambulance driver with the American Red Cross, came to Nina's aid and gave her the money for their fare to England. Although Edgar still had no papers except his birth certificate, he was allowed to enter the country as Nina's fiancé. She took him to her parent's home in Acton. They were utterly dismayed at the prospect of Nina's marrying a poverty-stricken foreigner who spoke no English, but they knew now that there was no point in opposing her will and her father reluctantly paid for their wedding licence. Three weeks later, on 12 October 1914, in an atmosphere of all-round gloom that was prophetic of their future life together, Nina and Edgar were married at Brentford Register Office.

8

Marriage

MARRYING Edgar had been a spontaneous, generous, even quixotic gesture. No doubt in those brief weeks at La Ruche, reading and drinking wine under the trees in the Cimetière Montparnasse, Nina had been in love. But it was the intoxication of the moment. She was dazzled as much by her idea of the artist's life and the total rejection of the conventional aspirations of her genteel background. The reality of poverty in two attic rooms in Camden Town wiped out the glamour of a Parisian summer and dampened even Nina's high spirits. An unaccustomed gloom set in as she realized that far from having saved Edgar by bringing him to England, marriage to him meant the loss of her own nationality so that she became an alien herself, subject to many restrictions. Perhaps most irksome was the regulation forbidding her to travel farther than five miles from her home without a permit, which entailed sitting in endless queues at the local police station. Their German-sounding surname gave rise to grave suspicions and Edgar adopted the name Roald Kristian.

Edgar's income, which had apparently come from a German uncle, was no longer accessible and the immediate problem was money. Nina turned once again to Roger Fry, who gave them both employment at his Omega Workshops. But during these first difficult months of the war, the Omega was barely struggling on, not even covering expenses, and Fry had serious doubts about its future. There were no important decorative commissions and very few artists working on a regular basis. The emphasis was on the decoration of individual objects and Nina thought highly of the batiks and painted boxes produced by Vanessa Bell and Duncan Grant. She always greatly admired Vanessa's beauty and used to try to imitate her marvellous deep voice. An exhibition of small objects suitable for Christmas presents was unexpectedly successful, but despite this revival of interest 1915 was a quiet year for the Omega. A new dressmaking venture initiated by Vanessa in the spring provided its only stable source of income.

Horace Brodzky, 1915

During the war the Omega became an increasingly important centre for meetings, exhibitions and performances of experimental theatre. It was one of the few places where publications and photographs from abroad were available. The notion of 'significant form' first propounded by Clive Bell, the idea that the narrative content and technical accomplishment of a work of art are secondary to its formal arrangement of line and colour, held sway among the artists associated with the Omega. Their fundamental agreement on aesthetic matters is demonstrated in a curious book of questionnaires kept by Fry called *The Connaught Square Catechism*.[1] As an after-dinner entertainment he would write down his friends' replies to a battery of questions about their artistic likes and dislikes. Cézanne, Picasso, El Greco, Holbein and Giotto were highly favoured by Nina and Edgar, while Vanessa Bell and Duncan Grant added Matisse and Piero della Francesca to the artistic pantheon.

Nina's talent had already been shown to lie in solidly constructed, rather low-toned portraits whose compositions displayed a strong awareness of formal considerations. Her stay in Paris had given her a greater confidence and sense of her own independent artistic identity and now she was back in London her work rapidly won a certain recognition. She showed two drawings in both the winter 1914 and summer 1915 exhibitions of the New English Art Club; and pencil drawings of a woman's head and a satyr with the Friday Club in February 1915. *Colour* magazine described them as 'most interesting, being something felt rather than something seen', and in May praised her as 'one of the few women artists of the contemporary movement'. In April, June and August it reproduced her self-portrait, the portrait of Dilys, and another of Louis McQuilland, the dandified poet and critic who was a contributor to the newly formed arts magazine the *Gypsy*, edited by Henry Savage. Allan Odle was its art editor and the first issue of May 1915 contained a boldly simplified pen-and-ink drawing by Nina called *The Velvet Coat*, depicting the back view of a man dressed in Bohemian style with long hair and a hat. Friends instantly recognized the tall, stooping, cadaverous figure of Allan Odle and the drawing was generally considered to be strikingly expressive.

The fact that a new publication like the *Gypsy* could still be launched alongside the barrage of patriotic propaganda was an indication of the extent to which life went on as usual despite the bombing. All the old crowd left in London still congregated at the Café Royal. If anything it was even livelier and noisier than it had been before the war. There was a huge influx of Russian, Belgian and French refugees as well as the clientele of the former German cafés and uniformed soldiers on leave. Nina and Edgar spent most evenings at the Café Royal over a fourpenny coffee before walking back to their rooms at 9 Malden Crescent to save the bus fare.

Horace Brodzky, 1915

The Velvet Coat
(Allan Odle), c.1915

On Thursdays they sometimes went to Lady Ottoline Morrell's soirées at her house in Bedford Square. The flamboyant Lady Ottoline was an untiring, generous and inspired hostess to the artistic and intellectual avant-garde. She had a genius for bringing people together and her net encompassed both Bloomsbury and the virulently anti-Bloomsbury D. H. Lawrence and his circle. Many of the Omega crowd went to her parties as well as Augustus John, Sickert, the Nash brothers, Bevan, Gilman, Ginner, Henry Lamb, and young Slade painters such as Gertler and his friends. Lady Ottoline encouraged everyone to dress up in her collection of Oriental costumes and dance to a mixture of Russian ballet music, Mozart, Brahms's *Hungarian Dances*, and music-hall tunes played by her husband Philip on the pianola. With her commanding height, strong features, coils of red hair and extravagant, almost fancy dress, Lady Ottoline was a wildly theatrical figure, much given to romantic self-dramatization. Some were repelled by her patrician manner, affected, drawling voice and prying intimacy. She was an easy target for ridicule and many who availed themselves of her hospitality did not scruple to malign her in private and caricature her in print. Nina could never bear Lady Ottoline. On one occasion at the Omega when she heard her mounting the stairs to the studio where she was working, she exclaimed, 'Oh God, not that old bitch!' and hurriedly hid herself, only to be discovered smoking behind a curtain by the ever-inquisitive Lady Ottoline.[2]

Lady Ottoline's house was not the only centre of gaiety in this early part of the war. With the arrival of Belgian refugees, Charlotte Street and Fitzroy Street took on a lively Continental atmosphere. There were many informal dances in the cafés which had sprung up, with a hat being taken round afterwards for the accordionist as in the French *bals musettes*. Roger Fry was very sympathetic to the Belgian cause and started the Omega Art Circle, which held a series of Friday evening concerts, plays and poetry readings to raise money and to introduce Belgian musicians and actors to English hostesses, who might then engage them to entertain their party guests. Apart from Fry's Bloomsbury friends and the indefatigable Lady Ottoline, many of the Omega's better-known clients came, such as the Duchess of Rutland, Lady Diana and Margery Manners, Iris Tree and Mme Lalla Vandervelde, the English wife of the Belgian Socialist statesman who was herself tireless in her fund-raising activities for the Belgians and a great supporter of the Omega.

Edgar seems to have established himself at the Omega remarkably quickly. On 15 January 1915 he staged a puppet performance of Debussy's *Boîte à Joujoux* with an orchestra of Belgians. He designed and made the scenery himself and cut the puppets out of cardboard with a knife. The evening was a great success and it says a lot for Edgar's ability that he was able to initiate such a project only a few months after his arrival in England. *Colour* reproduced a drawing by him in

January and the following month praised his talent for sculpture and woodcutting, which suggests that some of his work was on view at the Omega. The only known decorative works clearly attributable to Edgar are three small lampshade designs, whose frieze of interlaced winged dragons clearly shows the influence of early Celtic and Viking art, and two designs for rugs. One of the rug designs is abstract, based on a seated animal, while the other is of a stalking bear and has clear affinities with the work of the German Expressionist painter Franz Marc.

Quiet and studious, Edgar remains a shadowy figure who was considered rather mysterious by Nina's friends. Sickert wrote of his 'acute and informed intelligence'[3] and he was clearly very knowledgeable about artistic developments on the Continent. He and Nina read a great deal and went every day to the second-hand bookshops in the Charing Cross Road where they acquired a considerable library which included Baudelaire's *Œuvres Posthumes*, Casanova's *Memoirs*, and poetry by Laforgue, Chaucer and Blake. In December 1915 Edgar wrote and illustrated an obituary of the French poet and art critic Albert Aurier for the *Egoist*, and did a series of woodcut portrait heads to illustrate articles on contemporary poets, novelists, artists and critics, which were published between September 1915 and February 1917. *Form* magazine also reproduced seven of Edgar's woodcuts in April 1916 and 1917. They were mostly stark images of single animals, their highly simplified, elongated forms having something of the directness of primitive cave paintings.

Fry thought very highly of Edgar's talent and an exhibition of his woodcuts was held at the Omega in June 1915. It could well have been Fry's admiration for Edgar's work that prompted him to add the publication of fine illustrated books to the Omega's activities, an extraordinary step to take in view of the wartime paper shortage. The first Omega book to appear at the beginning of 1916 was an edition of Clutton-Brock's poem *Simpson's Choice*, with woodcuts by Edgar. Subtitled *An Essay on the Future Life*, it deals satirically with the arrival of the hero in Hell and his debate with his repentant brother, his former mistress and the Devil about the choice between good and evil. Apart from the abstract cover, beginning and end pieces, and decorated initials, Edgar did three highly stylized and sharply witty full-page illustrations of scenes and characters from the poem. They show an original sense of design and very effectively exploit contrasting surface textures. The second Omega book, *Men of Europe*, which appeared shortly afterwards, was a translation of poems from the young French writer Pierre Jean Jouve's *Vous êtes hommes*. It was a plea for the end of war, destruction and violence, with abstract designs by Edgar based on jagged scroll shapes whose harsh angularities underlined the tone of the poems.

In February 1916 Arthur Ruck, a private art dealer, commissioned the Omega to decorate a room in his house at 4 Berkeley Street. In March Vanessa Bell and Duncan Grant moved to Wissett Lodge in Suffolk, where, as a conscientious objector, Grant was engaged in agricultural work. Very few artists were available to assist Fry and he turned for help to Nina, Edgar and Dolores Courtney, who had studied in Paris when she left Brangwyn's and had most probably been introduced to the Omega by Nina. The four artists decorated one wall each of the Ruck room with scenes from contemporary London life. Fry's mural depicted a street scene with a newspaper stall and a woman mounting a stairway from the Tube, a London Underground sign being prominently displayed. Painted in pale colours, it juxtaposed broad areas of simplified geometric shapes. Dolores Courtney's mural, over the fireplace wall, showed figures in a London park. Her design was more complex, the wall being divided into four sections which cut through the figures in a manner suggestive of synthetic Cubism. No photographs exist of Nina's or Edgar's work, but according to Dolores Courtney,[4] Edgar's mural portrayed an industrial area of London in dark brown and beige colours; while Nina's, similarly restrained in tone, was of a street scene. To judge from Fry's and Dolores Courtney's murals, they had something of the two-dimensional quality of poster designs in their use of predominantly flat areas of almost unbroken colour in which relief was suggested by contour rather than modelling. One witness commented on the remarkable stylistic unity of the room: 'It is obvious in studying the different walls that the four artists concerned in the work have, without suppressing their individual personality worked in concert and aimed at modifying their designs in such a manner as to harmonise with the whole.'[5]

Fry was pleased with the room, and unusually and wittily incorporated an advertisement for the Omega into his mural in the form of a publicity poster on the news-stand. He invited more people than normal to the private view in May; and, as buyer for the Contemporary Art Society that year, proved his regard for Nina and Edgar's work by purchasing a still life by each of them. Nina exhibited widely throughout 1916, showing drawings, still lifes and portraits with the Friday Club, the London Group and the New English Art Club. She also joined Edgar and Dolores in an exhibition of Independent Artists at the Alpine Club Gallery in April, her *London Backyards* being praised as 'most accomplished'.[6] In September *Colour* reproduced her portrait of Horace Brodzky, who was the subject of several drawings by Nina.

The unity and harmony of purpose achieved by Nina and Edgar in the Berkeley Street murals was in striking contrast to the increasing discord of their life together. Boredom and gloom are the words most often used by Nina to describe her marriage: 'I was getting more and more bored with Edgar who was daily becoming more soulful, and spoke in parables which I had long ceased to

The Student (Dolores Courtney), 1917

The Little Tea Party (Edgar and Nina), 1916, by Walter Sickert

understand.'[7] In 1916 they sat to Sickert for a picture called *The Little Tea Party*, now in the Tate Gallery. It depicts Nina and Edgar seated together on a sofa with tea things on a table beside them. Nina, wearing a dark coat with a fur collar, one hand on her hip, the other holding a cigarette, stares straight out at the viewer, animated and self-assured. Edgar seems to be sunk into himself and stares ruminatively into the distance. Little rapport between them is indicated and Nina commented wryly that they looked 'the picture of gloom'.[8]

Edgar undoubtedly cramped Nina's style. They were often very poor as there was not always enough work at the Omega. Although one of Nina's uncles came to the rescue and paid their seven shillings and sixpence a week rent, there was very little left over for food. They lived on a diet of stew made from twopennyworth of bones twice a week, porridge and margarine. Even this meagre fare was shared with their neighbour, the Mexican painter Benjamin Corea. Sunday lunch at Nina's parents was often the only decent meal they had all week. Edgar held traditional views on marriage and expected Nina to stay quietly at home when he saw his friends. He preferred working at night and was possessive and jealous if Nina went out with other men friends or anyone showed too close an interest in her. What Nina considered Edgar's 'Victorian ideas'[9] became the source of many arguments between them. During one particularly violent row he flung a prized dish of butter at her, an expensive and rare luxury in wartime bought with the proceeds of the sale of a drawing. Nina was too dismayed to retaliate and ruefully told Winifred Gill: 'The dish was smashed but thank God the butter landed on a picture frame and I was able to scrape it off.'[10]

These were not mere surface squabbles but the sign of a deep-rooted incompatibility. There was no real bond between them. When, after a few months of marriage, Nina discovered that she was pregnant, Edgar was furious, blaming her entirely. He was completely unsympathetic to her condition and complained bitterly when she was taken unawares by early labour pains on a visit to friends. The next day, already in labour, Nina went to hospital alone on a bus. In later years she would tell the story of how she kept asking the conductor for her stop until he finally announced 'Queen Charlotte's Hospital – thank gawd!'[11] Nina was weak and undernourished and the baby, which was born two months premature, did not survive. As relations between Nina and Edgar deteriorated they spent more and more time apart. Edgar had made his own group of friends in Chelsea, whom Nina considered dull and boring, and he often stayed out for nights at a time. For Nina, marriage was an irksome tie that she increasingly disregarded, seeing other men freely as she chose.

Roger Fry himself was not proof against Nina's considerable charms. Working beside her on the Berkeley Street murals he had gradually become aware of her 'queer satyr-like oddity and grace'.[12] Bright and gay, bubbling over with amusing stories, enthusiasm and laughter, she swept away the cobwebs of his loneliness. Fry had never really got over the break-up of his affair with Vanessa Bell two years earlier and his replacement in her affections by Duncan Grant. Work was always a great antidote to pain for Fry and no doubt partly accounts for his feverish activity during these years: organizing the Omega and numerous exhibitions, experimenting with different painting styles, writing articles and lecturing, to say nothing of a succession of short-lived love affairs. His letters to Vanessa give a very frank account of the difficulty he had in coming to terms with life without her. He wrote on 15 June 1916:

> You are the only one I really want to talk to intimately so I'm developing bit by bit a habit of solitude. I go to the Omega in the morning to see to business with Winnie and then come back and paint all day till evening and now most often spend that alone. It's better than making believe with people and in a few years I'll have got such a crust that no one will break through. It may break down but it's my plan of life just now. It don't make me happy but it makes me more contented than trying to make other people do. Sometimes Nina and de Bergen come in and talk art.[13]

Nina also dropped in for little domestic rituals such as tea parties for Vanessa's children, and gradually she came to fill a gap in his life.

Despite the wide variety of Fry's interests, painting came first. Vanessa's relationship with Grant made him feel excluded from what to him always remained the charmed circle of artists. Fry took their work seriously and offered them valuable and appreciated criticism and support. He was deeply hurt that they would never accord his own painting the same degree of attention and felt, no doubt rightly, that they had a dismissive attitude to it. Nina did take his art seriously, and was able and prepared to give opinions and advice to which he gladly listened. The respect was mutual and Nina must have been flattered by Fry's genuine interest in her work. This artistic exchange was vital to Fry and more and more he found his thoughts turning to Nina. On holiday with his family and friends at Bosham in Sussex, he wrote to Vanessa on 5 August 1916: 'I'm rather longing after a week of this violent outdoor life for someone who cares about painting to talk to. I've tried to get Nina Hamnett down, but the police won't let her.'[14]

Over the next few months their relationship developed into an easy-going affair and Fry wrote to Nina, 'I am a great deal too old [?] for such a *volage* and too fascinating creature as you are. You are a dear to me all the same and it's always a bit of a surprise to me that you are . . . *Ton vieux satyr.*'[15] Tall and gaunt, of a care-worn, ascetic appearance, and looking older than his fifty years, Fry nonetheless astonished by his youthful enthusiasm and openness to new ideas. As Winifred Gill wrote: 'He was intoxicating company for the young. He really was interested in what you thought about things.'[16]

At this time Fry was devoting much of his artistic energies to painting still lifes in his studio at 21 Fitzroy Street. Virginia Woolf described it as 'an untidy room. He cooked there, slept there, painted there and wrote there. There was always an arrangement of flowers or of fruit, of eggs or of onions – some still life that the charwoman was admonished on a placard ''Do not touch.'' '[17] Encouraged by Fry, Nina painted still lifes too, and in November 1916 she exhibited at the Omega in a show devoted entirely to still lifes. Fry, Grant and Vanessa Bell all briefly experimented with abstraction and Nina's first still lifes show her tentatively following suit, using everyday objects such as a wine glass as the pretext for the juxtaposition of abstract planes. In November *Colour* reproduced a sparse, highly formal composition by her in which the cylindrical shape of a saucepan featured prominently in the foreground. This same saucepan appears on a table in the background of Fry's portrait of Nina now in the Courtauld Institute Galleries, which suggests that Nina worked alongside Fry in his studio. But these forays into a more abstract idiom were not among Nina's best works and it was not a path she was tempted to explore further. She did, however, sometimes

Still Life, 1917

include still life elements, such as a vase of flowers or a bowl of fruit, in her portraits in order to introduce greater variety and colour into her compositions.

Views of rooftops and the backs of houses, subjects much favoured by the Camden Town Group, were another new departure in Nina's work at this time. Influenced by Fry and French art, Nina's solution to the problem of translating perceived reality into paint was to concentrate on its underlying formal structure. In *Housetops*, illustrated in *Colour* in January 1917, the view from a window over back yards with washing hanging on a line is seen in terms of severely simplified geometric planes and volumes. Nina subsequently adopted a

The Stairway, 1916

less rigorously schematic approach and allowed greater emphasis to the particular individual qualities of the scene or still life before her.

Close contact with such a stimulating intelligence as Fry had an important beneficial effect on Nina's paintings and she produced some of her best work during this period. She continued to exhibit widely in the first half of 1917, showing a portrait of Dolores Courtney (entitled *The Student*) and *A London Square* at the Friday Club; a still life and *Landing Stage* with the London Group; and a portrait of the painter Adam Slade at the New English Art Club. *Colour* reproduced her portrait of *Louise* in April 1917 and *The Landlady** in August.

Nina remained primarily interested in what she termed 'psychological portraiture'.[18] Her portraits are strong, bold statements of character rather than exact likenesses. Features are simplified and exaggerated to express her concise view of the sitter's personality. The combination of fine draughtsmanship with well-defined modelling of forms gives her portraits an almost sculptural solidity.

* facing page 33

Her rather subdued palette is often relieved by well-placed details of colour that soften a tendency towards rigidity in her usually strongly frontal compositions. There was no feminine prettiness in Nina's work. Her meticulously precise, neat handling of paint and directness of style matched the forthrightness of her character.

During his association with Nina, Fry painted a series of portraits of friends such as Iris and Viola Tree, Maynard Keynes, Edith Sitwell, André Gide and Lalla Vandervelde, which rank amongst his finest work. Nina's influence can perhaps be detected in his stronger sense of design and subtler colour, as well as his adoption of her use of rough-textured hessian canvas. Just as Nina was not chiefly occupied with exact likenesses, so Fry was concerned with 'imaginative characterization'.[19] He successfully combined his interest in formal qualities with the sensitive expression of his sitter's personality by exaggerating certain revealing features and making the pose and design of the picture reinforce his interpretation.

Fry did several excellent portraits of Nina that capture her in a variety of moods. One small work shows her wearing a dark blue jersey and trousers, playing a guitar. Carefree and gay, she is the Bohemian forerunner of the sixties

Nina with a Guitar, 1917, by Roger Fry

hippie. In the portrait now in Leeds University, she appears graceful, attractive and ladylike, a delightful and charming companion. Her simple, brightly checked dress, with a full skirt falling from an empire-line bodice, was designed by Vanessa Bell in 1915 for the Omega. The picture was painted at Durbins, Fry's house near Guildford, where Nina went for weekends, either alone or with other artists such as Mark Gertler and Dolores Courtney. Photographs exist of Nina wearing the same dress with Fry's daughter Pamela. Pamela always enjoyed Nina's visits to Durbins and found her refreshingly different from Fry's Bloomsbury friends, who tended rather to ignore children. Unlike them, Nina did not take herself too seriously and was always natural, friendly and open. Pamela remembered her as a very vital, colourful person, who radiated her own pleasure in life. She loved to show herself off, yet could laugh at herself at the same time.[20]

When Fry rented Durbins to the Strachey family for just over a year in 1916, the evening entertainment took a decidedly literary turn. Lady Strachey would read Restoration plays to the assembled company and they all took turns to read aloud a passage from a book while the others had to name the author. Nina, who was rather intimidated by the Strachey wit and intelligence, surprised herself by correctly guessing a quotation from Oscar Wilde's pamphlet on Socialism, which she had read years before. When Fry painted Lytton Strachey's portrait on one of his visits to Durbins, Nina did several drawings of him too, one of which is now in the National Portrait Gallery.

Fry's portrait of Nina in the Courtauld Institute Galleries is one of his most penetrating and successful works.* In her dark polo-necked jumper and skirt, sleeves rolled up ready for work, she seems serious-minded, self-possessed and independent, very much of the breed of new woman. Fry also did a painting of Nina nude, in which a brightly coloured Omega rug features prominently, as well as a series of nude drawings in pen and ink. Strangely, Nina never seems to have painted Fry, although she did do a drawing of him crouching nude, very reminiscent of Gaudier-Brzeska in style.

Nina displayed another side of her versatile personality when she took part in the so-called Monster Matinée at the Chelsea Palace Theatre, given in aid of Miss Lena Ashwell's Concerts for the Front on 20 March 1917. It was a great social event and Society ladies, stage personalities and various members of the artistic community vied with each other to join in. Nina appeared as a black cat in a costume, designed by George Wolf Plank who did covers for *Vogue*, which was so tight that she had to be sewn into it. Her particular qualification for her role was her ability to purr like a cat with her mouth shut, a talent she retained until

---

Opposite Nina and Pamela Diamond (née Fry) at Durbins, 1917
* See half-title

Nina, 1917, by Roger Fry

The Ring Master, c.1919

Lytton Strachey, *c.* 1917

the end of her life. The Matinée took the form of a history of Chelsea with little sketches about Rossetti, Whistler and other artists, ending with the grand finale of Mrs Grundy and the John Beauty Chorus of almost forty girls dressed as Augustus John models in costumes designed by Carrington and made by the Omega. The girls slouched on and arranged themselves around the stage in typical John poses, singing the refrain:

> John! John!
> How he's got on!
> He owes it, he knows it, to me!
> Brass earrings I wear,
> And I don't do my hair,
> When I walk down the street,
> All the people I meet
> They stare at the things I have on!
> When Battersea-Parking
> You'll hear folk remarking:
> 'There goes an Augustus John.'[21]

The show was generally considered a huge success and so much money was raised that the performance was repeated in June at the Lyric Theatre. But there were some dissenting voices, not least that of Roger Fry. Thoroughly disgruntled, he deemed it 'fatuous and feeble',[22] and left before the end without seeing himself caricatured by Edgar, who according to Lytton Strachey, did him to perfection.

Edgar turned his hand once more to puppeteering and produced a curtain-raiser to Lowes Dickinson's morality play *War and Peace*, performed at the Omega in aid of the Belgians. Edgar's puppets were made of flat, jointed cardboard, about two feet six inches high and worked by strings from above. Winifred Gill recalled that the piece 'consisted of a pas-de-deux between a nymph and a satyr. The duplicated programme was in French and all I remember was that the nymph danced "avec une telle intention" which was amply manifest. The scenery was beautifuly designed.'[23]

Whether from apathy or principle, Edgar had never bothered to register himself as an alien, despite repeated urgings by Nina. One senses in his conduct in both Paris and London a certain anti-authoritarian stand, a refusal to conform to bureaucratic patterns of behaviour. Asked by a district visitor what his religion was, his reply of 'Hedonist'[24] was a dangerous and suspect sign of independence on the part of a foreigner in wartime. After a warning which he ignored, Edgar was arrested in April and tried at Marylebone Police Court for not registering. Nina did not go to the trial and when she heard that he had been sentenced to three months' hard labour, she was merely relieved to be rid of him for a while. She certainly did not repine and only visited him once during his prison term. When, at the end of three months, Nina learnt that Edgar was to be deported to France to serve in the Belgian Army, she was not too sorry. She had enjoyed her regained independence and frankly did not want him back. She cried a few tears of sentiment for the youthful hopes of the past as she waved him good-bye at Waterloo, and never saw him again. He sent her letters from time to time, and after the Armistice wrote asking her for £5, saying that he loved her as much as ever, but she did not reply. She made enquiries about the possibility of obtaining a divorce, but faced with the legal difficulties, expense and lack of any compelling reason, she did not pursue the matter and remained legally his wife until she died. Her marriage to Edgar was the one thing Nina always regretted.

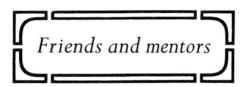

9

Friends and mentors

Nina threw herself into the gay round of wartime London. Gladys Hynes, her old friend from Brangwyn's who worked at the Omega, went to stay with her in Malden Crescent and they often spent the evening at the Café Royal, which closed early during the war. When it shut, the artistic and literary crowd all crammed into a tiny café run by an unsavoury Armenian behind the Lyric Theatre in Shaftesbury Avenue, where the crème de menthe frappée was exchanged for strong black coffee, Russian tea and Turkish delight. A tame white rabbit wandered about among the customers and the talk went on until midnight.

Nina had met Lady Constance Stuart Richardson, who was famous for dancing in a tigerskin at the Palace Theatre before the war, and they often went out together with officers of all nationalities. Nina's portrait of her in a flowing red robe and black turban was shown at the National Portrait Society exhibition in May 1917 and bought by Michael Sadler. It prompted John Salis, the art critic of the *New Witness*, to comment that: 'In Miss Hamnett's work one always feels a definite struggle to "express" which marks her portraiture well above that of the "herd".'[1]

The war gradually wrought a distinct change in the tenor of social life and much of the old simplicity disappeared for ever. Richard Aldington, Imagist poet and literary editor of the *Egoist*, observed that

Before the war *les jeunes* were perfectly happy to dine simply and to spend the evening in talk on nothing more expensive than tea and cigarettes. But as the young men began coming home on leave in khaki, they wanted more violent and expensive amusements, good dinners, theatres, dancing, girls. I do not say it was the artists and writers who did this . . . but somehow the majority began to set a more hectic standard which persisted until long after the war.

Very few were content with art any more; they had to have art and champagne.[2]

The Tour Eiffel, a high-class French restaurant in Percy Street, catered to the more expansive tastes of the time. It was a favourite haunt of Augustus John and Sickert, and became the unofficial headquarters of Wyndham Lewis and his Vorticist allies. When Lewis decorated a private upstairs dining-room with abstract panels and ornaments in the summer of 1915, the Tour Eiffel became an important show-piece as well as a meeting-place for the avant-garde. Nina went there whenever she could afford it or if someone rich took her. Roger Fry, on holiday with his children in the summer of 1917, wrote to her reproachfully: 'I was glad to get your card – a beastly little thing *quand même* and I think you might take a scrap of paper to the Tour Eiffel and scribble on it between the drinking bouts and the flirtations with Guevara and Nelson, oh most confirmed roisterer that you are.'[3] He worried that she was going the pace too violently and urged her to 'work hard and do things that will fill me with curious delight. And don't become the greatest of Café Royalists.'[4]

Nina's headlong rush of pleasure continued unabated. There were parties almost every night, all night, and in one week she went to five. Many of the old formalities were dispensed with, and gatecrashing became common. Nina often went to parties with the tall and willowy Marie Beerbohm, who was a faithful supporter of the Omega. Sensitive and nervous, her fragile femininity was in striking contrast to Nina's more robust personality. Since the death of her brother in the war, Marie lived in terror of the air raids and sought constant distraction. She clearly irritated Carrington, who described the mixed company at a party given by Augustus John in his studio in Mallord Street, Chelsea, for a local barmaid who was leaving:

> Joseph, a splendid man from one of those cafés in Fitzroy Street, played a concertina, another man a mandoline. John drunk as a King Fisher. Many dreadfully worn characters, moth eaten and decrepit who I gathered were artists of Chelsea. Nina. MacEvoy, Evan [Morgan]. Beerbohm female. Geoffrey [Nelson]. Un petit garçon from the Slade . . . some appalling pimps of the military and naval tribe. Dorothy Warren, and a few more fitchews unknown . . . It is always rather amusing to watch a party die, and to see the pairing off . . . MacEvoy and Nina. John and the Barmaid.[5]

The 'petit garçon from the Slade' was the young actor and painter Edward Wolfe, who had arrived from South Africa at the end of 1916. He was taken to the party by Geoffrey Nelson, a good friend of Nina and ex-student from the

Torahiko Khori, *c.*1917

Slade who had gone back to work there on leave from the navy. Nina and Wolfe first met at this party and became firm friends, Fry later reporting that Wolfe had 'a touch of the usual complaint – a certain softness in the head on the subject of Nina H.'[6] They often modelled for each other and Wolfe painted a still life of a group of Omega objects in her studio in 1918. Nina introduced Wolfe to the Omega when she became bored with copying Fry's designs for a large order of painted candleshades commissioned by Sir Ian and Lady Hamilton, and suggested to Fry that Wolfe would be the ideal person to do them. He soon found the task just as monotonous as Nina and made slight variations to the designs to keep himself amused. Fry was delighted with Wolfe's inventiveness and declared him 'a perfect genius for candleshades'.[7]

Sickert carried on the tradition of the pre-war Fitzroy Street Group 'At Homes' by keeping open house on Wednesday afternoons at the Frith, his cavernous, dimly lit and dusty studio at 15 Fitzroy Street. He liked the company to be as mixed as possible and Marjorie Lilly, who shared a studio in the same house, recalled that, 'On a good day there might be Spaniards, Americans, actors, old pupils, dilettantes, the world of Mayfair, a sprinkling of French, besides the *quartier* and a never ending stream of khaki.'[8] It was most likely at one of these parties that Nina met the successful young Japanese dramatist Torahiko Khori, whose portrait she painted at this time. His work was first performed in

London in 1917 and was translated into English by his close friend, the poet and artist Hester Sainsbury, who later married Frederick Etchells.

Nina was in her element at Sickert's large gatherings and liked nothing better than bringing together people of different backgrounds and interests, whispering such clues about them as 'he's Slade . . . second year' or 'he's FO . . . very cagey' or he's Army, *stage* Army'.[9] Osbert Sitwell, who first met Nina at Sickert's, wrote about her that, 'Generosity is so marked a feature of her character that she longs to introduce her friends to one another, to make presents of them in the same manner in which in those days she gave away drawings by Modigliani and Gaudier-Brzeska as though they were twopenny prints.'[10] Nina's mother and bemused brothers sometimes came to these parties and Nina made a special effort to put them at their ease. Shy and modest, her mother was clearly alarmed by her unconventional offspring and felt very out of place in such unfamiliar surroundings. Nina would have liked to have seen her sister Helen there too and was upset by her apparent coolness. She was astonished rather than estranged by their differences in temperament and would tell friends, 'She *likes* clocking in . . . Can you believe it? She gets to the office by nine and leaves at six.'[11]

Nina's social skills were very well developed and Marjorie Lilly commented that she

> could hardly be accused of self-effacement but neither was she assertive; she had the good manners that spring from utter unself-consciousness, boyish, direct, and not without dignity. She had decided views on the consideration that members of a polite society owed to each other and she deferred charmingly to opinions and ideas that were not her own; for her part, she welcomed the newest theories about everything but you were not expected to do the same and she chose her friends from different cliques, stipulating as it were that they should be good of their kind rather than that they should be of her kind.[12]

Nonetheless, Nina's high spirits could easily turn into wild mirth and caused Sickert's long-suffering wife Christine to mutter about her uproariousness: 'How I wish Nina wouldn't get so excited at parties!'[13] Even Sickert could be startled by Nina's more flagrant flaunting of conventional behaviour and shared her father's scandalized reaction to seeing her coming out of the Fitzroy Tavern hatless and carrying a jug of beer.

Nina was one of the privileged circle invited to Sickert's breakfast parties. Always in good spirits in the morning and spry after his early swim, he thought breakfast the most important meal of the day. Sickert loved cooking almost as

Nina, c.1916, by Walter
Sickert

much as he liked dressing up. He took delight in donning a chef's white hat and
jacket, and preparing and serving breakfast to friends such as Osbert Sitwell,
Alvaro Guevara, Aldous Huxley and the tramp poet W. H. Davies. The
conversation would range widely but was sure to come round at some point to
two topics of enduring fascination for Sickert: the identity of Jack the Ripper and
the Tichborne claimant. The latter had been in the headlines when Sickert was a
boy; the case involved a man who claimed to be the long-missing Roger Charles
Tichborne, heir to a large estate in Hampshire. After two trials the pretender
was declared to be Arthur Orton, a butcher's son from Wapping, and
imprisoned. Sickert, however, remained convinced that he was the rightful
heir. Breakfast passed all too quickly. While Nina smoked a large cigar, Sickert
entertained the company with stories about famous artists and writers he had
known, such as Whistler, Degas, Charles Keene, Toulouse-Lautrec, Beardsley
and Wilde. At ten o'clock, when the large bowls of coffee were empty, he sent
his guests reluctantly home and got down to work. Sometimes Nina would stay
and pose for him for a short while.

The same group of people might meet again for dinner at the elegant house shared by Osbert Sitwell and his younger brother Sacheverell in Swan Walk, Chelsea. With their sister Edith, the Sitwells were a self-contained literary movement. They first came to wider public notice at the end of 1916 with the publication of the annual poetry anthology *Wheels*, which was edited by Edith and included verses by all three Sitwells as well as contributions from Wyndham Tennant, Iris Tree and Nancy Cunard. The Sitwell trio were aristocratic rebels against the philistine hordes, with a marked talent for self-publicity and a flair for controversy, their more frivolous antics providing a welcome antidote to Bloomsbury earnestness.

Tall and distinguished in the uniform of the Grenadier Guards, Osbert was a witty and urbane host. He was far more outwardly conventional than the eccentric-looking Edith, who regally dispensed strong tea and buns at her own literary salon in her spartan flat in the Moscow Road, Bayswater. Nina first wittily captured Edith's distinctive features in a rather caricature-like drawing of 1915. It seems probable that she was present when Edith posed for Fry in 1918 and the drawings that Nina did of her then, one of which was owned by Sickert, had a greater subtlety and display a sensitive response to her sitter's personality.

Nina always enjoyed the dinner parties at Swan Walk, where the food and wine were excellent and the other guests might include Van Dieren, Arnold Bennett, Nevinson, Fry, Lalla Vandervelde, Clive Bell and the Icelandic playwright Haraldur Hamar, known simply as 'Iceland'. He was never seen without a copy of his unperformed masterpiece, whose cast numbered some 300 characters, tucked under his arm. On the rare occasions when he had any money he was extravagantly generous and once presented Osbert Sitwell with a drawing that he had bought from Nina. Dressed in a golden evening dress, with a wreath of autumn leaves around her head which made her look like 'a dissipated Bacchante after a little champagne',[14] Nina joined in the playing of charades after dinner and once acted Salome, with Robert Ross as Herod. Sickert never took part in these revelries but was occasionally persuaded to give a private performance of *Hamlet* in which he imitated the voice of each of the characters in turn.

Over the next few years Nina drew and painted many of those present, including Sickert, Alvaro Guevara, Haraldur Hamar and the Sitwells. Sometimes, as in the case of W. H. Davies, the sitters objected to the revealing character of Nina's portraits. Nina got on very well with the shy nature poet and did several drawings and paintings of him. Davies had spent his early years in England as a vagrant, and had tramped the roads doing odd jobs and begging in

---

Opposite Edith Sitwell, 1915

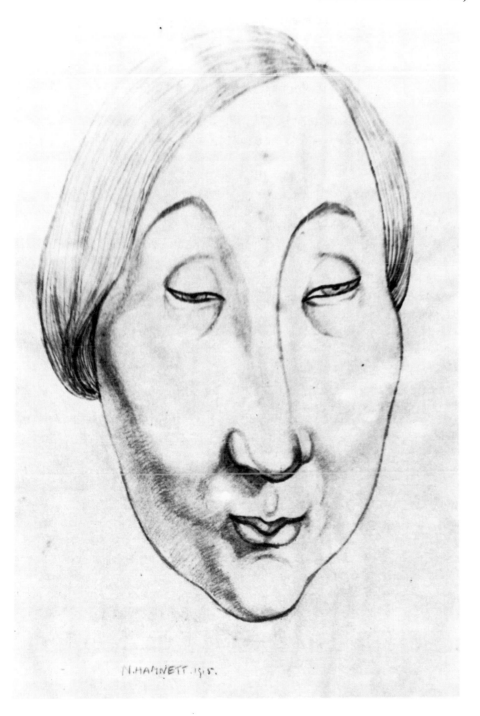

N.HAMNETT. 1915.

America and Canada, where he lost a leg 'jumping trains'. Now a well-known and respected Georgian poet with a civil-list pension, he had a strong sense of the proprieties and confessed to Augustus John that when he wanted to go on a pub-crawl he always went to Clapham or somewhere he was sure of not being known. He was highly aggrieved by a painting that Nina did of him seated at a table with a glass and bottle of port in front of him, and thought it made him look 'like a gaunt sick wreck of a drunkard, who was in the act of drinking himself to death'.[15] He complained to Edith Sitwell: 'You know, Nina really ought *not* to have done it . . . She ought *not*. It doesn't do for a man in my position – and it was Nina who bought the port!'[16]

Nina was working hard and rapidly consolidating her position in the English modern movement. She showed eleven works, mainly portraits, still lifes and London scenes, in Fry's exhibition 'The New Movement in Art', which was held in Birmingham from July to September 1917, and in a modified form in London at Heal's Mansard Gallery in October. It was far less radical than Fry's earlier Post-Impressionist shows, the selection strongly reflecting his personal taste.* The common factor amongst the artists was friendship with Fry and the influence of Cézanne. Clive Bell criticized the omission of work by Stanley Spencer, Lewis, Bomberg, Roberts, Matisse, Picasso and other important contemporary painters. Fry himself admitted that the show was very restrained: 'The whole effect is very discreet and yet gay and lively of course; except for Gertler, we are fearfully tasteful.'[17] Nonetheless the general press reaction was still one of hostility and mirth.

The air raids were at their height in London during the autumn of 1917. There was a warning while Fry was hanging the show at Heal's and everyone was shepherded down into the basement for an hour. He wrote to Vanessa: 'It seemed an absurd and boring proceeding and spoilt my lunch. People have been very much shaken – Walter Sickert . . . is however much pleased, as the place where he teaches has good cellars where he sits and smokes and drinks with his pupils and gets a guinea for doing so.[18] The denizens of Fitzroy Street managed to make light of the raids and turn them into an excuse for gathering together in cellars for impromptu parties. As they became more inured to danger – and the barrage became more effective – they took to sitting on roofs and drinking wine while they watched the bombs falling.

Since Gaudier's death Nina had stayed in touch with Sophie Brzeska, who had

* Of the seventy-eight exhibits, twelve were by Fry and twenty-three came from his own collection. Two-thirds of the show was by one-time employees of the Omega including Vanessa Bell, Duncan Grant, Gaudier-Brzeska, Frederick Etchells, Dolores Courtney and Roald Kristian (Edgar de Bergen). The rest was by French artists such as Derain, Doucet, Friesz, Gris, Lhote, Marchand, Vlaminck and Brancusi.

become even more nervous and eccentric. In September, anxious to escape the daily air raids in London, Nina gladly accepted Sophie's invitation to stay with her at her cottage at Wotton under Edge in Gloucestershire. To start with all went well. Sophie was pleased to break her solitude and enjoyed having a companion with whom she could discuss art and literature. They went for long walks, talked and worked together, picked blackberries and made jam. In her first rush of pleasure Sophie wrote admiringly in her diary about Nina's intelligence, broad-mindedness and unexpected commitment to her work. She poured out her innermost thoughts and feelings to Nina, explaining her strange personal philosophy at length. She certainly had some odd views and feared the evil influence of the moon, going to great lengths to avoid looking at it. The more insistently confidential Sophie became, the more Nina withdrew, unwilling to reciprocate her cloying intimacy. She felt even less enthusiasm for Sophie's poetry than for her personal revelations. When she first arrived Nina tried her best to be accommodating and listened politely while Sophie recited her verse. But this did not satisfy Sophie, who complained that Nina only praised her more amusing and slighter efforts, passing over in silence the earnest expressions of her soul. Later Nina did everything possible to prevent Sophie reading her poetry, and would try and distract her by singing music-hall songs whenever a poem seemed imminent.

Sophie violently resented what she felt was Nina's dismissive attitude to her work and all her old jealousy and hostility soon reasserted itself. It was not long before she was once again railing in her diary against Nina's supposed English reserve, insensitivity and arrogance, and criticizing both her and her work for their coldness and soullessness. She took revenge on Nina in petty ways. They had agreed that Sophie should provide the food while Nina would pay for drink. Obsessively suspicious, Sophie watched Nina like a hawk. Convinced that she poured more wine for herself, Sophie retaliated by not offering her a milk drink at night when she took one, and washing Nina's plates and cutlery with less care than her own.

Nina felt deluged by Sophie's torrent of words, which went on well into the night. Even when she had retired to her attic bedroom to sleep on a sofa that was so short her feet stuck out over the edge, she could not escape. The room had no door and Sophie would stand at the bottom of the stairs, loudly continuing her monologue. One morning in the early hours she demanded to know if Nina would have gone off with Gaudier if she had had the chance. Nina shouted back that she would, and felt some alarm at the ensuing silence. But Sophie, her suspicions confirmed, merely went to bed. If anything, Nina found her stay at Wotton more unnerving than the threat of the bombs, and Sophie commented that Nina sighed deeply, slept badly and looked unwell, all of which she attributed to her regret about Edgar's having left for the war. Nina was immensely relieved to leave Sophie after two weeks and return to London, where the air raids had stopped. With the money she had earned from the sale of three of her pictures to Michael Sadler in Birmingham, she moved from Camden Town to a top-floor studio with a bedroom and kitchen at 18 Fitzroy Street, close to Fry at number 21.

1917 was a quiet year for the Omega. There was a show of children's art and another of 'Copies and Translations' of past art, mainly the early Italian masters. In April, *Colour* magazine published an article by Fry in which he extolled the merits of artists as interior decorators: 'our artist may be able, merely out of the contrast of two or three pure colours applied in simple rectangular shapes, to transform a room completely, giving it a new feeling of space or dignity or richness.'[19] The article was illustrated with a sketch by Nina of a proposed Omega interior which closely related to Fry's description of the decorations carried out for Lalla Vandervelde's flat at Rossetti Garden Mansions, Chelsea.

Nina contributed to the first mixed-subject exhibition of recent paintings by Omega artists in November. In the same month she also showed three portraits and two drawings, one of a grocer's shop in Camden Town, with the London Group, of which she was elected a member. Her work was widely praised in the daily press. The critic of the *Globe* remarked on 'Miss Hamnett's strenuous personalities on canvas';[20] while John Salis singled out her portrait of Haraldur Hamar for particular comment: 'It is the best thing she has yet done. There is an air of steady progression in Miss Hamnett's work which is very stimulating, and this presentation of the Icelandic playwright is a very thorough piece of work, carefully composed and intensely seen.'[21] The same critic described the portrait she exhibited at the winter New English Art Club show as 'excellent. It has the rare power of drawing one across the room.'[22]

Nina and Fry saw a good deal of each other at this time. Their relationship was sufficiently well established for Vanessa Bell to invite them both to stay at Charleston in October, but the visit did not take place. Although familiar with Bloomsbury, Nina was never a fully fledged member of the inner circle. She did, however, accompany Fry on social occasions such as dinner in Soho with the Bells, Virginia and Leonard Woolf, Saxon Sydney-Turner, Barbara Hiles and 'a party such as might figure in a Wells novel'.[23] Fry never considered his affair with Nina to be of the deeper kind and Vanessa always remained his ideal woman. Nina, however, satisfied his need for 'someone who can talk art and sympathise and criticise'[24] as well as providing 'the kind of intimate companionship in little things' for which he craved.[25]

But Nina was not the person to enjoy a comfortable, domestic relationship for long. In February 1918 a shocked and hurt Fry wrote to Vanessa announcing the

Nina, 1917, by Roger Fry   Nina, 1917, by Roger Fry

sudden end of their affair, which had lasted happily for more than a year:

> I was rather upset when I got back to find that Nina had picked up a young man
> of 18 a drunken sodomite of pleasant manner and weak character with whom
> she was actually living. . . . She's incredibly light and easily turned and acts
> without any reflection and will probably have a bad time as a result of this
> escapade as well as being reduced to poverty. It's all very awkward as I have to
> work in the studio next door and see her casually and yet never to talk to really
> . . . I have as well a good deal of physical jealousy. I never expected fidelity,
> but in this case it looks as though she were so wrapped up as to want to throw
> me over altogether . . . I think she's been rather excessively selfish and
> inconsiderate in the way she's done the thing but I daresay that's only the
> inevitable reaction to the pain it's caused me.[26]

Nina's affair with the anonymous young man was no more serious or long-lasting than any of her other flings. She was highly promiscuous, but sexual liberation was merely one aspect of her rebellion against convention and her quest for personal independence. Underlying this was a basic sexual coldness, even indifference. She told her friend Gladys Hynes: 'Can't see anything in it myself . . . But they seem to like it so I let them get on with it'.[27] There was nothing romantic or idealistic about her approach to sex and she remarked to the same friend on another occasion: '(So and So) said the other day, "You love me with your body, I wish I could think that you loved me with your soul" . . . What the hell do you suppose he meant?'[28]

By May, Fry had re-established friendly contact with Nina and wrote to Vanessa: 'Nina came down for a night; she's very friendly again and I know now exactly what I can expect and feel much less hurt about it. *Elle est vraiment putain* but a very nice one and one ought to accept that as a type of character *comme une autre* and not be amazed at it or demand what it can't give. I suppose I shall learn some philosophy by the time I am impotent.'[29]

Despite his harsh words, Fry did not succeed in banishing Nina from his thoughts and sent her frequent poems, letters, and a long disquisition on the subject of unsuccessful love in the aggrieved tones of a rejected lover. He could still write to her in June 1918 that she was

> the most fascinating, exciting, tantalising, elusive, capricious, impulsive, beautiful, exasperating creature in the world . . . Oh what letters I would write you from my hermitage, how I would combine amusement with instruction and obscenity with philosophy and how pleased I would make you with yourself if only . . . there were just that minimum of response without which it's impossible. I can't do it all myself – but what waste – for I feel in such a vein to make you think yourself incredibly lucky and happy – *tant pis*.[30]

Nina and Fry continued to see each other from time to time until the end of 1918. Fry did his best to accept the limitations of their relationship and not be too oppressively demanding. He wrote to her in July after she had visited him at Durbins: 'You were so charming (for once, as you warned me) yesterday and so beautiful (as always) that I can't get you out of my head.'[31] He composed the following *Ronde de nuit* to her:

> I cannot get to sleep at all
> For conjuring to mind your face,
> And now that I've become its thrall
> I have to bless you, if a place

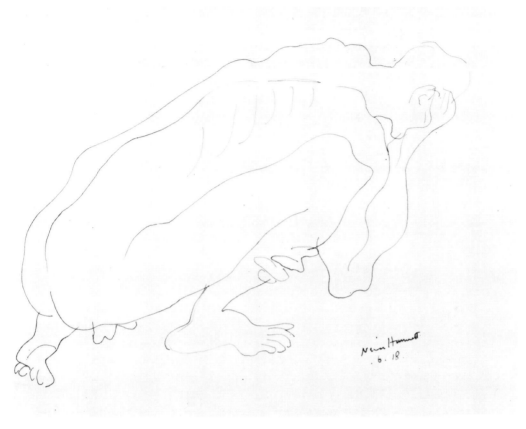

Roger Fry, 1918

By virtue of your gentle grace,
Therein, be mine, however small.
I cannot get to sleep at all
For conjuring to mind your face

And all its beauties I must trace
As each one's image, I recall
Let me not quite from favour fall,
Yet surely I'm in evil case
I cannot get to sleep at all.[32]

As Fry's influence waned with the end of their affair, Sickert regained the ascendancy over Nina, resuming his long-held role of friend, confidant and mentor. He always maintained a special interest in Nina and said she should be locked in her room and beaten to make her work. But Nina's gay round of party-going continued unabated and she kept open studio for her friends on Thursday evenings, when a Spaniard played the guitar to entertain them. Like Fry, Sickert was concerned that she was frittering her energies and wrote to her in avuncular tone from Bath, where he spent the summers of 1916, 1917 and 1918:

> You are young and can stand a lot but you won't always be. Save your precious nerves. You must not be perpetually in a state of purposeless excitement. The grounds must be allowed to settle and the coffee to clear . . . Don't stand any nonsense from your men friends and lovers. Keep them *tyrannically* to their settled hours — like a dentist — the hours that suit you — and them so far as possible. Don't give any one any rights. Exact an absolute obedience to time *as the price of any intercourse at all*. Don't be a tin kettle to any dog's tail, however long.[33]

Sickert need not have worried, for despite her hectic social life, Nina was clearly working very hard. In May she exhibited a drawing and portraits of Mary Butts, Edith Sitwell, C. J. Hope Johnstone and the poet Wilfred Childe with the London Group. Paul Konody wrote in the *Observer* that they showed 'more restraint than is her wont. Her remarkable gifts have never been as fully revealed as in her portrait of Miss Mary Butts.'[34] The poet and novelist Mary Butts was the great-granddaughter of Thomas Butts, the friend and patron of William Blake. She was the same age as Nina and like her was also in full revolt against her family background. Her dramatically pale face and flame-gold hair matched her passionate personality. In her intelligence and imagination were both at high pressure. She lived in an atmosphere of constant intellectual and emotional turmoil, overwhelming her listener with her ardent and chaotic enthusiasms and indignations.

Sickert wrote to Ethel Sands in 1918 that Nina had 'grown up but still has a little XIVe Arr. + Roger provincialism to get rid of'.[35] Sickert gave Nina much advice about painting techniques and tried to convince her of the merits of working from carefully squared-up drawings rather than from life. Nina experimented with his method but found it irksomely laborious and the results disappointing. There is a finished oil of the landscape painter Ethelbert White and his wife Betty playing the guitar and banjo which clearly shows the grid of lines used in the squaring-up process. Nina was evidently unhappy with this procedure and uncharacteristically had trouble with the proportions of the figures and their relations to each other. The work lacks her usual deftness of touch and assurance of composition, capturing none of the gaiety of her subjects.

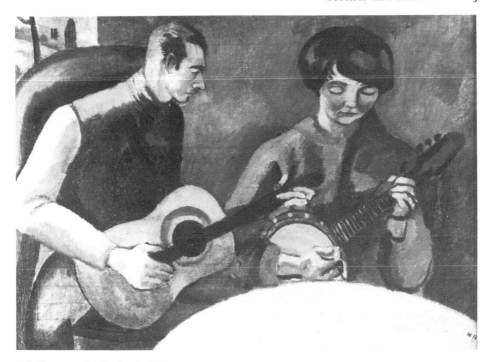

Ethelbert and Elizabeth White, c.1918

No Fitzroy Street party was complete without Ethelbert White – often joined by Claude Marx – singing and playing a whole range of folk songs, dances and flamenco, which Betty would perform for the company.

Despite Sickert's strictures against painting from life, he admired Nina's work and admitted that it inspired him with 'what the Germans call ''einen Kolossalen Respekt'''.[36] In June 1918 she held her first solo exhibition on the premises of the *Cambridge Magazine* in King's Parade, Cambridge. She showed some thirty works, including eight portraits, seven still lifes, drawings and watercolours. Sickert wrote an article in the magazine by way of an introduction to the exhibition, stressing her talent as a draughtsman:

Nina Hamnett has shown at every stage of her rapid and somewhat turbulent development as a draughtsman and painter the possession of unmistakable power. An imperious instinct in the choice of her influences, a generous and frank surrender to such influences, and an almost indecent gluttony for work have placed her in a position that is, for an artist of her age, sufficiently brilliant. . . . The work begun under Messrs. Cope and Nicol was re-inforced by influences as far removed as Gaudier-Brzeska, Modigliani, and Segonzac. And drawing incessantly with these masters has made of her a producer of drawings that may rather be called sculptor's than painter's drawings, in the sense that the form of the figure is studied in contour and the modelling mostly apart from relation to any pictorial background. I cannot see her drawing not leading her to sustained practice in sculpture, sculpture being merely the multiplication by a theoretic infinity of the sharp silhouette that her uniform and sensitive line defines with such expressiveness and such startling virtuosity.[37]

Also in June a further exhibition of Nina's work opened in London at the new Eldar Gallery in Great Marlborough Street. Apart from three portraits and a landscape in oils, the rest of the fifty-two exhibits were drawings, consisting mainly of portraits, figure studies and nudes. In the preface that Sickert wrote to the catalogue he again praised Nina's draughtsmanship and went on to discuss her talents as a painter:

From her earliest exhibited canvases Nina Hamnett has shown herself a painter by temperament, with a normal eye for sober and harmoniously related colour. Her portraits are not those of an employé. She seems to have no disposition to enter into competition with the valetaille of the already somewhat over-stuffed Society super-goose. Like Hogarth, she picks her sitters, rather than suffers them gladly to pick her, so that in the end her gallery of portraits is likely to form an interesting sequence. The critical acumen and learning of Roger Fry has influenced her most usefully. She probably owes to him as much as to any one the habit of thinking correctly in terms of the painter's art.

Following on the success of this exhibition Nina showed a portrait, a still life and a study of roofs with the Allied Artists' Association in July, but she was critical of the generally low standard of the other exhibitors.

While Sickert's wife Christine went on ahead of him to Bath to prepare things for the summer, he remained in London, taking Nina out to breakfast at the Euston Hotel and lunch at the Café Royal, and showing her all his favourite haunts in Camden Town. When he left for Bath he sent her a characteristically ebullient telegram on his arrival: 'Bonjour Nina, Bath spiffing',[38] followed by a series of letters full of practical advice about painting and life, work in progress, books read, jokes and gossip about fellow painters. He good-humouredly referred to himself as her 'uncle': 'What did I say. Who's clever. Who's always right. Stick to your Uncle and your Uncle will pull you through.'[39] Although the

Reclining Man, c. 1918

extravagant gallantry and easy sexual bantering of Sickert's letters to Nina sound too intimate for innocence, it was his usual style to his favourite women followers and he wrote in a similarly flirtatious vein to Enid Bagnold, who declared that it was just 'airy love'.[40]

Sickert believed that an artist should always have two studios, one tidy and conventional 'to receive non-hogwash in as a matter of business and a pigstye as much as you like for private use'.[41] He was delighted that Nina used the Whistler – his studio at 8 Fitzroy Street – to paint portraits while he was away and wrote to her, 'You will be obliged to remain in it. Dear Angel you can burn all my furniture and throw my pictures out of the window if only you will take care of yourself and your nerves.'[42]

Sickert loved the peace and elegance of Bath and urged Nina to join him:

I am dying all obvious selfishness apart, for you to come to Bath. It will rest and amuse and refresh you and week for week it will cost you less money than in

> London. . . . You could work in these gardens and orchards in perfect peace.
> Such roofs, such roses, such contorted walls . . . Such fresh, bracing
> air. . .[43]

He pressed his case, purchased a painting from her for £15 and went to great
trouble to find her suitable lodgings in a row of workmen's cottages half way
down Beechen Cliff. He described the view out of her window in excited terms:
'From the bed it looks as if someone had chucked the roofs of the whole town in
at the two windows with the Abbey in the middle and the tower of your old
school on the horizon. It takes one's breath away.'[44] Nina did not need very
much persuasion and left for Bath with high expectations of a gay time with
parties and outings.

Fry was rather jealous of Nina's spending time with Sickert and wrote
reproaching her for not writing to him: 'I suppose it was all too thrilling and dear
W. S. too engaging.'[45] This was quickly followed by a new rondeau which he
declared was 'deeply expressive' of his sentiments:

My only love, my mistress and my joy
Since now I'm bound so far from you to stay
Nothing I have my sadness to allay
But memories of you, my mind's employ.

Hope only can my spirits now up-buoy;
In such wise must I pass my time away,
My only love, my mistress and my joy,
Since now I'm bound so far from you to stay.

Now sadness will my tired heart destroy
Which only longs to be with you alway
Nor can I have it back, whate'er I say,
Till with your youthful beauty I may toy,
My only love, my mistress and my joy.[46]

When Nina did write, Fry must have been reassured by her letters which suggest
that she was having a less than ecstatic time in Bath. Sickert thought that like
himself, Nina wanted to devote herself to painting. His established routine in
Bath was to get up at six, draw outdoors till eight, then go to his studio where he
would breakfast and paint until he swam at midday. After lunch he slept until
four, had tea at his studio and did some more work until seven when he returned
home for dinner with Christine. Nina only saw him at five-thirty, when she

would watch him paint sketches of the river and Pulteney Bridge and listen to him discoursing on his methods. She wrote to Fry: 'He . . . spends at least two hours daily at tea-time in holding forth. I always say "yes" and go home and do the opposite. He admits he can understand nothing of modern art. I understand that he doesn't, but why he doesn't I don't see. I am giving him all the available literature on Rimbaud which thrills him.'[47] Nina impatiently rejected Sickert's painstaking techniques: 'W. S. now paints on four small panels a day & paints them in ink colour black and tan boots colour, the architecture is getting more & more minute & laborious. I sit beside him in a garden the last sitting after tea. How silly he is!'[48]

Left to her own devices all day, after her meeting with Sickert Nina returned to a solitary supper in her lodgings and went to bed. Her only amusement was to dine with the Sickerts twice a week. She found Christine 'very odd, very nice but awfully jealous of him I think & leads a rotten life. I wouldn't put up with him for five minutes, not as a husband certainly.'[49] Nina spent Sundays entirely alone as Sickert did not go to his studio. Not surprisingly, she rapidly became bored and disenchanted with the quiet life she led in Bath. She needed the stimulus of contact with other people to work and hated the enervating climate, which as in her school-days made her feel ill.

Sickert did not restrict his lectures to painting and evidently felt that Nina should present a more conventional appearance to the world. When Nina reported Sickert's latest strictures to Fry, he wrote back in horrified tones:

No please don't listen to W. S. about clothes do for God's sake be yourself in that. You have made a very piquant and amusing and characteristic figure of yourself my dear and a damned lovable one – however I needn't bother you have too much character for it not to come through anything and as it's your character I'm in love with I needn't worry. Any more than I do about your painting.[50]

Sickert never visited Nina's lodgings so did not know that she was ignoring his injunctions to work from squared-up drawings and was doing a portrait of her landlady, the wife of a policeman.[51] Nevertheless, he did have some influence on her work in Bath and the picture's unusually detailed depiction of the sitter's interior, complete with patterned wallpaper, lamp, teacup and telescope, suggests that Nina was heeding Sickert's insistence that a figure exists in relation to its surroundings. The portrait has clear affinities with certain Camden Town Group interiors and bears comparison with Harold Gilman's *Mrs Mounter at the Breakfast Table* painted in 1916. Its very schematic composition, based on a rigid grid pattern of horizontals and verticals, highlights the severity of the sitter's features as she stares uncompromisingly straight out at the viewer. The picture, which was bought by Fry, thoroughly disgruntled *The Times* critic who described it as 'so impersonal that it makes one feel one is looking at some queer animal in its own private cage at the zoo. Here, again, is a human being painted as if not by a human being, but with purely abstract curiosity.'[52] In contrast, John Salis called it 'an excellent analysis of a certain type of English woman'.[53]

Nina also did some views of roofs from her window but for the most part she was very dissatisfied with her work in Bath and had to be persuaded by Sickert not to destroy it. Thrown back almost entirely on her own resources, feeling ill and depressed, Nina became increasingly desperate. Finally, deciding that death must be preferable to spending another day in Bath, she left at the end of five weeks.

Sickert had decided to retire from his teaching post at the Westminster Technical Institute in Vincent Square, and he and Augustus John recommended that Nina should replace him. Sickert thought that Nina was 'one of the curious people who will always influence gangs of others'[54] and was sure that she was well suited to teaching. He advised her to be amenable and compliant with the authorities: 'I am convinced that once the students have had a fortnight's experience of you, you will create an enthusiastic following, because, firstly you have been through so much and secondly because you have so much intellectual vitality and students quickly feel that.'[55] Nina took three evening classes in Life drawing a week and had to hire and pose the models as well as teach. At first she was very nervous and wore a large grey hat rammed down over her eyes which she never took off, but as she became more confident she relaxed and drew with the students. The numbers in her class soon swelled from five to thirty and she made a point of getting to know them all. One of Nina's most diligent students was a very beautiful elderly lady who always dressed in a neat white apron and worked very hard. She was Gertrude Kingston, the famous actress and founder of the Little Theatre for whom Shaw wrote *Major Barbara*. They had a great liking and respect for each other and Gertrude was to prove a loyal supporter of Nina.

Nina was still involved in the Omega and some idea of her relative importance can be gauged from a letter Fry wrote to Vanessa estimating the possible earnings of each of the artists: Grant £400; Wolfe £300; Nina £250; Fry £250; Vanessa £200 and other artists £500.[56] Although these figures represent a considerable increase on the Omega's actual takings, they show Nina in a surprisingly strong position. Dressmaking remained the Omega's most reliable source of income and Nina had suggested to Fry that Mlle Gabrielle Soëne, a good friend of Modigliani who was living in poverty in Paris, should be brought over to take charge of it. Her designs were enthusiastically received by Fry and dresses by her were exhibited with Fry's pottery downstairs at a mixed show of paintings by

Life Class at the Westminster Technical Institute, 1919

Omega artists which opened in October 1918. Nina contributed the portrait of her landlady in Bath, a second portrait of Haraldur Hamar, an *Acrobat*, and some drawings. John Salis praised her work in glowing terms:

> For some years now one has been watching the steady progress of Nina Hamnett, she is like a snowball rolling down a hill, and one can see no reason why she should stop rolling. One feels that as she has done so she will go on, adding year after year more insight and more subtlety. Her colour has made great strides in the last year.[57]

In November Nina exhibited five works with the London Group – studies of roofs in London and Bath, a portrait of Edward Wolfe, a head of a Negro and a drawing. The show prompted Virginia Woolf to write to her sister Vanessa Bell: 'Nina Hamnett does roofs; why are you artists so repetitious; does the eye for months together see nothing but roofs?'[58]

The highlight of autumn 1918 was the unexpected arrival in London of Diaghilev's Russian Ballet with its new stars Lydia Lopokova and Massine. For two months the company shared the bill with music-hall turns at the Coliseum, delighting audiences with their popular production of *The Good Humoured Ladies*, based on Goldoni's comedy of the same name with music by Scarlatti and simple, Guardi-inspired décor by Bakst. Nina did not think the dancing was up to pre-war standards but the very presence of the Russian Ballet in London after four years of virtual cultural isolation seemed like a portent of peace. As indeed it was.

On 11 November Nina was walking along Tottenham Court Road when she saw the word ARMISTICE written up in large letters. She did not know what it

Armistice Day
Celebrations (From
The Silent Queen)

meant until she read further on that fighting would stop at eleven-thirty that morning. The war was over and there was only one way to celebrate. Rushing to the bank to withdraw some money, she bought two bottles of champagne and made her way with Geoffrey Nelson to Trafalgar Square where the crowds were already going mad, linking hands, dancing, singing and laughing. All down the Strand windows were flung open and paper rained down on to the street. The packed buses, spilling over with cheering passengers, ceased to take fares and abandoned their normal routes, following the whim of the driver. Lorry-loads of singing and yelling factory girls drove slowly along to the accompaniment of hooting motors and police whistles. Taxis were crammed full and often carried an extra few people on the roof.

Nina threw herself into the celebrations. Lunching at the Tour Eiffel, she went on the Café Royal, where the toast was to the Kaiser. She battled her way through the surging crowd to the flat of the barrister and art collector Montague Shearman in the Adelphi, where a riotous party was in progress. Everybody seemed to know everybody else. Bloomsbury was there in force: Duncan Grant, David Garnett, Lytton Strachey, Carrington, Mary and Jack Hutchinson; a contingent from the Russian Ballet – Diaghilev, Massine, Lydia Lopokova – the Sitwells and Gertler. Augustus John was cheered when he entered in uniform accompanied by some land-girls in leggings and breeches. There was an ever-changing sea of faces. Henry Mond, the chemical manufacturer, wearing just a singlet, was banging on the pianola, clutching a tumbler of whisky in each fist. As the night grew hotter, people threw champagne over him to cool him down. Everyone danced, even Lytton Strachey.

The celebrations went on for a week. Then, finally, the war really was all over.

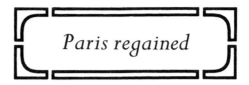

10

Paris regained

L ONDON was swept up in a delirium of revelry and euphoria. 'Christmas came riotous with parties . . . The motto of Chelsea and Fitzroy Street was . . . "on with the dance, let joy be unconfined." ' [1] In the brief post-war boom there was a great excitement and optimism in the air and it was easy to ignore the inconveniences that the continuation of wartime restrictions and rationing imposed on everyday life.

Early in 1919 Nina moved to the top floor of a house at 37 Great James Street in Bloomsbury. But she soon regretted her decision, finding her new accommodation dark and depressing, and missing the friendly camaraderie and bustle of Fitzroy Street. She continued to teach three evenings a week at the Westminster Technical Institute and went to Life classes at St Martin's School of Art on the other two nights to draw from the model. Her talents as a portrait painter were officially recognized by a commission to paint Major-General Bethune Lindsay for the Canadian War Memorials Fund, which had been set up in 1917 to provide a visual record of the Canadian war effort. Frederick Etchells described the resulting work, now in the National Gallery at Ottawa, as 'a solid and largely successful "official" portrait of a somewhat corpulent officer.' [2]

Hardly a month went by without work by Nina being exhibited and favourably reviewed. However, her portrait of Edith Sitwell in a rainbow jacket provoked a controversial response when it was shown with a portrait of Osbert Sitwell and a drawing of Alvaro Guevara at the National Portrait Society in February 1919. The conservative critic of the *Tatler* declared himself staggered by her Futurist frock and 'kaleidoscopic breasts', [3] while Clutton-Brock proclaimed in *The Times* that it was 'a serious work in the midst of much frivolity'. [4] Also in February, *Colour* reproduced a particularly accomplished still life of 1917,* depicting a milk jug and French paperback book painted in richly glowing blues, yellow, brown and ochre, comparing it to 'a piece of good prose . . it has . . . a definite

* See page 93

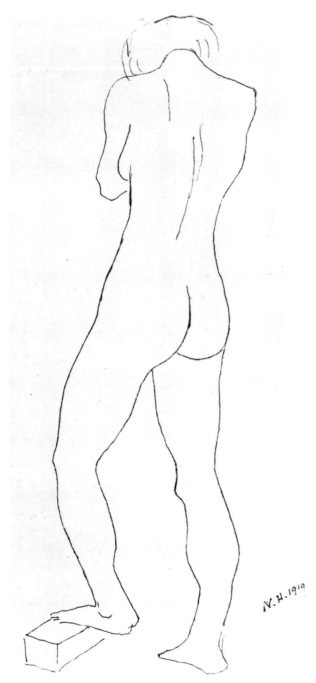

Nude, 1919

Anthony Butts

rhythm, and in form, colour and texture it is beautifully consistent.' The critic of the *Cambridge Magazine* singled out her portrait of W. H. Davies at the London Group exhibition in April, where she also showed a still life and three watercolours. In July she exhibited three portraits with the Allied Artists' Association, including one of Sickert and another of Anthony Butts, Mary Butts' nineteen-year-old brother, a wealthy and extravagantly amusing dilettante who was for a time a pupil of Sickert. Her *Interior* and *Life Class* at the New English Art Club summer show prompted one critic to exclaim, 'How this young lady does sail full tilt with her pictures, trusting confidently in her sensations which seem so little at fault!'[5]

Nina's rapidly growing reputation and her wide acquaintance amongst artists made her a natural choice to join the editorial committee of *Coterie*, one of the

Anthony Butts, *c.*1919

liveliest of the new avant-garde magazines which appeared after the war. Largely
devoted to poetry, it was edited by Chaman Lall, the other committee members
initially including T. S. Eliot, Tommy Earp, Richard Aldington, Aldous
Huxley, Russell Green and Wyndham Lewis.* *Coterie* was first published in May
1919 from the Bomb Shop, Frank Henderson's famous left-wing bookshop with

* Apart from the committee members, the better-known contributors numbered Roy
Campbell, the Sitwells, Iris Tree, H. D., John Gould Fletcher, Amy Lowell and Herbert
Read. The illustrations were by a mixture of Nina's friends such as Sickert, Adrian Allinson,
Allan Odle, John Flanagan, Modigliani, Gaudier-Brzeska, Ethelbert White and Geoffrey
Nelson; Wyndham Lewis's Vorticist associates William Roberts, Lawrence Atkinson and
Bomberg; and the École de Paris, including Dearin, Kisling, Zadkine, Archipenko, René
Durey, Rubczak, Zawado and Mendjizky.

Nina Hamnett,
Self Portrait, 1918

scarlet shelves in the Charing Cross Road, and ran for seven issues until the end of
1920. A drawing by Nina of a café scene was featured on the cover of the
Christmas 1920 issue and a seated female nude and a self-portrait also appeared
during the magazine's short life. Another drawing by Nina of a short-haired
saucy-looking vamp was used on the cover of *Ten Sonnets* by George Harcourt
Johnstone, a contributor to *Coterie*, published in 1921 by Basil Blackwood.

After the long war years there was a great eagerness to discover what had been
happening abroad. Paris was still the centre of the modern movement and the
Diaghilev ballet provided an important focal point for all the most aggressively
avant-garde tendencies in music, art and choreography. When the Russian Ballet
returned to England in the summer of 1919, bringing productions of Massine's
La Boutique Fantasque with sets and costumes by Derain and *The Three Cornered
Hat*, designed by Picasso, London had what Osbert Sitwell called 'the
excitement of seeing truly modern works of scenic art upon the stage'.[6]

Diaghilev's example inspired Osbert and Sacheverell Sitwell to aspire to the
role of impresarios to the avant-garde in London. They joined forces with the

Anthony Butts, Paris 1921

Street Corner Conversation, c.1916, with Lytton Strachey in the centre

Polish-Parisian art dealer Zborowski to mount an exhibition of Modern French Art at Heal's Mansard Gallery in August.* Crowds thronged to the gallery and a good many works were sold on the opening day. The exhibition was well received by sympathetic critics such as Roger Fry, Clive Bell and Tommy Earp but the vitriolic reaction of the general public recalled the furore caused by Fry's pre-war Post-Impressionist shows. One outraged visitor wrote indignantly to the *Nation* that the whole collection was 'a glorifying in prostitution'.[7] Modigliani's work, exhibited for the first time in England, proved to be the sensation of the show. His elongated swans' necks provoked such constant and vehement derision that Osbert Sitwell observed

> out of this rage . . . it would have been possible at last to extract a mathematical formula, the heat of the anger seeming to be based on the number of times the neck of the given Modigliani could be multiplied to make the neck of the person protesting. Certainly, the thicker the neck, the greater the transports of its owner, and the thicker still would it become, swelling from fury.[8]

For artists and amateurs however, the exhibition was a welcome opportunity to catch up with the latest artistic developments and it made Nina long to return to Paris as soon as she could.

There were plenty of other visiting attractions that summer. One of the most popular was the Southern Syncopated Orchestra, which acquired something of a cult status among Nina and her friends. They went twice or three times a week to the Philharmonic Hall near Oxford Circus to hear a non-stop two-hour programme of Negro spirituals joyfully delivered to tumultuous applause. The orchestra's success was a foretaste of the immense vogue for black musicians that was to sweep the twenties. The star of the show was Mrs Reavis, whose Gauguinesque beauty so captivated Nina that she asked her to pose for her and invited Epstein to draw with her. Nina became quite friendly with Mrs Reavis and she was one of the few white people invited to a reception given on 8 August at the Albert Rooms in honour of distinguished African visitors to London. Nina met the President of Liberia and listened to speeches about conditions in Africa before the orchestra played and she joined in the noisy, uninhibited dancing.

In October Nina held her second exhibition at the Eldar Gallery. It included portraits, landscapes – studies of roofs, bridges, canals and a mill – several still lifes and a quantity of nude and figure drawings. The *Burlington Magazine* praised

*It included, among others, paintings by Picasso, Matisse, Derain, Vlaminck, Modigliani, Lhote, Friesz, Marcousis, Léger, Survage, Ortiz, Kisling, Utrillo, Suzanne Valadon, Soutine and Dufy as well as sculpture by Zadkine and Archipenko.

Woman Reading,
c.1919

her as 'one of the most interesting of the younger generation of British artists';[9] while Frederick Etchells, writing in the *Cambridge Magazine*, admired her 'direct feeling for character', wittily comparing her to 'an avid spider' who 'pounces on every vital trait of her sitters'. He particularly liked the nude studies, which he thought presented 'a body of sincere and personal observations and a real achievement in the use of pen line'.[10] David Garnett and Francis Birrell included Nina's painting of *The Canal* in their anthology of modern art published in 1921, which placed great emphasis on the importance of design.

Despite so much success and activity, Nina was becoming increasingly bored with life in London, which seemed like a provincial backwater in comparison with Paris. The initial post-war excitement had worn off and been replaced by an atmosphere of dull apathy. Nina's friend Douglas Goldring, a writer and contributor to *Coterie*, commented that

> After the Armistice those who could do so had every inducement to cross the Channel. London was grim, gloomy, depressed, shabby, overcrowded and expensive. Dora and her misbegotten progeny reserved most of the good

The Canal,
c.1919

things of life for the profiteers, who could evade her restrictions, drinks were dear, pubs opened late and closed early, and financial depression soon followed on the brief post-war boom.[11]

Nina craved the hectic gaiety of Paris and wrote at the time of her exhibition at the Eldar Gallery: 'If I had some money and not my class I should leave at once (go abroad) and not return for at least five years. Perhaps I shall if I make some money out of my show.'[12]

In the event, Nina did just that. When her teaching term finished at the end of March 1920 she took the train to Paris where she stayed once again at the Hôtel de la Haute Loire. She went straight to the Rotonde to ask about her old friends and joyfully rediscovered Wassilieff, Zadkine and Brancusi. Not all the familiar faces were there, however, and she was saddened to hear the tragic details of Modigliani's death from tubercular meningitis in January. But if he died like a pauper, he was buried like a prince and the whole shocked quarter turned out *en masse* to follow his funeral procession.

Although Nina was thrilled to be back in Paris and wore out a pair of shoes in three weeks visiting all her favourite haunts, she could not help noticing how drastically Montparnasse was changing . The wartime political and geographical upheavals had brought a new wave of exiles from Eastern Europe, while the devaluation of the franc against other currencies meant that artists and writers, visitors of all kinds, poured into Montparnasse from the four corners of the earth, eager to enjoy themselves and throw off the dark shadow of war. Many Americans had had their first taste of life abroad on active service and the introduction of prohibition in the United States made Paris all the more alluring to those anxious to escape the twin horrors of American puritanism and rampant consumerism. People left their inhibitions at home and came to enjoy the legendary freedom of Paris. Skirts were shorter, cars and crowds proliferated and the new jazz was heard everywhere, heralding the post-war era. With the influx of affluent foreigners, Montparnasse was losing its old village atmosphere and smartening up to cater to the tastes of the newcomers. It was no longer a tranquil backwater reserved for artists. Many of the old quarterites such as Picasso, Derain, Chagall, Soutine, Foujita and Zadkine had become well known and prosperous and moved away. Only those like Kisling and Pascin, who enjoyed the brouhaha of constant fête, remained.

Nevertheless, Paris could still work its old magic and it seemed to Nina as if history was repeating itself when one evening, sitting at the Rotonde with Beatrice Hastings, her attention was caught by a badly dressed young man with long fair hair. Beatrice told her that he was a talented Polish artist and once again obligingly provided the introductions. Wartime restrictions were still in force and when the Rotonde closed early at ten-thirty they went off to someone's studio where the Pole sang songs and played the guitar. He was quite unlike any of Nina's friends in London and reminded her so much of the happy times in Paris before the war that Nina knew she would fall in love with him and invited him to visit her in the studio she had borrowed from Zadkine's wife.

There was no longer any question of Nina's returning to the drab life of London. At the end of three weeks she went back briefly to hand in her resignation at the art school and borrow some money. She also submitted two drawings, a watercolour of Alvaro Guevara, and paintings of a *Circus* and *The Ring Master** to the London Group show which opened in May. The boldly simplified figures and flat, bright colours of the circus pictures were a new departure in Nina's work and the critic of the *Atheneum* praised her 'remarkable eye for silhouette and . . . singular facility of touch'.[13]

Nina hurried back to Paris and her Pole, moving into his bug-ridden hotel near the Avenue d'Orléans. She gave him all her money to look after and spent most of her time painting roofs out of the hotel window, which were much gayer than the rooftops she had done in England. She never knew, and did not ask, what

* facing page 97

the Pole did during the day, only seeing him in the evening when they had dinner together at a small workmen's restaurant nearby.

A few weeks later he suddenly ran off without warning with a wealthy English woman friend of Nina's, leaving her penniless and heartbroken to cry on Wassilieff's shoulder and borrow money from Zborowski and friends in England. Nina was forced to recognize that there was no going back to the days of pre-war innocence. She cursed her stupidity in having given the Pole all her money but ruefully put it down to experience and enjoyed his discomfiture when he was in turn abandoned by her friend, who was as much of a man-hunter as he was a fortune-seeker.

Nina had plenty of friends in Paris to distract her, such as Marie Beerbohm, Nancy Cunard, Evan Morgan, the painters Cedric Morris and Lett Haines, and the wealthy and witty poet and critic Tommy Earp, ex-President of the Oxford Union, famous for his hair *en brosse* and very mannered, high, quavering voice. The English were there in force at this time, eager to take advantage of the fact that the pound bought three times as much in France as in England. Gertler, on his first visit to Paris in April 1920, wrote to Carrington that in one day he had seen Roger Fry, Duncan Grant, Vanessa Bell, St John Hutchinson, Epstein, Iris Tree with her husband Curtis Moffat, and Nina.[14] The Café Parnasse next to the Rotonde, and the Dôme opposite, became the main meeting-places after Libion was forced to give up the Rotonde during the war to pay a fine for trafficking in American cigarettes. Its new proprietor asked ladies not to smoke or appear hatless on the terrace and made his lack of sympathy with artists quite clear. The Restaurant Baty, underneath the Hôtel de la Haute Loire, was a favourite eating-place and many of the old crowd went there, such as Zadkine, Kisling, Léger and Blaise Cendrars. With its baskets of oysters stacked outside and sawdust-covered, tiled floors, it rivalled Rosalie's in popularity in these early post-war years. Those of Nina's friends who had money were always very generous to her and after dinner at Baty's they usually did a round of all the cafés in Montparnasse, where they drank a lethal concoction called Pernod (Susie) Suze Fine, consisting of Pernod, gentian and brandy. There were endless parties which frequently ended up in the small hours among the flowers and cabbages at Les Halles.

The episode with the 'abominable Pole'[15] forgotten, Nina had moved to a hotel opposite the Gare Montparnasse and was working again. She had got to know one of his friends, the Polish Waclow Zawadowski, called simply Zawado, who was a talented painter of portraits and flower studies. A year younger than Nina, he had first come to Paris in 1912 to see the masterpieces in the Louvre, and spent the war years in Spain. Although he was not himself Jewish, he soon met many of the Polish Jewish artists who flocked to Paris before the war and was

Zawado (From *Laughing Torso*)

a good friend of Zborowski and Modigliani, whose studio he was now living in. Zawado was greatly attracted to Nina and she liked him very much. He was small and sturdy with a moustache and did a good imitation of Charlie Chaplin in the baggy corduroy trousers he always wore. When he told her she could come and work in his studio, Nina gladly accepted his offer even though she was very self-conscious about her painting, which was much more sombre in colour than the brilliant canvases she saw all around her in Paris.

Zawado quickly became very fond of Nina and after a short while suggested that they should get married and spend the summer in the South of France. Nina had to confess that she was already married, which was of no consequence to her although it gave the more scrupulous Zawado pause for thought. When he finally decided that it did not matter very much, Nina was politic enough to pretend that she was making a great sacrifice for his sake. She sold a few drawings and joyfully set off with him for the South. As the weather grew hotter, the sky bluer, and she saw olive trees and bright flowers from the window of the train, she thought that she was approaching paradise. After a long and excruciatingly uncomfortable journey on hard wooden benches, they arrived at Port Vendres at eight in the morning and walked about four miles along the cliffs to the tiny fishing village of Collioure, where the main occupation was salting and packing the locally caught sardines. Matisse had spent many summers painting there and Foujita and his wife Fernande Barrey were staying in the house Matisse had lived in, overlooking the bay. They welcomed Nina and Zawado and found them a large room in a narrow street near the sea, with a primitive charcoal-burning stove and an alcove with a bed. The only sanitary arrangements consisted of a bucket in another small recess, but Nina and Zawado were delighted with the room and quickly settled into a routine.

Nina was dazzled by the harsh southern light and the proliferation of strong colours – the blue of the sky and sea, the brightly painted fishing boats, the pink, green and white houses, and the purple shadows. She felt too daunted by the unfamiliar light and landscape to paint anything, fearing that whatever she did would look like a coloured photograph. Zawado encouraged her, saying that it did not matter what she painted, the important thing was simply to work. She followed his advice and after a few days began to feel confident enough to attempt a landscape. By the end of a week she and Zawado had found so many subjects that interested them that they painted one motif in the morning and another after lunch, Nina sometimes spending the afternoon drawing at the local café.

However, it was not all work. The Foujitas and Zawado tried to teach Nina to swim and after a week of determined effort she did manage a few triumphant yards – but then promptly sank. They went for picnics in the nearby countryside, where Nina astonished Fernande by insisting that they bury their rubbish so as not to spoil the landscape. There was little sympathy between Nina and Fernande, who frankly admitted that she had been a street-walker and model before her marriage to Foujita, whom she shouted at most of the time in her deep, gruff voice. Fernande brought out the hearty, no-nonsense side of Nina's character. On one of their excursions to an Arab castle they had to jump across a moat, a prospect which filled Fernande with such terror that she was in a fainting condition when she was finally persuaded to cross. Nina could barely contain her irritation at this display of feminine feebleness and made pointed remarks about education at the Royal School for the Daughters of Officers of the Army, the British Empire, courage, sport and so on. The contrast between them was graphically highlighted when they set out to cross the mountains into Spain for a fête day. Fernande appeared dressed in her best clothes and high-heeled patent-leather shoes, taking along some espadrilles for walking; while Nina wore a sensible corduroy land-girl's skirt and coat with copious pockets, and looked so typically British that the Spaniards screamed *Inglese!* as soon as they caught sight of her. However déclassé, Bohemian and outrageous Nina became, the values of her class and time were deeply ingrained in her and quickly reasserted themselves when put to the test. She never lost a certain respect for class; if anything, she was always far too susceptible to grand names and titles.

The Foujitas left after two weeks and Roubczak, a Polish artist friend of Zawado, arrived with his wife. They spent gay evenings together at the local café where an uproarious, risqué cabaret was performed on Fridays, Nina claiming that the songs were so indecent they shocked even her. On fête days a band dressed in Catalan costume would appear in the square and everybody danced in the streets until midnight. By the end of their three-month stay the grapes had ripened and wine presses were set up in the street. Before they left there was an orgy of tasting of the raw, new wine and they spent their last days in an alcoholic haze. The patron of the café treated them to a farewell Catalan breakfast of anchovies in oil and garlic, sausages and olives washed down with such vast quantities of red and white wine that afterwards they were in no state to contemplate leaving. Instead, they went for a long, silent walk to try to sober up, but abandoned the attempt after three miles and lay down in a row to sleep on the sea-shore.

Nina had uncharacteristically enjoyed her period of quiet domesticity with Zawado, whom she found kind and sympathetic, and when they arrived back in Paris she moved into his studio at 8 Rue de la Grande Chaumière. It was on the top, third floor of a dark, old, rickety wooden building reached by a long winding staircase. The studio was exactly as Modigliani had left it and consisted of two long rooms with bare floorboards, no gas or electricity, and only a coke stove on which to cook. Parts of the walls had been painted in broad washes of different colours to serve as backgrounds for paintings. It was sparsely furnished with little more than a brown wooden chest and Modigliani's old work table. Despite the lack of comfort they worked hard in their adjoining rooms. Nina painted still lifes and drew from the model in the afternoon at the next door Académie Colorossi. Zawado was always very encouraging and gave her helpful advice. Nina respected his judgement and felt he knew far more about painting than she did. When it was too dark to work they would sit each side of the table and read French classics by the light of an oil lamp, watched over from the shadows by one of the copies of Modigliani's death mask given them by Zborowski, a ghoulish *memento mori* with its drooping jaw. Nina found the cavernous, ramshackle building very sinister and was certain that she heard Modigliani's footsteps pacing the studio at night.

Two of Modigliani's old friends, Abdul and Ortiz de Zarate, who lived in the studio beneath, often came and spent the evenings with them talking over a bottle of wine. Abdul's full name was Abdul Wahab Gilani, although most people in the quarter called him simply the Arab. He was a member of one of the most aristocratic families in Tunis, descended from the last Emir of Almera, and as a Muslim he did not drink at all when he first arrived in Paris in 1911. But he had soon met Modigliani and spent nights at a time drinking and smoking hashish with him until his wealth and elegance, though never his charm, were completely evaporated. As faithful friends of Modigliani, he and Zawado had the sad task of watching over the body of his young mistress Jeanne Hébuterne when she committed suicide shortly after his death. Nina and Zawado were often very short of money and on one occasion neither they, nor Abdul nor their cat had anything to eat for three days. Help came from an unexpected quarter. As Zawado was turning the pages of one of Modigliani's philosophy books he discovered a hundred-franc note which Jeanne must have hidden away against a rainy day. The impoverished Modigliani had not forgotton to leave his old friends a legacy after all, and the three of them rushed off to eat and drink his health, taking the cat with them.

Nina was quite pleased with the fifteen or so paintings that she had done in Collioure and in the autumn she decided to try to sell them in London. She went via Dieppe so that she could visit Sickert, who had moved there at the end of the war. The recent death of his wife Christine had been a great blow to him and he was living alone with his cook and gardener at the Maison Mouton, a converted inn on the outskirts of the village of Envermeu, about ten miles from Dieppe. One could never tell what Sickert's latest disguise would be and this time he met her wearing a sailor's cap, oilskins and a red spotted scarf. To Nina's dismay, Sickert was horrified by her latest work and hated it. The reaction in London was not much more encouraging. She only managed to sell two works and left three landscapes and a still life at the Independent Gallery for a mixed show in February 1921. Nina was very disheartened. It was her first real set-back and she cursed the South of France, later coming to the conclusion that she had no affinity with its light and landscape.

Back in Paris she continued work on a series of watercolours of cafés and gardens. She especially liked the Luxembourg Gardens and went there every day to do drawings which she painted from memory in her studio. They looked very bright and gay when they were shown together at the Independent Gallery in June 1921. Nina went over to London for the opening and the reviews were very complimentary. Edward Holroyd, writing in the *New Statesman*,[16] thought that she was a shrewd observer and praised her sensitive ability, patent sincerity, and pleasing colour and composition. The critic of *The Nation and The Atheneum* was similarly enthusiastic about her 'sense of silhouette and pattern, attractive stylistic facility, and . . . obviously quite real comprehension of the nature of the modern painter's art.'[17] But despite such a favourable reaction Nina was

Paris Café, 1921

disappointed to sell only one work for seven guineas during the whole exhibition, although most of the paintings were bought later.

Nina returned to Paris as soon as the show closed and happily resumed her café life. There was a constant stream of familiar faces and endless, little-needed causes for celebration. Zawado thought, quite rightly, that Nina's English friends were a bad influence and led her astray. He did not join in her nocturnal revelries but patiently awaited her return home in the small hours. Aleister Crowley came to Paris from time to time in search of suitably solvent recruits for his Abbey of Thelema at Cefalu in Sicily, where he instructed his disciples in his own brand of occult science in which sex, drugs and drink played a large part among the magical rites. Crowley always ensured that he would not go unnoticed amongst the crush of eccentric geniuses crowding Montparnasse and appeared on the terrace of the Dôme in a variety of eye-catching disguises, wearing full Highland regalia on one occasion, a grey velour hat and black frizzy wig with his face heavily and badly painted on another. Nina viewed him with a mixture of healthy scepticism and tolerant affection, writing to a friend that 'The celebrated Aleister Crowley is here filled with magic dressed in a black cloak belonging to the Italian Army and trying to convert people to his doctrine about how to make geniuses or turning sow's ears into silk purses!'[18] She saw Crowley quite often and took people to visit him at his hotel in the Rue Vavin, where he shocked one of her women friends by casually using the lavabo as a lavatory in front of them. Crowley's hostly qualities included palm-reading and serving a lethal cocktail called Kubla Khan No. 2 – a mixture of gin, vermouth and a potion that he liked to pour with a dramatic flourish from a small black bottle which was labelled poison, and was in fact laudanum. Nina got on very well with both Crowley and his 'Scarlet Woman', the tall, gaunt, red-haired Jewess Leah Faesi, and they tried to persuade her to join them in Cefalu. It is perhaps because of this that Crowley became obsessed with the idea that Zawado was trying to kill him and took to carrying a great iron staff at all times to protect himself.

Nina had known Crowley too long to be impressed by his theatrical mystifications and found the people who gravitated towards him dull and boring, never understanding how he could tolerate them. She had heard far too much about the goings-on at Cefalu from Mary Butts, who had spent the summer of 1921 there with her lover Cecil Maitland, for it to hold any interest for her. They had returned to Paris with their health permanently undermined by the terrible climate, bad food and insanitary living conditions, and Mary had acquired a life-long drug habit. She was full of stories of having been offered goat's excrement – or the Host of the Eucharist in the religion of Crowleyanity – and of seeing the Scarlet Woman copulating with a goat. When, immediately afterwards, Crowley cut the goat's throat so that its blood spurted over Leah's bare back, she asked Mary what she should do, and received the laconic reply, 'I'd have a bath if I were you.'[19] Nina felt she knew something about the dangers of the Abbey when in November 1921 she tried to dissuade Betty May, another old friend from the Café Royal, from going to Cefalu with her new, fourth husband, the brilliant twenty-year-old Oxford graduate Raoul Loveday. They refused to listen and Nina's dire warnings proved all too prophetic, for Loveday died at the Abbey a few months later from enteritis.

Nina met up again with the Chilean diplomat and cosmopolitan dilettante Tony Gandarillas, to whom she had first been introduced at the Sitwells' house. He was living in a large apartment in the Avenue Montaigne with the young English painter Christopher Wood, and lavishly entertained smart Society and fashionable artists. They knew many people in common and he often took Nina out with Christopher Wood and various friends. Viva King, one of the wartime Café Royalists who was in Paris for a few months in 1921, remembered an occasion when the four of them were returning home in a taxi in the early hours of the morning and were quarrelling so violently that the driver stopped dead in consternation in front of the Louvre. An anxious gendarme immediately appeared to find out what they were up to, saying, 'C'est très drôle de s'arrêter comme ça au milieu du Louvre', but was reassured that they were harmless when

Nina replied with unconscious humour in her heavily accented French, '*Oui, c'est très drôle.*'[20]

The most fashionable meeting-place in Paris for artists and Society alike was a small bar and restaurant called the Gaya in the Rue Duphot, on the Right Bank close to the Madeleine. It had been opened in February 1921 by the tall, blond, young Alsatian, Louis Moyses. He knew scarcely anybody when he first arrived in Paris from Charleville but he had a valuable introduction to the brilliant pianist Jean Wiener, who agreed to play for him at the Gaya. Moyses's fortune was made when Wiener asked Darius Milhaud, who had been a fellow student of composition at the Conservatoire, to suggest to his friend Jean Cocteau that he adopt the bar as his headquarters. Cocteau did not hesitate. It was just what he was looking for and the small, white-tiled bar became the nightly gathering-place for his extensive coterie, which included painters, poets and musicians such as his young protégé the poet Raymond Radiguet, Jean and Valentine Hugo, Paul Morand, Lucien Daudet, Marie Laurencin, Irène Lagut, Marcelle Meyer and the group of young composers known as 'Les Six' — Georges Auric, Francis Poulenc, Arthur Honegger, Louis Durey, Germaine Tailleferre and Darius Milhaud. The delighted Moyses decorated his bar with coloured posters bearing the names of his distinguished new clientele.

News of the Gaya spread quickly and smart Society flocked there to see and be seen and to hear Wiener, accompanied by the American Negro Vance Lowry on banjo and saxophone, pass without any transition from fashionable ragtime and fox-trots to Bach. Marie Beerbohm, who was a great friend of Radiguet, first took Nina to the Gaya and introduced her to Cocteau. She was dazzled by his wit and brilliant conversation and charmed by Radiguet. They acted as hosts, going from table to table greeting the guests, who might include André Gide and Marc Allegri; Diaghilev, Kochno, Picasso and Misia Sert; Mistinguett, Volterra and Maurice Chevalier; Satie and René Clair; Picabia, Tzara and Poiret; Anna de Noailles and Marcel Herrand; Princess Violette Murat and Yvonne Georges; Léon-Paul Fargue and Jacques Porel. When the visitors left, Cocteau and his friends had the place to themselves and he would roll up his sleeves and play drums in improvised jazz sessions with Milhaud, Marcelle Meyer, Wiener and Vance Lowry.

The Gaya was not equipped to deal with its sudden popularity. The bar and restaurant, inconveniently situated on either side of an entrance leading to apartments above, were always so crowded that people had to be turned away and the street was jammed with cars. Moyses quickly realized that he needed larger premises and on 15 December 1921 he moved to 28 Rue de Boissy d'Anglas, still in the quarter of the Madeleine. The new bar was called the Bœuf sur le Toit after Cocteau and Milhaud's famous ballet of the same name, subtitled

The Nothing Doing Bar. Cocteau invited Nina and Marie Beerbohm to the unofficial opening of the Bœuf, where they joined him for champagne with Radiguet, Marie Laurencin, Brancusi, Picasso and his wife Olga. Nina enjoyed herself immensely and arrived back in Montparnasse with Brancusi and Radiguet just in time to buy some cigarettes at the Dôme before it closed at two. Brancusi, in spontaneous party mood, impulsively suggested that they should all three go to Marseilles that instant. Nina did not take him seriously and went home to Zawado; but Brancusi and Radiguet, still in his dinner-jacket, went straight to the station and took a train south, spending two weeks in Corsica. Nina cursed herself for not going with them and regretted it even more when Cocteau showed her a telegram at the official opening of the Bœuf on 10 January 1922 saying what a marvellous time they were having.

The Bœuf consisted of a large room with two rows of tables and a piano and the bar at the far end. The pale tan cloth-covered walls were dominated by a huge canvas by Francis Picabia which bore the title *L'Œil Cacodylate* and a realistically painted eye. Picabia asked all the visitors to sign their names on the canvas and anything else that might come into their heads. Cocteau's signature was embellished with the flourish 'Couronne de melancolie'. As Valentine Hugo held the brush in her hand, she confessed to Picabia that her heart was beating, and he told her to write exactly that; while Jean, finding nothing to say, merely signed his name and uttered a Gallic 'Voila!', which Picabia insisted he add to the canvas. The painting was the perfect expression of the Dadaist spirit, of everything that was anti-art, and it became a permanent calling-card of those who passed through the Bœuf. They were many. If the Gaya had been a success, the Bœuf was a sensation, winning a leading place in the legend of Paris in the twenties. Everybody went there, even Marcel Proust, if only once. Nina and Marie were frequent visitors, especially in the first year when the only other English were their friends Nancy Cunard, Iris Tree, Evan Morgan and Tommy Earp. As Cocteau said later: 'The Bœuf became not a bar at all, but a kind of club, the meeting place of all the best people in Paris, from all spheres of life – the prettiest women, poets, musicians, businessmen, publishers – everybody met everybody at the Bœuf.'[21]

Artists and writers, composers and dancers, and the *beau monde* which patronized them, all crowded in to savour the special atmosphere of the Bœuf and to hear the Belgian Clement Doucet, who had replaced Wiener at the piano, play the latest jazz numbers from ten in the evening until two in the morning without ever looking at the keyboard, more intent on chatting with his friends or reading the latest detective story propped up on his music stand. Yvonne Georges, the famous Belgian cabaret singer and diseuse, who was strikingly beautiful with her Eton crop and immense, expressive eyes, would transfix the audience with her tender, melancholy renderings of popular songs in her deep, grave voice. There was a very special intimacy amongst the regulars at the Bœuf, a relaxed mixture of elegance, wit and humour. Everyone knew everyone else and spoke freely to each other and the staff across the tables. The Bœuf became, in Jean Hugo's words, 'le carrefour des destinées, le berceau des amours, le foyer des discords, le nombril de Paris'.[22] Nina was well known for her repertoire of English folk songs, music-hall favourites and sea shanties. Jean Hugo remembered her sitting at the bar of the Bœuf with a small guitar, singing her ever-popular version of 'Nautical William':

'Where am I going to sleep tonight?' said Bollicky Bill the Sailor.
'You may sleep within my bed, Sir,' said the fair young lady.
'There's no room for two in a bed,' said Bollicky Bill the Sailor.
'You may sleep within my thighs, Sir,' said the fair young lady.
'What shall I find between your thighs?' said Bollicky Bill the Sailor.
'You shall find a nice pincushion,' said the fair young lady.
'I have a pin that'll just fit in,' said Bollicky Bill the Sailor.[23]

Nina first met Eric Satie at the Bœuf. He had been friendly with Cocteau since they had worked together during the war on *Parade* for the Russian Ballet, and the experimental, whimsical nature of his music made him the adopted father figure of Les Six. He was a melancholy, solitary man who lived in poverty in a single room without even a proper piano in the working-class suburb of Arcueil, carrying a hammer to protect himself when he returned home late at night after his forays into smart Society. Satie looked the perfect *bon bourgeois* with his pince-nez and goatee beard, and was always dressed in a dark suit, waistcoat and wing collar. He wore a bowler hat and carried an umbrella from his vast collection at all times, whatever the weather. But beneath his conventional appearance Satie had a malicious wit and quirky humour, and he found Nina very amusing. They got on extremely well and Nina saw him almost every day at the Dôme or the Bœuf. Her wealthy women friends generously gave her their cast-off evening clothes so she was always able to go out in great style and she enjoyed dancing for Satie in a magnificent long, tight-fitting, gold-spangled dress that made her feel like Salome performing for Herod.

Nina also became friendly with Princess Violette Murat, who was a descendant of Napoleon's famous Field Marshal Ney, Prince de la Moscova. She was an enormous mountain of a woman, then in her sixties, and Proust is supposed to have remarked on first seeing her that, 'She looks more like a truffle than a violet.'[24] The Princess was a heavy drinker and lesbian, familiar to all the bartenders and taxi drivers in Paris. Her preference for the opium pipe and other drugs was as well known as Cocteau's. She spoke English well and had many English friends including Augustus John, who commented of her, 'What didn't she know of the ins and outs of Paris?'[25] The Princess took an immediate liking to Nina and became one of her main financial supports.

The Princess invited Nina to stay for a few days at her converted farmhouse near Versailles. She was very curious to meet the eccentric English novelist Ronald Firbank, who was then living in Versailles, and Nina arranged a visit, assuring the Princess that there was sure to be plenty to drink. But when they arrived Firbank was cold sober and seized with one of his customary fits of shyness. He said nothing but rushed over to his writing desk and snatched up a stuffed bird of paradise which he presented to the astonished Princess. Undismayed, she invited him to lunch the next day. Firbank finally appeared in a very old barouche when they were already at the dessert stage, and to Nina's intense mortification he refused either to eat or speak, but pressed a copy of his latest book into the hands of the Princess and rushed away. The Princess did rather better in her attempts to entertain Nina, and Coco Chanel, Van Dongen, and the famous Comédie Française actress Cécile Sorel were among the guests who stayed for cocktails and dancing.

Marie Beerbohm introduced Nina to her friends François de Gouy and Russell Greeley. They knew many of the hard-drinking English crowd and were often at the Bœuf with Princess Violette Murat, Tony Gandarillas, Cocteau and his circle. François de Gouy d'Arcy – he always dropped the later addition to his name – was half-French, half-English. He was a fascinating and witty talker, well known for his exquisite taste and knowledge of the fine arts, architecture and antiques. His early mentor had been the Marquis de Broc, a friend of his English mother, who taught him about architecture and furniture of the seventeenth and eighteenth centuries. Alphonse Khan, the famous collector and connoisseur, completed his artistic education by initiating him into modern painting and de Gouy was one of the first to admire the Douanier Rousseau. De Gouy had been very good-looking when young and was living with Russell Greeley, a wealthy American from Boston, who was himself a talented amateur portrait painter. They sat drinking all day and most of the night at their ground-floor flat in the Rue de Condé in a beautiful ivy-covered eighteenth-century house built around a courtyard with a fountain in the middle. Nina and Marie were invited to cocktails with Cocteau, Radiguet, Stravinsky, Diaghilev and Yvonne Georges. Nina brought her guitar and entertained the company with some of her favourite songs such as 'She Was Poor but She Was Honest', 'The Servant Girl in Drury Lane' and 'The Drunken Sailor'. Despite her reputation as a *grande malheureuse*, Yvonne Georges had a strong sense of humour and, dressed in cushion covers with a pair of kid gloves arranged on her head, sang and acted in an imaginary play with Cocteau and Radiguet. They had a riotously funny evening and after dinner retired to the Bœuf.

Through the Princess Nina met many rich people whom she hoped would commission portraits, as she was desperate to make some money. The wealthy Tony Butts came to Paris often and Nina did a watercolour of him seated at a café terrace in 1921.* On one of his visits with his mother he invited Nina, Douglas Goldring and another young painter, Harry Jonas, to a superb lunch with champagne and oysters at Foyot's. Nina's hopes ran high when they all went back to her studio in a taxi. She managed to produce a passably clean chair for Tony's mother and displayed the entire contents of her portfolio. After a while, when no move had been made to purchase anything, Nina whispered to Goldring to go out and buy some champagne. This resulted in the conversation becoming decidely livelier but still no sales. At the end of a very jolly afternoon Nina bowed them out with the manners of a duchess, which as Goldring commented,[26] she always had at her command. Nina automatically assumed the role of social equal and hid both her urgent need for money and her subsequent bitter disappointment when none was forthcoming.

Fortunately, others had a more sympathetic awareness of her situation and did their best to help her. One of her most loyal friends was her former pupil Gertrude Kingston, who was something of a feminist and regretted the fact that people were more keen to help second-rate men painters than Nina. She tried to remedy this in her own small way and whenever she passed through Paris she always took Nina out for a meal and either bought a picture or gave her a loan which she never expected to be repaid.

Another very staunch lifelong supporter of Nina was C. K. Ogden, the editor of the *Cambridge Magazine*, whom Nina had first met at the time of her exhibition at the magazine's art gallery in 1918. Ogden was a man of terrific energy and originality who is best known as the inventor of Basic English, but his immense and varied learning covered the fields of philosophy, psychology and linguistics. During the twenties he co-translated Wittgenstein's *Tractatus Logico-Philosophicus* and wrote with I. A. Richards the influential *The Meaning of Meaning* as well as being an art critic, bookseller and antique dealer. An eccentric kleptomaniac with a genius for raising capital, he sported an artificial cigarette with a bulb at the end which glowed red, listened to records backwards, and had such an aversion to nature that he installed an ozone machine in his flat rather than subject himself to the elements. His friends remembered his secrecy and elusiveness, his impish sense of humour, and his unfailing willingness to assist them in any way he could. Ogden's help for Nina took many forms: writing about her and reproducing her work in the *Cambridge Magazine*, buying pictures himself or selling them to others, trying to arrange exhibitions for her and

* facing page 128

James Hepburn,
1922

lending her money. While Nina was in Paris he also performed numerous small services for her such as sending her books, dealing with her framers in London, and showing photographs of her work and press-cuttings to potentially useful people. He suggested that she should do line drawings of leading artistic personalities for a projected book, and with this in mind she drew James Joyce, Radiguet, Epstein, Sickert, Brancusi, Ford Madox Ford, Aldous Huxley, Derain and Frank Harris amongst many others. The book never materialized, but quite a few of the drawings were published in magazines and newspapers such as the *Paris Times*.

Portraits remained an unending source of fascination for Nina. She declared, 'I am more interested in human beings than in landscapes or in still lifes. That is why I live in Paris and sit in cafés . . . My ambition is to paint psychological portraits that shall represent accurately the spirit of the age.'[27] Many of her friends obliged by posing for her. Anna Wickham was in Paris to recover from the tragic death of her four-year-old son. She was accompanied by her eldest boy, the fourteen-year-old James Hepburn, who had the distinction of beating

Rupert Doone, 1922–3

Crowley at chess in an unguarded moment at the Dôme, much to the latter's intense irritation. Nina painted both James and his younger brother John when he came over on a visit. She greatly admired the Ariel-like beauty and mercurial temperament of the young ballet dancer Rupert Doone, who had modelled for painters in London to pay for his tuition. Nina very much wanted to paint him, but as she could only afford to employ him to sit for a few drawings she solved the problem by getting him a job posing for the portrait class at the Académie Colorossi for a month and going there to work. Nina graciously submitted to the criticism of the Professor and the resulting portrait was full of elegance, highlighting Rupert Doone's fine, elongated features. She also introduced him to Christopher Wood, who often hired models and generously invited Nina to draw with him in his studio. Christopher Wood took a great liking to Rupert Doone, who subsequently became part of his and Tony Gandarillas's social circle.

Apart from friends, Nina painted portraits of any extraordinary and unusual-looking people who caught her attention. She was fascinated by a tall stranger who always sat alone every evening at the Café Parnasse wearing a monocle, top hat and tail coat, with white spats and a cane. He introduced himself as Georges Manuel Unwin, a Chilean who had come to Paris to study opera singing, and loudly burst into an aria from *I Pagliacci* to demonstrate his talent before confessing that he had only one other change of clothes and earned his living as a Cooks tourist guide. Immensely vain and conceited, he was flattered to pose for Nina. She seated him with his legs crossed holding his hat and stick, with a richly coloured red and blue Moroccan rug in the background. Her guitar hung on the wall behind and she placed a white pot of flowers at his feet. The portrait was over five feet high and was one of her most ambitious and successful works. She found painting his top hat with its dark shadows a great challenge, and as she used no black in her palette but only dark blue, the portrait was in a much higher key than usual. As always with Nina, the touches of colour were skilfully placed to unify the composition and relieve the predominantly dark tones.

She sent this portrait along with two others, including one of Mme Walter Duranty, the wife of the American journalist, to the 1921 Salon d'Automne, which was one of the most vital showcases for contemporary art during the twenties. Nina was very encouraged that all three works were hung together on the line in André Lhote's room and received mentions in the French press as well as a favourable review in Polish. The painting of Georges Manuel Unwin also attracted attention when it was shown with several other of her portraits at the *Daily Express* Women's Exhibition at Olympia the following year. The *Observer*'s critic Paul Konody praised them as a remarkable group and commented that 'even those who are repelled by their rude directness will have to admit in each single case the penetrating characterisation which brings out the typical as well as the individual in each sitter. Miss Hamnett's art savours slightly of caricature.'

Nina showed a portrait of William Burgess at the 1922 Salon d'Automne and in 1923 exhibited a painting of the Tunisian servant of one of Zawado's friends. He was a very tough character with a cast in one eye who would appear late at night on the terrace of the Parnasse or the Dôme and stand silent as a statue waiting to take his employer home. Nina found painting him a rather unnerving experience as he sat so motionless that she had to ask him to rest every quarter of an hour to prevent herself becoming hypnotized.

One night at the Bœuf Nina met Lucien Vogel, who offered to give her an exhibition at his gallery in the Rue St Florentin behind the Place de la Concorde. She showed her watercolours of Paris cafés and gardens, the work she had done in Collioure, various portraits and some drawings. Nina was not familiar with the French custom of greasing a critic's palm to obtain a good review and was noisily outraged when the writer and editor Waldemar George demanded 2,000 francs for including her in an article about English painting. She indignantly refused, with the result that she received no press notices. All her friends came to the private view and Cocteau murmured appreciatively and diplomatically that her paintings were '*plus vrai que le vrai*'.[28] But the fact was that Nina's work was too realistic for Parisian tastes and she sold little, although quite a few were bought in the weeks following the show.

By this time Nina had moved out of Zawado's studio and was living in a small hotel. She knew that she had behaved badly to him, often staying out half the night — or indeed all the night — with any man who took her fancy. Nina was famous for discovering beautiful young men whose charms were not so immediately apparent to other eyes. Homosexuality was very prevalent amongst Nina's circle of friends and it has been said that Nina and Nancy Cunard were lovers. It is possible; such liaisons were very much *à la mode*. Sex did not mean a lot to Nina and was never much more than a companionable gesture. One of her friends, who married Abdul, commented that

> Nina had affairs with all sorts of awful people but didn't appreciate Zawado really or anybody else[29] . . . Nina slept more or less with anyone who was of any apparent interest at all but just like having a glass of wine with a friend — I mean she was apparently completely frigid — she told me once that she had never felt anything.[30]

Nina hated knowing that there was someone at home waiting for her return to whom she was even vaguely accountable. However, she remained very close to Zawado, who was always very kind and patient, and continued to work in his studio throughout her stay in Paris.

Away from Zawado, who had had some slight steadying influence on her, Nina took to staying out more and more and was often in no state to work the following day. She wrote to Ogden on one of his visits to Paris, apologizing for not meeting him as arranged:

I went straight home to bed, the only place for me. I was very well paid out by the Bon Dieu for my disgusting behaviour by getting into all kinds of trouble and finally forgetting entirely thank God the object of my affections who turned out to be even worse than I feared . . . I do hope you will forgive me and if I am ever rude or drunk crash me over the head with a bottle if not with an umbrella. Reform has set in for some time.[31]

11

Café society

Nina was the best-known British woman painter in Paris. She appeared in Michel Georges-Michel's novel about the quarter, *Les Montparnos*, in which he described her as '*une sorte de Gibson-girl de faubourg, qui travaillait habillée en homme, pantalon de velours de charpentier et chemise bleue*'.[1] There was no more animating figure among the Anglo-American community than Nina. Douglas Goldring characterized her as

> in command of our 'bridgehead' in Montparnasse[2] . . . Not only did she 'know everybody', but her friendliness, high spirits, inexhaustible good humour and . . .. charming manners, made her the perfect unofficial hostess for the Quarter. She took newcomers under her wing, uttered those magic words of introduction without which the Anglo-Saxon seems unable to make contacts, even in France, and in every sense of the word showed herself an admirable 'mixer'. To Chambon, the proprietor of the Café du Dôme, her popularity and sociable gifts – though probably he never realised it – were worth a fortune.[3]

Nina was equally at home with the Anglo-American crowd as she was with her grand French friends and slipped easily from world to world. She was quite an accomplished actress and as the day progressed she played her entire repertoire of roles. In the morning she was the serious painter in an old pair of trousers and a workman's shirt, briskly passing by the café terraces where her friends lingered over their *café au lait*, consenting to pause for one drink only before rushing off to work. By early evening she was happy to relax over an aperitif but she would soon disappear to dress for dinner with her rich and titled friends – 'swells . . . who "smelled of money"'[4] – returning elegantly gowned to sip a cocktail aloofly and allow herself to be admired before going off to her rendezvous. By midnight,

Nina in 1920

sated with champagne and caviare, she would be back in the quarter to recount her adventures, confident that her hosts were about to buy a picture or commission a portrait. Depending on her mood, she would then be ready for a round of all the bars and nightclubs in the neighbourhood.

One of the most popular of the new American bars was the Dingo in the Rue Delambre, where Nina and Flossie Martin, a pretty and jolly former chorus-girl from New York with a loud, infectious laugh, were rival centres of attention. Nina was often to be found there and at Pizzuli's, a small Italian restaurant opposite, famous for its excellent cheap ravioli, entertaining her friends with songs such as

> We went down to Buenos Aires
> Where all the men are fairies . . .[5]

She was always surrounded by a group of admirers with resounding titles and well-known names. According to Jimmy Charters, the famous Jimmy the Barman, 'It became rather a joke at the Dingo, for the telephone would ring constantly for Nina, and the waiter would announce in a loud voice that the Prince of Something or the Count de Z wished to speak to Miss Hamnett.'[6]

Nina, Flossie Martin and Kiki, the full-blown Burgundian model painted by most of the celebrated artists of the quarter, were each in their different way contenders for the title of Queen of Montparnasse. They had in common a mutual passion for American sailors. When the crews of the USS *Pittsburgh*, *Memphis* and *Detroit* were on leave, Nina was to be seen parading the quarter dressed in a sailor's uniform, surrounded by an attentive group of admiring *beaux* who liberally treated her to drinks. She became great friends with a fat electrician from the *Pittsburgh* called Neil O. Cahan, who impressed her by making more noise when drunk than anyone she had ever known and paid her for painting his portrait. When he was not on leave himself, he sent his friends for her to entertain and show the sights. They even used to turn up later when she was back in London, asking for her at the Fitzroy Tavern.

Kiki was to the Jockey what Nina was to the Dingo. The Jockey, named after Miller, a retired jockey who had an interest in it, opened on the corner of the Rue Campagne Première in 1923 and quickly became the most fashionable nightspot in Montparnasse. Hilaire Hiler, an American painter and expert on costume, decorated the outside with flat, brightly coloured figures of cowboys and Indians; while inside it was small and cramped like a saloon bar in a western, with a low, cracked ceiling and splintered floor, the walls plastered with tattered posters, cartoons and limericks. The tiny dance-floor was jammed tight with people. Crowds thronged to hear the latest jazz-blues numbers sung by the

Nina
by Ferjac

ex-cowboy Les Copeland with Hiler on piano and Bangs, the Negro drummer. Twice a night Kiki gustily performed a selection of Apache songs, making full play with the bawdy parts. Her speciality was 'Les Filles de Camaret':

Les Filles de Camaret se disent toutes vierges
Mais quand elles sont dans mon lit
Elles préfèrent tenir ma vis
Qu'un cierge — qu'un cierge — qu'un cie-er-ege.

Mon mari s'en est allé a la pêche en Espagne
Il m'a laissé sans un sou
Mais avec mon p'tit trou
J'en gagne — j'en gagne — J'en gagne — gagne-e.[7]

Kiki's songs made Nina's look like nursery rhymes and the crowd roared for more whilst she passed round a hat.

Although the Jockey was far less salubrious than the Bœuf, it attracted the same mixture of artists in work clothes and elegant *gens du monde*. It was very popular with Americans and many of the original quarterites went there, such as Kisling, Pascin, Foujita, Van Dongen and Derain, as well as Cocteau, Radiguet, Aragon and Crevel, and any number of *poules* and gigolos. There was a constant interchange and flow of traffic between the Jockey and the Bœuf. Jimmy the Barman told the story of the memorable occasion when Nina and Hiler arranged to take Frank Harris, recently returned from America, to meet Cocteau at the Bœuf, thinking that two such important literary figures should know each other. When they entered the Bœuf Cocteau was standing at the bar talking to a friend. He turned and greeted Nina and Hiler effusively, but when they introduced Harris he merely nodded and said, '*Ah, oui, bonjour monsieur,*' and turned his back without even shaking Harris's proffered hand. Harris retreated, spluttering with indignation 'Who is this man! . . . Does he know who I am! Does he! The idea!'[8]

Much as Nina enjoyed her popularity, in her more sober moments she felt she was not making any real progress in her work and wrote to Ogden that she was 'fed up with this rotten quarter and being always drunk'.[9] She met an aspiring young American writer called Frank, who was tall with large blue eyes and always dressed in old-fashioned knickerbockers. He spoke and danced like Groucho Marx and Nina found him very amusing. When he offered to take her to Douarnenez in Brittany for August, she was delighted at the prospect of escaping the distractions of Paris.

They stayed in a small, cheap hotel on a high cliff about half a mile from the port and regaled themselves with course after course of the excellent food and wine. While Frank sat outside a café reading *Ulysses* and drinking vermouth cassis, Nina worked. She felt far more at home with the light and landscape of Brittany than she had in the South and found many subjects which interested her. She drew the local sailors and women in their black dresses and white caps, and painted a portrait of Frank.

As self-respecting denizens of Montparnasse they made a thorough investigation of all the cafés, where they did full justice to the local cider and calvados, and danced with the sailors to a penny-in-the-slot piano. They bathed from a large deserted beach a few miles from Douarnenez and made expeditions to other towns along the coast such as Concarneau and Pont Aven, which had been famous artists' colonies in the last century. At Concarneau they were dismayed by the sight of a row of old ladies and gentlemen lined up painting the boats. Pont Aven was worse, full of stuffy English colonels and their families who were shocked when Nina and Frank held hands at lunch and joined in dancing reels and quadrilles in the street on a fête day. Nina thought Frank was one of the nicest young men she had ever known and was very sorry when they had to return to Paris, as he was leaving for America. She hated seeing people off at railway stations, and shook hands with him outside his hotel before running up the Boulevard Montparnasse to the Dôme.

Nina quickly managed to sell some of her Brittany drawings, which consoled her a little for Frank's departure. With the money she earned she was able to afford a model and set to work at once in the studio she still shared with the long-suffering Zawado, who had missed her while she was away. Her friends at the Dôme and the Bœuf welcomed her back and she resumed her old life of late nights and drinks. One evening she downed eleven cocktails with Ronald Firbank and had to go home to be sick.

In September, Princess Violette Murat invited Nina to join her for the last week of her cure at Vichy and then to motor south to stay with her brother-in-law Prince Lucien Murat in Juan-les-Pins, which was just becoming a fashionable summer resort. Nina thought Vichy was an utterly dismal town full of bad-tempered, liverish people. She did her best to enter into the spirit of the place and to keep the Princess company knocked back her mug of Vichy water from the Celestin Spring in one gulp, trying to convince herself that it had more kick than the bottled version. But it certainly was not *eau-de-vie* and Nina was very relieved when they set off on their cultural and gastronomic tour south. The Princess proved to be a marvellous guide as she had studied architecture at the Sorbonne and was very knowledgeable about French history and art. They found old friends and good drinking companions everywhere they went. At Nîmes they chanced upon François de Gouy and Russell Greeley; at Avignon they came across Tommy Earp with his wife; while at Aix-en-Provence they met Darius Milhaud, who showed them Cézanne's house and garden and his most famous motif, the Mont Sainte Victoire.

Prince Lucien Murat's house at Juan-les-Pins was built in Gothic style with a crenellated tower like a castle, its walled garden leading down to the sea. Nina was in her element amidst such grand surroundings and among people with such resounding titles. She could not resist writing to Ogden: 'You will be amused to know that I am here staying in the villa with three Princess Murats, a Russian Count and Countess, and a Baroness who fought in the war as a Russian soldier and got the St George's Cross.'[10] She omitted to mention that there was in fact no room for Violette and herself, and they had to stay next door in a house owned by an Austrian countess. Nina found the place very sinister, and her room, which had a padded door with a barred window let into it, reminded her of a cell. One night she woke up in a state of complete terror and found herself staring fixedly at the window leading into the conservatory beyond. It was several minutes before she was calm enough to turn on the light and was mystified because she found nothing to explain her fear. It was only when they were leaving that they were told the house was haunted. Nina was all too glad to escape its oppressive atmosphere and join her friends on the nearly empty beach. They took their meals with the Murats, and François de Gouy and Russell Greeley often came over from Nice in the evenings for barbecues in the garden.

The high point of Nina's stay was being taken for tea and cocktails with Rudolf Valentino and his wife, whose parents lived in an enormous house in Juan-les-Pins. Nina and her escorts, Sir Hugo de Bathe and the Russian Count, swept up to the house in two motor cars and were ushered into an imposing marble hall with life-sized bronze statues. After the introductions Sir Hugo mentioned Nina's talent for singing sea shanties and a delighted Valentino immediately sat her down at the large grand piano in the middle of the room. Ever game, Nina swallowed some whisky and proceeded to astonish and amuse everyone with her songs. She must have been an agreeable change for Valentino as she hardly ever went to the cinema and had never seen any of his films. Nina found Valentino charming and got on very well with him, although she did not think he was as good looking in real life as in his photographs. Far from being struck dumb by his beauty, she kept everyone laughing with stories about herself.

Nina vastly enjoyed her forays into smart Society and airily described her nerve-racking drive along the Lower Corniche to Monte Carlo with Prince Murat, who drove at break-neck speed around the hairpin bends. This was all heady stuff for Nina and it was with great reluctance that she returned to Paris and penury at the end of five weeks.

Paris had rapidly become established as the centre of the American literary avant-garde. Writers such as Gertrude Stein, Ernest Hemingway, Scott Fitzgerald, E. E. Cummings and John Dos Passos all lived there, and there were a host of small English-language publishing houses and little magazines, as well as Sylvia Beach's influential bookshop and lending library, Shakespeare and Co. The hard core of the American expatriate community who haunted the Montparnasse cafés and nightclubs included Jane Heap and Margaret Anderson, editors of the *Little Review*; the *Broom* crowd – Harold Loeb, Kitty Cannell, Alfred and Dorothy Kreymbourg; Bill Bird of the Three Mountains Press; Nina's great friend Robert McAlmon, writer and publisher of *Contact Editions*; the dramatically elegant novelist Djuna Barnes; Clothilde Vail and her painter-brother Lawrence Vail, who was married to Peggy Guggenheim; the photographer Berenice Abbott and her friend the sculptor Thelma Wood; writers and journalists Harold Stearn, Malcolm Cowley, Janet Flanner, Solito Solano; and the beautiful and witty painter and poet Mina Loy.

One of the champions of the new American writing was the fifty-year-old Ford Madox Ford, the former editor of the *English Review* and a distinguished and prolific novelist himself. Nina had read and admired his books and found him very amusing and interesting. She was friendly with both Ford and Stella Bowen, the talented painter with whom he lived. In December 1923 Ford launched the short-lived *Transatlantic Review*, which quickly became one of the most important English-language magazines in Paris, publishing new work by Joyce, Hemingway, E. E. Cummings, Pound, McAlmon, Gertrude Stein and Antheil. The visual arts were not neglected and a drawing by Nina of a Life class appeared in June 1924 along with reproductions of Picasso, Brancusi and John Storr.

Ford was immensely sociable and an inveterate party-giver. He had a fund of stories about the many famous writers he had known, such as Conrad, H. G. Wells and Henry James, and he delighted in playing the grand old man of English letters to aspiring youth. In appearance he was a typical upper-class Englishman, bulky with a ruddy face, thatch of blond hair, droopy walrus moustache and multiple chins. Either because of asthma or through having been gassed in the war, he wheezed, gasped and snorted as he presided over his Thursday afternoon tea-parties at the offices of the *Transatlantic Review* on the Ile St Louis. On Tuesdays he invited all his friends and supporters to a *bal musette*, a little

The Drawing Class, 1923 (reproduced in *Transatlantic Review*)

workmen's dance hall with a small Auvergnat orchestra near the Place de la Contrescarpe. Later, when his funds ran out, he held large informal parties with music provided by an accordionist at his studio in the Rue Notre Dame des Champs which Nina had found for him, regretting that she could not afford it herself. Ford and Stella Bowen were very kind to Nina and bought her drawings. She always spent Christmas Day with them as they kept up the English traditions. After lunch at Le Nègre de Toulouse, a smart restaurant in the Boulevard Montparnasse, they gave a children's tea party for their young daughter, complete with a Christmas tree and Santa Claus. Nina did not like children very much and, instead of joining in the party games, preferred to sit by the punch talking to Gertrude Stein, whom she had first met before the war when she had been taken to see her famous collection of paintings by Picasso and other modern artists.

Nina and Ford decided that it would be a good idea to hold fortnightly gatherings of the many talented English-speaking foreigners in Paris. Ford organized the first meeting at Lavenue's, with Joyce as the guest of honour. When he failed to appear at the appointed hour, William Bird was sent to fetch a protesting Joyce, who disclaimed all knowledge of the arrangement. It was an ominous start to the evening and the anticipated sparkling intellectual exchange conspicuously failed to materialize, leading Joyce's wife Nora to remark acidly in one of the silences, 'Jim, what is it all ye find to jabber about the nights you're brought home drunk for me to look after? You're dumb as an oyster now, so God help me.'[11] A miraculously sober Flossie Martin tried in vain to liven up the proceedings but Nina, sensing that the party had fallen flat, tittered over her drink before discreetly disappearing when she spotted the American writer Bob Coates, whose red hair she found irresistible.

Although the evening was a dismal failure it did not stop Joyce from remarking that Nina, whom he always referred to as Miss Hamnett, was 'one of the few vital women'[12] he had ever known. Nina had met Joyce before with Ford and saw him whenever she was taken to the Trianon, where he always dined. She was completely charmed by Joyce and much appreciated his old-fashioned manners and courtesy towards women. On a later occasion, when Nina happened to see Joyce in the bar during the interval at the Swedish Ballet, she brought off the extraordinary social coup of introducing him to Valentino, much to the astonishment of both parties who were almost speechless with amazement.

The American influx into Paris reached its height in 1924 when the steamship companies introduced the new tourist third class. Would-be artists, students, tourists, schoolteachers and businessmen came over in their droves. Scores of fresh-faced young Americans speaking little or no French sat at the café terraces, eating specially imported breakfast cereals and ham and eggs, sipping iced water and reading American newspapers. Ernest Hemingway, whose novel *The Sun Also Rises* did so much to glamorize the quarter's hard drinking and casual sexual encounters, observed the changes with dismay: 'Montparnasse became rich, prosperous, brightly lighted, dancing-ed, shredded wheated, grapenuts-ed or grapenutted (take your choice, gentlemen, we have all these breakfast foods now) and they sold caviare at the Dôme.'[13]

The transformation of the Rotonde, the cradle of the original Montparnasse, heralded the new era. The revamped Rotonde was officially opened in December 1923 with a speech by Gustave Kahn and all the pomp and ceremony befitting the cultural monument it had become. The new, brightly lit Rotonde was tripled in size, its extensive terrace absorbing the neighbouring Café Parnasse. On the ground floor there was a bar, a grill room and a brasserie; whilst upstairs was a large dance-floor with a jazz band, where the evening clothes worn by the visitors were as extravagant as the price of the drinks. In recognition of its glorious artistic past the walls were adorned with quantities of second-rate paintings. The Dôme, the official headquarters of the American colony, was not slow to follow suit and was completely redecorated the following year in jazz-age style, its interior partly papered in a strident dazzle design of bright orange and purple, with coloured glass lights let into mirrors. Outside, painted low relief plaques depicted the delights of café life to be found within.

The old crowd felt ill at ease in the modernized Dôme and crossed the road to the newly opened Sélect, which was elegantly decorated in art-deco style and had the great advantage of staying open all night. Apart from the usual contingent of American literary expatriates, the regular group at the Sélect included Mary Butts and her friend Mary Reynolds, a quiet, intelligent lady with a Mona Lisa smile and prematurely white hair who lived with Marcel Duchamp; Cedric Morris and Lett Haines; Rupert Doone and the young English painter Robert Medley; Isadora Duncan's devoted secretary Alan Ross MacDougal; Cocteau's friends Jacques Stettiner, Jean Aran and Raoul Leven; Kisling, Foujita, Zadkine, Wassilieff and, of course, Nina.

In January 1924 Nina went to London with Yvonne Georges and Princess Violette Murat, who was visiting Tony Gandarillas at his house in Cheyne Walk, accompanied by her pet white rat. Yvonne was engaged to sing in the Midnight Follies at the Hotel Metropole and since she knew no one in London, the Princess offered to pay Nina's expenses if she would look after Yvonne and stay with her. Yvonne needed all the moral support that Nina could muster. When she woke up at nine-thirty on her first morning in London it was so dismal and foggy that she declared her intention of leaving immediately. But Nina knew the remedy and disappeared to Soho, where she procured a bottle of pre-war absinthe, the *Matin* and some Maryland *jaunes*. A few glasses of absinthe made London look distinctly brighter and they left to rehearse with Nina acting as interpreter. After the first house, which was a great success, Yvonne wanted to see some local colour and Nina whisked her off in a taxi to Dirty Dick's in the City, where the bar was festooned with stuffed cats and rats, policemen's helmets and giant keys, all with a thick covering of dust. Nina explained that Dirty Dick had been the son of a rich eighteenth-century City merchant and had acquired his name because when his fiancée died he swore never to wash or clean his house again. Yvonne stood in her sensational stage make-up amidst the bank clerks, sailors and old ladies, blissfully munching sandwiches and drinking port until she suddenly realized that she was due back for the evening performance in twenty minutes. They had only a ten-pound note, a great deal of money in those days and viewed with grave suspicion by the bartender and manager, who refused to change it. A policeman directed Nina to the Great Eastern Hotel, where she breathlessly explained their predicament and ran back to Yvonne with the change, managing to deposit her at the stage door just in time. Nina certainly earned her trip to London, but she only stayed long enough to sell some drawings before leaving Yvonne and the Princess and returning to France.

For those interested in the arts, Paris was still one of the most exciting and vital places to be. Almost every day there was a new exhibition, a recital of the latest music by Les Six, a Dadaist manifestation, the première of a new play or ballet, or a fancy-dress ball in Montparnasse. The high point of 1924 was the Soirées de Paris, mounted by the wealthy Maecenas, Comte Étienne de Beaumont, a serious patron and devotee of modern art, theatre, music and dance, as well as host of some of the most extravagant costume balls of the decade. During the six-week season which opened in mid-May at the Théatre de la Cigale in Montmartre, Beaumont presented six ballets and two plays, bringing together some of the best modern talents such as Cocteau, Paul Morand, Tristan Tzara, Braque, Derain, Picasso, Marie Laurencin, Jean and Valentine Hugo, Darius Milhaud, Sauguet, Satie and Massine.

Cocteau's adaptation of *Romeo and Juliet*, with Marcel Herrand and Andrée Pascal in the title roles, was one of the sensations of the series, largely due to Jean Hugo's startlingly original stage designs. The costumes and sets were entirely black, only the brightly coloured linear decorations painted on the dark background being visible to the audience. Several of Nina's friends were involved in the production. Cocteau himself took the part of Mercutio, while Yvonnes Georges had a great success as Juliet's nurse and Rupert Doone, who was briefly Cocteau's lover, danced in a miniature ballet inserted into the piece. Nina went to see it with the visiting English art critic Paul Konody and thought it was great fun, although she was not entirely sure that Shakespeare would have approved. Her rather proprietorial attitude towards the Bard was perhaps not unconnected with the fact that her Warwickshire surname was said to have originated from the Christian name of Shakespeare's son, Hamnet, and the waiters at the Dôme always called her Mlle Hamlet. After the performance Nina and Konody went with Cocteau, Yvonne Georges, de Gouy and Greeley to drink champagne at Zelli's, an American-style bar in Montmartre with a jazz band and large dance-floor frequented mostly by English and Americans. It was not the most salubrious of places but Nina had been there before with Lady Cupid Michelham and the fearless Princess Violette Murat.

Nina herself made a small but significant contribution to a new work by the Ballets Russes, *Les Matelots*. She spent the summer with François de Gouy and Russell Greeley at the small villa they had rented overlooking the sea at Le Canadel, a few miles from Hyères. Le Canadel was a very isolated spot consisting of little more than a strip of land about a hundred yards wide on a slope between the sea and pine-covered hills. The surrounding countryside was uncultivated with just a few small houses and vineyards by the coast. There was only one shop, which was also the local post office and café, and even that could only be reached by walking along the sea-shore or in a single file along the narrow railway line that ran at the bottom of the garden behind the house. As there were only two trains a day and the road was so bad, continuously twisting and turning along the coast and criss-crossing the railway line, it was simpler to go by boat to the nearby villages. But despite its remoteness, life at Le Canadel was far from quiet. Tony Gandarillas and Christopher Wood were staying in the neighbouring villa and they all took meals together and saw each other every day. Other friends were nearby. Cocteau was at Villefranche; Kisling and his wife were at St Tropez; while Tzara and his companions were living just along the coast. Christopher Wood complained of the impossibility of getting any work done because of all the friends, like Yvonne Georges, who kept turning up for the day or to stay.

Georges Auric arrived from Monte Carlo where he had been working with Diaghilev on the music for the new ballet about sailors, *Les Matelots*. He had written the first two acts and was coming to stay with de Gouy and Greeley to finish it. Nina had often met Auric at the Bœuf but did not know him well and was rather awed by him. The twenty-five-year-old Auric was already one of Diaghilev's favourite composers. With his plump features, mischievous eyes, lock of hair forever falling over his forehead, and small pursed lips, he still had the amiable air of an overgrown child prodigy. Nina was dismayed when, the day after his arrival, de Gouy and Greeley went off to inspect a property that they were thinking of buying near Cannes, leaving her alone to entertain Auric. He refused all her invitations to walk or swim and insisted on spending the day

Georges Auric, 1924

composing at the piano. Nina was somewhat at a loss and wandered among the orange trees and freesias in the garden, where she was surprised to hear a gramophone record of 'Je cherche Titine' being played over and over again. Intrigued, she decided that Auric was either very interesting or else had gone suddenly mad, and returned to the house to discover which. The Russian butler served them cocktails and by lunchtime they were on very good terms, Auric explaining that he had run out of ideas for the last act of his ballet. He could not have consulted a greater expert on sailors than Nina, and after lunch she whistled him her entire repertoire of sea shanties. Auric was enchanted and quickly devised musical accompaniments. When de Gouy and Greeley arrived back the next day they were astonished to find their guests in such rollicking good humour.

Auric had the inspiration he needed and cleverly wove all Nina's songs into his composition. Nina did a line drawing of him before he left and promised to say nothing to Diaghilev about the origin of the piece. When the ballet opened in June 1925 with Serge Lifar dancing the leading role, it was a great triumph. At the première a smiling Diaghilev came up to Nina in the interval to enquire, 'And how is the fair young lady?'[14] – a direct reference to the words of 'Nautical William' which was clearly recognizable in the finale.

In all Nina stayed some nine weeks with de Gouy and Greeley at Le Canadel. At the end of her visit they spent a few days in Nice during the carnival, seeing Cocteau, Milhaud, Poulenc and Stravinsky every day at Chez Vogade, the favourite meeting-place in the Place Masséna. Nina immensely enjoyed the spectacle of the carnival, which she thought was like some great pagan festival, and she and her friends wore painted masks and joined in throwing confetti. Afterwards they wandered through the back streets and drank and danced with sailors in a bar. Nina had one last drink at the Hôtel Negresco, the luxurious bastion of the Anglo-American colony, and left for Paris the next day.

Nina had done very little work in the South and did not show in the 1924 Salon d'Automne. However, she was not forgotten in England and an illustrated article on her portraiture by Mrs Gordon Stables appeared in the October issue of *Artwork*. The writer praised the 'mordant biting quality' of Nina's portraits, her 'unerring flair for detecting the mainsprings of human purpose', and went on to discuss her methods: 'A peculiar sense of unity, an unusual skill in welding lines and planes into a single, expressive and rhythmic whole, an innate feeling for values, underlie the quality which gives to Nina Hamnett's work its distinctive force . . . she achieves . . . a remarkable sense of "tactile values".'

Gratified though Nina must have been by this fulsome recognition of her talents, it changed little. Money was often very short and commissions few. Nina certainly had her moments of bitter despondency and disillusionment with Paris life, but she had immense resources of optimism and resilience. A drink, a loan of twenty francs, a meeting with a titled person or some new young man, were sufficient to restore her high spirits and *joie de vivre*. Yet Nina was not without a streak of harshly ironic realism. Despite her need to be liked and admired, the more she gloried in her immense social success, and the more she frittered her talent in oceans of drink and casual debauchery, the clearer-eyed she became about the futility of it all.

Two figures above all others caught the mood of Paris in the twenties: Van Dongen and Pascin, both hugely successful, worldly artists. Van Dongen was the most fashionable painter of what he himself aptly called the cocktail epoch, composed as it was of all colours and classes. His elongated, elegant figures embody the stylish sophistication as well as the soulless, hectic dissipation of the jazz age and exude an aura of jaded cynicism. Van Dongen was seen in all the smartest places – riding in the Bois de Boulogne, dancing the foxtrot at the Bœuf, at the races, in the casino in Cannes and at Deauville. Wherever he went he was besieged by people clamouring to commission portraits by him. *Le tout* Paris, New York, Venice, Deauville – or as he nonchalantly put it, '*Le tout* what-you-will' – flocked to his Monday evening receptions at his large, sparsely furnished house in the Rue Juliette Lambert, where he had two enormous studios for working and showing his pictures, and a bright red dining-room decorated with panels of nudes. Here he welcomed a dazzling array of the rich and famous – royalty, *gens du monde*, writers, journalists, financiers, actresses, artists and models. Nina had a permanent invitation to Van Dongen's soirées, where she loved to show off her collection of evening clothes. The entertainment was lavish and Nina thought his parties the best she had ever been to. Sometimes the musicians from a *bal musette* would play, a famous music-hall singer might perform, celebrated guests such as Josephine Baker were persuaded to do a party piece, and there was always dancing to the latest jazz records. Such were the rewards of a Society portrait painter who well knew how to flatter and please by slimming his sitters and enlarging their jewels. But by the end of the twenties Van Dongen's work had lost much of its charm as it conformed increasingly to his own tried and tested formulas.

The Bulgarian-born artist Pascin was king of a different kind of Montparnasse nightlife, preferring to depict the secret world of the *maison close*. His voluptuous drawings and watercolours of plump girls erotically posed in transparent chemises, sensuous negresses, nightclub and brothel scenes were in great demand and commanded huge prices. Always deliberately drunk and indifferent to smart Society, Pascin needed an atmosphere of constant fête and revelry. His studio at 36 Boulevard de Clichy was full of young girls, models of all colours, strangers picked up casually on the street, artists, gypsies, and a crowd of hangers-on – parasites with no liking or interest in his work, only in the money he so freely squandered on orgies of drink and drugs. Almost every evening he had ten or fifteen people to dinner and as many as forty on Saturdays. Pascin would then take his entourage in a fleet of taxis to do a tour of the nightclubs of Montparnasse and Montmartre, invariably ending up in a brothel. Amidst all the commotion and uproar around him Pascin remained a slight, solitary and melancholy figure, correctly dressed in a dark suit and bowler hat.

Nina went to Pascin's parties from time to time and although the door was usually opened by a naked girl she always thought their reputation for wickedness was vastly overrated. One night when she was dining with Pascin and some friends in Montmartre, he was shocked to discover that she had never been to a brothel and promptly took her off to the Belles Poules near the Boulevard Sebastopol. They explained that they only wanted to draw and sat down at a table to drink some wine with their chosen companions. Nina selected a large redhead from the eighteen heavily painted girls who paraded their charms before them clad only in socks and high-heeled shoes. By the end of the evening all the *filles* crowded round and Nina did a drawing of each of them, which they folded up and stuffed in their socks to keep. Despite his great fame and success, Pascin committed suicide in 1930 at the age of forty-five, surfeited with excess, feeling he had burnt himself out. His life was almost a symbol of the inner emptiness which lay beneath the glittering surface of the 'twenties.

1925 saw the apotheosis of the jazz age, when black mixed as freely with white as artist with aristocrat. Pascin was one of the creators of the Negro vogue which swept Paris in the twenties. He was amongst the first to go to the Bal Nègre in the Rue Blomet, an unassuming café frequented by immigrants and old colonials from the French West Indies. On Saturdays and Sundays a remarkable West Indian clarinettist played jazz and there was traditional dancing and colonial songs. When the Surrealists, who met in a café across the road, discovered the place, the Bal Nègre quickly became as popular and as fashionable as the Bœuf or the Jockey, and the original humble clientele was forced to go elsewhere.

Another Negro nightclub much favoured by the smart set was Bricktop's in Montmartre, which stayed open until the last customer left. Nina did a drawing of Bricktop, the dusky Ada Smith whose dyed orange hair was her trademark. Tough and shrewd, she was the daughter of an Irish-Negro policewoman from Chicago. She knew all her customers by name and when not energetically performing the latest jazz-blues songs and Cole Porter numbers she would take up her usual place at the cashier's desk from where nothing escaped her. While visitors drank and danced the Charleston and the Black Bottom she supervised every aspect of the running of the club: adding up accounts, calling out requests to the orchestra, indicating to the waiters which tables needed service, skilfully and firmly dealing with difficult and tough customers and staff alike. Bricktop was so celebrated that when Cole Porter took her to the Paris Opera Ball eyebrows were raised only by the fact that she was wearing the same Molyneux creation as Princess Marina of Greece.

If Bricktop was the most famous hostess of the black cabaret world, Josephine Baker, the slim mulatto dancer from St Louis, was its greatest star. The public's first glimpse of her in the *Revue Nègre* at the Théâtre des Champs-Elysées caused a sensation. She made her entry naked except for a pink flamingo feather between her thighs, carried upside-down doing the splits on the broad back of a black giant. Mid-stage he swung her in a slow cartwheel to the floor, where she stood quite still like an ebony statue to thunderous applause. The audience was transfixed by the raw, primitive rhythms of the jazz musicians and the spectacle of Josephine shaking, slithering, contorting herself in all directions, blowing out her cheeks and crossing the stage on all fours like a sleek wild animal. Overnight she became the toast of Paris and her slicked-down hairstyle with its kiss-curl like an upside-down question mark on her forehead was the latest fashion, even giving rise to a new French verb, *bakerfixer*. To the public Josephine appeared as an exotically alluring savage. On-stage she adopted her famous skirt of uptilted bananas and painted her fingernails gold. Off-stage she wore a snake called Kiki coiled around her neck and later daily stalked the Champs-Elysées with her pet leopard Chiquita.

The most fashionable way to end an evening in the late spring and summer of 1925 was at the International Exhibition of Decorative and Industrial Arts, whose pavilions stretched along the quays of the Seine between the Pont Alexandre III and the Pont d'Alma. The exhibition was neither as contemporary nor as international as it claimed to be, since it had originally been planned for 1915 and pavilions designed ten years previously were erected as the last word in modernity. Britain's contribution was very small, while America and Germany, home of the influential Bauhaus, were not represented at all. The greatest attraction proved to be not so much the pavilions themselves, which for the most part were backward- rather than forward-looking, but the Bœuf sur le Toit's barge moored along the quayside. Poiret also had three barges lavishly decorated by Dufy: *Amours*, a nightclub-restaurant; *Délices*, which housed a theatre; and *Orgue*, where he displayed his luxurious *objets d'art*, furnishings and fabrics. It was a vain attempt by Poiret to turn the tide of fashion away from the modern, easy elegance of Chanel back to his own brand of exotic opulence. But while the crowds came to look and the socialites to sip his champagne, they were not quick to buy. The future lay with the neon-lighted world of mass production and publicity, stridently symbolized by the Eiffel Tower with its brightly coloured neon decorations and advertisement for Citroën emblazoned down one side.

Nina exhibited a nude and a landscape at the spring 1925 Salon des Indépendents. However, the rackety life she was leading was taking its toll. Roger Fry, on a visit to Paris in May 1925, evidently saw her on a bad day and wrote to Helen Anrep:

We had café at the Dôme and, of course, Nina Hamnett appeared. Oh Lord! what a collapse. I suppose her endless *petits verres* and her endless *coucheries* have at last begun to tell, but she's really repulsive. However I shall go tomorrow and see her work and also the work of Zawado, the Pole she lives with and maltreats in every way. He would have saved her if she would have let him, but her vagrant lusts were too strong and she was always going off with a new genius.[15]

Nina was herself well aware of the debilitating effects of her late-night life. She seized the opportunity of escaping Paris when Ferdinand Tuohy, a large, attractive Irish journalist and writer who was always laughing, invited her to spend the summer with him and his girlfriend Kinko at their cottage on Bréhat, an unspoilt island off Brittany. Nina immediately felt at home there and did many watercolours of the landscape and drawings of sailors and the local women with their black poke-bonnets tied under the chin. When they were not working they bathed and made expeditions in their little two-seater Citroën, taking turns to sit on the folded hood at the back. At Concarneau the line of old ladies and gentlemen painting seemed not to have moved since Nina's last trip to Brittany, and they tried to avoid the usual tourist spots, visiting Morlaix, an old town with fine carved houses where the poet Tristan Corbière had lived, and stopping at many churches with very old painted statues of Breton saints. They drove across wild moorland and hills, going as far as the Point du Raz, the westernmost part of France, where the inhabitants of the remote villages spoke only Breton. After five weeks Nina's money ran out and she very reluctantly returned to Paris. As the train approached Chartres the sun was setting and she never forgot the sight of the spires of the cathedral rising up against the purple sky and fields of golden corn.

Nina was becoming very bored with life in Paris and being always broke. De Gouy and Greeley had bought the house that they had been to see when she was visiting them and invited her to join them there as soon as she could. Nina was extremely frustrated as she could not leave Paris until she had enough money to pay her hotel bill. Providentially, Dreydell, an Englishman who had bought some of her drawings before, arrived in Paris and purchased a still life for 1,200 francs. He also took four or five pictures back to London to sell for her and promised to try to arrange an exhibition of her work. Nina was overjoyed to be a free woman again and immediately wired de Gouy and Greeley to say that she was on her way. The ever-devoted Zawado saw her off at the station and she travelled south in a third-class compartment appropriately full of Breton sailors.

Her friends met her at Cannes and they motored to Clavary, their ninety-acre estate near Grasse. Nina was delighted with it. The house, which had been built about 1802, was on the top of a steep hill surrounded by pine trees and mimosas, above terraces of olive trees and jasmine. At the rear there was a man-made lake with a small island planted with mimosa trees; beyond lay a field of irises and a view of the sea at Esterel. From the front the house looked over a valley and distant snow-capped mountains. Clavary became de Gouy's masterpiece, a monument to his idiosyncratic taste. The hall and the staircase were decorated with *trompe-l'œil* cornices and mouldings; white rocaille console tables adorned the dining-room; and the smoking-room was paved with a mosaic by Picasso. De Gouy was particularly proud of the Bamboo bedroom, which had a wicker bed and was decorated with eighteenth-century wallpaper of a Henri Rousseau-type landscape with huge trees and large snakes and alligators coming out of the water.

Life at Clavary was leisurely and civilized. In the morning the friends breakfasted in their dressing-gowns before going for a walk over the estate. Nina then did a little work and joined the others for pre-lunch cocktails on the terrace in the warm sun. De Gouy and Greeley had a wonderful French cook who prepared such good and plentiful food that they usually slept most of the afternoon. Nina's hosts never bothered to change in the evening but she insisted on dressing up and enjoyed grandly sweeping up and down the wide, winding staircase in her cast-off finery. Before dinner they always had caviare, which it was Nina's special job to spread thinly on toast. Afterwards they retired to the

Francis Poulenc,
1926

Landscape in Provence, 1926

smoking-room to be entertained by de Gouy, whom Nina thought the most intelligent and well-read person she had ever known, regretting that his highly developed critical sense inhibited his talents as a painter. He attempted two portraits of her but was so dissatisfied with them that he finished neither.

Francis Poulenc came to stay at Clavary for a few weeks while Nina was there. She was very pleased as she knew him quite well and much appreciated his mixture of buffoonery and seriousness. Like his contemporary Auric, Poulenc was a disciple of Satie and a great admirer of Cocteau. He had first attracted Diaghilev's attention in 1921 with his score for the Swedish Ballet's *Les Mariés de la Tour Eiffel* and he commissioned Poulenc to write the music for *Les Biches*. He composed all morning at the piano while Nina worked happily in the sun. She painted a pear tree in blossom and two pictures of farmhouses surrounded by olive trees, which owed something to Cézanne and showed her artistic affinities with Bloomsbury more clearly than her portraits. Poulenc sat to Nina for an hour every day and she did drawings and a portrait of him. De Gouy took the greatest interest in the work of both, offering advice and supervising the choice of flower that Poulenc should wear in his buttonhole for his portrait. Eventually they settled on a pinkish-purple wild anemone to offset his grey-green suit.

Nina and Poulenc shared a taste for bawdy popular songs. Poulenc's latest work was the *Chansons gaillardes*, composed to a set of boisterous seventeenth-century drinking choruses and love songs. He was very interested in Nina's sea shanties and amused himself inventing accompaniments for them. Indeed, Nina and the homosexual Poulenc got on so well that their friendship gave rise to an amusing anecdote recounted by Jean Hugo: 'The Bamboo room, with the jungle wallpaper, was given to Nina Hamnett. While she was there, Poulenc . . . came to Clavary. His compliments were often emphatic. *"Oh! cette Nina!"* he said, *"je l'aime! Je l'adore!"* "Let's go up to my room," said she. He was very frightened. Of the jungle, we may suppose.'[16]

As always, life with de Gouy and Greeley was a constant round of pleasure with visits to Grasse, Nice and Cannes; lunch-parties and dinners with friends such as Cocteau, Stravinsky, Honegger, Mme Jasmy Van Dongen, the dressmaker Nicole Groult and Mme Porel, daughter-in-law of the great actress Réjane. They often saw Francis Picabia, who lived in the sumptuous Château de Mai at Mougins, near Antibes. Apart from being an artist he was a wealthy and flamboyant showman, poet and novelist as well as a connoisseur of fast cars, yachts and women. In his role as Dadaist he and Satie collaborated on *Relâche* for the Swedish Ballet, taking their curtain call at the première in 1924 in a small Citroën car. Picabia came to lunch at Clavary with Marthe Chenal, the famous opera star who had sung the 'Marseillaise' on the steps of the Madeleine during the war. Nina thought she was very beautiful and greatly admired her mass of deep red, Medusa-like curls. Although she refused to sing for them at lunch, she invited them all to a box at the Casino in Cannes where she was performing *Carmen*. Nina flaunted a magnificent long, white, beaded dress and quantities of fake gold and pearl costume jewellery showered on her by her escorts. After the opera they joined Chenal for supper and Nina danced with Picabia.

De Gouy considered himself something of an authority on the subject of feminine deportment and he found a ready pupil in Nina. She loved putting on the grand style and riding in Chenal's Hispano-Suiza, even if there was always an element of play-acting in it for her. Chenal hired a motor boat and took Nina, Poulenc, Picabia and his wife to lunch at a restaurant on Ste Marguerite, a small island opposite Cannes. They sat by the sea under the shade of some trees and ate lobster before returning to the Casino at Cannes. Chenal bought Nina a month's

Nina, *c.*1923

season-ticket to the gaming-room, but she preferred to watch rather than play, fascinated by the intense faces of the serious gamblers.

Nina could evidently carry off the *grande dame* manner with panache, at least well enough to convince the sixteen-year-old Francis Rose who was staying at Villefranche, where Cocteau held court to his circle of friends and admirers at the Hôtel Welcome. Nina, perfectly dressed by Chanel courtesy of her rich friends, visited Villefranche with Mary Butts. Francis Rose was astonished by her neatness:

> She gave me the impression of a slick fashion drawing of the period. During the two days that she stayed at the Welcome she painted a picture, and this picture was as neat and regulated as her paints, her clothes, and her tidy room. One could not imagine her in the Bohemian set of Augustus John or even travelling with the untidy, dramatic Mary Butts. She left us to join the smart set of Lady Juliet Duff, Lord Berners, and Lord Alington who were in Cannes with Daisy Fellowes.[17]

Nina was plainly on the razzle in a big way and was enjoying herself enormously. She was even more buoyed up with optimism when she received a letter from Dreydell saying that he had arranged for her to have an exhibition at the Claridge Gallery in April. She returned to Paris without delay, staying only long enough to collect her work for the show. Zawado accompanied her to the Gare St-Lazare and she set off for London, full of hope and confidence for the future.

12

London Bohemia

NINA stayed at the cheap and friendly Hôtel de l'Étoile in Charlotte Street, where there were three or four bedrooms above the restaurant, and the French atmosphere and *petit déjeuner* softened the blow of returning to England. Her exhibition opened at the Claridge Gallery in Brook Street on 13 April 1926. The fifty paintings and drawings on view consisted mainly of portraits, café scenes, still lifes and landscapes done in the South of France and Brittany. Individual works, particularly the portraits, were very good and five were reproduced in the *Sphere*. But seen as a whole the show was something of a disappointment to those who had considered her one of the most promising painters of her generation. For left to her own devices amidst the multifarious distractions of Paris, without the challenging and stimulating company of artistic mentors such as Roger Fry and Sickert, Nina had not significantly developed her style and technique.

Roger Fry clearly felt that she had failed to fulfil her potential and wrote in *The Nation and The Atheneum*:

> She has a very genuine native talent. She seizes at once on the general characteristics of a head or of a gesture, and has a quick, easy notation in firm and fluent lines. This alert and slightly disillusioned, but never ill-natured, awareness of the general character and situation of human beings around her never fails her. On the one hand, she has never exploited it for a sentimental or popular appeal, but on the other hand she has lacked the ambition which her talent required and merited. . . From the very beginning she had the wit to pick out from among contemporary idioms of painting those which suited her native gift of observation, and no further curiosity either about appearances or character has impelled her to make her statements either more penetrating or richer. What she feels most she can express in her pen

and wash drawings of scenes in cafés, or in the general statement of a head upon canvas. The further elaboration in her large oil paintings, which to do her justice she never pushes very far – they are never laboured or tiresome – really adds nothing personal to this first impression.[1]

Despite such critical reservations, the exhibition generated a lot of interest and Nina did very well. Edward Marsh bought her portrait of Rupert Doone and in all she made some £50 or £60, more money than she had seen for a long time. There were other causes for optimism. The show attracted the attention of Seymour Leslie, a young cousin of Winston Churchill, who with Ethel Sands' brother Morton ran the Chelsea Book Club, where they stocked the latest French and English literature, and gave tea parties for young writers and composers. Seymour Leslie liked Nina's work so much that he commissioned her to illustrate his first novel *The Silent Queen* and obtained an advance for her from the publishers, Jonathan Cape. She also did a complete set of decorations for the Isola Bella restaurant in Soho.

Nina basked in her minor celebrity and with no thought for the future entertained her friends royally to lunch and dinner at L'Étoile, a much more modest establishment in those days than now. There were plenty of parties and familiar faces from Paris, such as Robert McAlmon, appeared to add to the gaiety. New nightclubs had opened in Nina's absence, one of the most popular being the Cave of Harmony, run by Harold Scott and Elsa Lanchester. They staged a midnight cabaret with revivals of Victorian music-hall songs and performances of rarely seen one-act plays by, among others, Aldous Huxley, Pirandello and Chekov, followed by dancing until two in the morning. London also had its own answer to the antics of Cocteau and his friends. Nina joined the excited and enthusiastic crowd which included Diaghilev, Augustus John and the young Cecil Beaton at the Chenil Galleries in April for the second public peformance of Edith Sitwell's poetic entertainment *Façade*, with music by William Walton. It was one of the key works of the 1920s, characterized by the Sitwell's special brand of patrician humour and irrepressible sense of fun. The performers and the orchestra were hidden behind a drop-curtain painted by Frank Dobson and Edith declaimed her wittily rhythmical verse through a Sengerphone – a kind of megaphone – which protruded through the open mouth of a huge mask in the centre of the curtain. London was proving to be far more enjoyable than Nina had expected and she decided to remain in England for the moment as she had no real reason to return to Paris.

The General Strike broke out on 3 May, two days after the closure of Nina's exhibition. Her visits to anarchist meetings with Gaudier far from her mind, Nina was largely indifferent to politics and merely relieved that her show had not been jeopardized. Flushed with her success, she was in buoyant mood and treated the whole thing as a great lark. She went to the first night of an opera at Covent Garden with the young Sir Leigh Ashton, who was a special constable for the duration of the strike and wore his police cap and coat over his evening clothes and carried a truncheon. Tension ran high as everyone enthusiastically joined in 'God Save The King' and wondered if a riot had taken place outside. Nina, resplendent in a cast-off evening dress given to her by Lady Cupid Michelham and Woolworth pearls, felt just as grand as everyone else and thoroughly enjoyed the excitement.

But when life returned to normal, Nina soon began to find London dull. Much as she proclaimed her relief that there were no really late clubs to tempt her to stay out all night, she missed the easy camaraderie and liveliness of Montparnasse. In an attempt to recreate something of the spirit of a Paris café Nina, Augustus John and Tommy Earp decided to adopt the Fitzroy Tavern as a meeting-place for seeing friends and doing business, and it rapidly became a focal point for artists and writers.

The Fitzroy Tavern was a largish pub on the corner of Charlotte Street and Windmill Street with a sawdust-strewn floor and a mechanical piano, its walls adorned with First World War recruiting posters. It was run by the large and genial Papa Kleinfeld, who was renowned for his kindness and generosity. Having arrived from Russia with just fourpence in his pocket, he knew what poverty was and could always be relied on for a loan when times were hard. Augustus John wrote that Kleinfeld 'though he had the simplicity of a child, was no fool. If I knew the Yiddish for ''gentleman'' I would use it to describe Mr Kleinfeld.'[2] Each year the customers of the Fitzroy Tavern collected enough money to send the local poor children on a visit to the seaside. Kleinfeld had devised an ingenious method of inducing his clients to part with their money. They wrapped their coins in paper and fastened it to a dart which they then threw at the ceiling, where it would remain if properly aimed. 'Charity thus became a popular game of skill. Nina Hamnett, although she might often miss the target herself, encouraged this practice, for she was the soul of generosity.'[3]

On Monday evenings there was a loan-club meeting at the Fitzroy. Nina, herself a member, liked to sit in a corner and draw quick sketches of the procession of old men and women in bonnets and shawls who would file down the long saloon bar each week to give their sixpences to the daughter of the house, getting the money out at Christmas. Many of these drawings were later included in the deluxe edition of Nina's autobiography, *Laughing Torso*.

A perfect evening for Nina might start at the Fitzroy Tavern and be followed by an invitation to dinner at the Restaurant de la Tour Eiffel. More expensive than the other restaurants in the neighbourhood, the Eiffel Tower was the favourite gathering-place of High Bohemia throughout the twenties and appeared in several of the literary embodiments of the period, such as Michael Arlen's novel *Piracy* in which it was thinly disguised as the Mont Agel. Like the Étoile, the Eiffel Tower was also a small hotel and Nancy Cunard, who often stayed there, wrote a long poem 'To The Eiffel Tower' published in 1923, in which she described it as 'our carnal spiritual home'. Elsewhere she affectionately referrred to the proprietor as 'dear, sophisticated, generous, drunken Rudolf Stulik'.[4] He was a corpulent, moustachioed Austrian Jew from Vienna, who had taken over the Eiffel Tower before the war. Previously a chef in a big hotel in Monte Carlo and with Kitchener in Egypt, Stulik liked to give himself an aura of mystery by hinting that he was the product of 'a romantic, if irregular attachment, in which the charms of a famous ballerina had overcome the scruples of an exalted but anonymous personage'[5] – rumoured to be the Emperor Franz Josef.

The main restaurant was a small and simply decorated L-shaped room with eight or nine tables, each with a white tablecloth and red lampshade, arranged around a three-tiered trolley piled high with fruit and rare delicacies. A huge brass urn filled with hydrangeas and ferns dominated the room and brass pots overflowing with abundant greenery hung from the ceiling. The walls and every available space were covered with bric-a-brac and pictures painted by Stulik's many artist clients, including Nina, David Bomberg, Bernard Meninsky and Jacob Kramer, who painted a portrait of Nina at this time.* Upstairs were two private dining-rooms: the Vorticist room, and another described by Viva King as 'far cosier and full of mahogany, plush, Nottingham lace, antimacassars and pots of aspidistras'.[6]

Undoubtedly something of a snob, Stulik delighted in entertaining the rich, famous and titled. But he had his own personal method of subsidizing talented young artists. According to Tristram Hillier, who was just starting his painting career in the mid-twenties,

> Stulik maintained a ratio of charges based upon what he estimated to be the wealth of his clients. For the fashionable, who liked to gather at night in what they imagined to be a Bohemian atmosphere, his prices were astronomical, but for the likes of myself, once accepted as a friend of the house, there was always a good *plat du jour* of some kind at a modest price, and generally people of interest to talk to or famous ones to watch with respectful awe.[7]

Augustus John, alone or with his models, was one of the restaurant's most colourful attractions, but there was always a host of fashionable beauties, celebrated actors and actresses such as Tallulah Bankhead, even royalty. The

* See frontispiece

Right Rudolf Stulik at the Eiffel Tower

Below The Eiffel Tower

(Both from *The Silent Queen*)

wealthy dilettante Lord Napier Alington gave frequent large dinner parties there, and regulars included many of Nina's friends such as Michael Arlen, Horace de Vere Cole, Tommy Earp, Evan Morgan, Marie Beerbohm, Viola and Iris Tree, the Irish-Polish pianist and composer Lady Dean Paul (Poldowski) and her daughter Brenda, and the beautiful concert pianist Harriet Cohen, whose portrait Nina painted. Ronald Firbank became the subject of one of Nina's favourite anecdotes. She recalled:

> One night in the Eiffel Tower I was sitting at a table with Ronald and at the next table arrived a very drunken American. The waiter said 'What would you like to eat — beef steak à la John or beefsteak and onions?' 'No', said the American, 'I don't want any of your gawd damn onions.' Ronald, overhearing, shrugged his shoulders, pressed his hands to his face and said, 'Try violets.'[8]

Stulik's favoured clients treated the Eiffel Tower more like a club than a conventional restaurant and were allowed in by the hotel entrance after closing time to spend the last part of the evening drinking there. Although Stulik had no spirit licence, the two tail-coated waiters, Joe and Frank, served drinks of all kinds until the guests decided to depart. As the hour grew later Stulik would often sit down at a table and regale the company with tales of his past life in his broken English, liberally treating his customers to drink. Sometimes things got out of hand and one evening a conspicuously drunk Nina was persuaded to leave the restaurant by a side door at least three times, only to return a few moments later by the main entrance. A waiter was finally ordered to escort her home, no ill-feeling being created on either side. Nina's old friend Edward Wolfe immortalized one such drunken exit in an amusing drawing which captures her staggering, splayed-leg gait as she was helped out.

In the small hours of the morning Stulik would make valiant attempts to persuade the lingering revellers to depart. Robert McAlmon recalled that

> Every night Rudolph went through his category of invitations, asking us to leave so that he could go to bed. It was 'Ladies und chentlemen, ve close.' After that he would become fraternal and plead with us as a brother. 'Brudders and sisters, go to ped. I vant to sleep.' He would finally let his head fall on his chest, and snooze. After another bottle of champagne had been drunk by the rest of us, Rudolph would awake with a start. 'De sooner you go de bedder I ligk you. Ged oud, blease,' he would declare decisively.[9]

The Café Royal was still a favourite meeting-place, where for the price of a drink

A Drunken Girl Went Home One Night by Edward Wolfe, *c.*1928

one could be sure of seeing people one knew. But by the mid-twenties it had undergone considerable changes. When the authorities decided to rebuild Regent Street, reconstructing John Nash's quadrant so that all the buildings would conform to the Piccadilly Hotel, the old Café Royal was also demolished and rebuilt. Work was begun in 1922 and carried out piecemeal so that the Café did not have to close, the new Café Royal being officially opened in 1928. The much loved Domino Room was transformed into a smaller Grill Room; and the Brasserie, with its slick modern décor, had none of the atmosphere of the Domino Room it replaced. Nevertheless, if only for nostalgic reasons, the Café Royal retained its hold over artists' affections. The writer Rhys Davies

At the Café Royal, 1929, by William Gaunt
Seated from left to right are Alan Clutton-Brock (*Times* art critic), Frank Dobson
(sculptor), Cecil King (artist), Charles Ginner and Nina

remembered seeing Nina there: 'When I first met her, in the Café Royal, she
gave me out of her worn handbag one of the Bath Oliver biscuits she had dropped
into it at a party the night before; at another time she fished prawns out.'[10]

Rhys Davies was a fellow contributor to the revived *New Coterie*, which was
published from the tiny, chaotic Progressive Book Shop in Red Lion Square,
under the general editorship of the Czech poet Paul Selver. This time the
emphasis was on prose rather than poetry.* A drawing by Nina of the head of a
Negro was published in the summer 1926 issue of *New Coterie*, and a Chartres café
scene of 1923 in the autumn.

Nina enjoyed doing the illustrations to *The Silent Queen*, which was a
humorous, semi-autobiographical novel, recounting the hero's adventures in
Europe and America working for an engineering firm that manufactured the new
technological marvels of the twentieth century. The Silent Queen itself was the
last work in modernity – a silently flushing WC. For the most part Nina's

* Work appeared by H. E. Bates, Tommy Earp, Louis Golding, Douglas Goldring, Robert
McAlmon, Liam O'Flaherty, T. F. Powys, Hugh MacDiarmid and Nancy Cunard. William
Roberts designed the cover and illustrations were included by Augustus John, William
Rothenstein, Bernard Meninsky, Frank Dobson, Pearl Binder and Jacob Kramer.

illustrations were quick, witty sketches whose subject-matter included pre-war street scenes, a burning zeppelin, Armistice day celebrations, the terrace of the Rotonde, a boxing match at the Blackfriars Ring, the pier at Greenwich, and various views of London. The Eiffel Tower appeared in the novel as The Big Wheel and Nina did several drawings of the cluttered interior of the restaurant with Stulik seated at a table.

Nina was always attracted to places and objects with any kind of oddity value such as Dirty Dick's and Madame Tussaud's and once when Sickert offered to buy her a birthday present, she chose a very realistic wax head of a woman with elaborately coiffured real hair, eyebrows and lashes that she had seen displayed in a hairdresser's window. When Seymour Leslie took her to draw at the Crystal Palace, which she had not visited since she was a child, Nina developed an instant, passionate enthusiasm for the massive Victorian glass construction with its giant corridors, deserted terraces, and man-made lake with huge replicas of prehistoric monsters. Seymour Leslie described it in his novel as

Britain's lumber room! There are canary birds in gothic cages, the temple at Luxor, the Alhambra, the Doges' Palace, a court of stuffed stags from Balmoral. And in the Aisles of Pure Art are statues of bronze, marble and plaster, all over-sized . . . Queen Victoria as Boadicea, Mr John Bright making eyes at a Canova nymph, General Gordon on a camel, the Maid-of-Saragossa, Una-and-the-Lion, and a stuffed buffalo that had wandered in by accident from the very un-Natural History Aisles.[11]

Nina often went to the Crystal Palace to draw and included a pen-and-ink sketch of General Gordon on his camel in *The Silent Queen*. The fifteen illustrations varied quite considerably in quality and Nina was evidently far happier drawing from life than from her imagination. They are most successful when she was working in a familiar genre, and the café and restaurant scenes are the most fully realized.

Nina quickly got through the money she had been paid for the drawings and by the autumn she was seriously in debt and desperately trying to sell some work. She wrote to Ogden: 'I will certainly send you some drawings and do try and sell them. I have a picture at the Goupil Gallery Salon and six drawings at the Brook St Gallery. Poulenc, Auric, Lambert, Dobson and two watercolours. Also the Arts League of Service has taken my stuff so I suppose I ought to sell something somewhere.'[12] She wrote later: 'I am still here. Very broke . . . will have a very nice still life of yellow orchids at the Claridge Gallery in the company of Bonnard, J. E. Blanche, Duncan Grant and everybody . . .'[13]

Short of money, Nina became very restless and bored in London. She found

Café scene (From *The Silent Queen*)

temporary relief in her renewed friendship with the composer Philip Heseltine, whom she had known since before the war. In the intervening years he had grown a neat ginger beard and transformed himself into 'the lusty, roystering, mysterious, swashbuckling, drinking, wenching Peter Warlock of popular legend'.[14] He had a scholarly interest in early English music and traditional folk songs, and attempted to revive something of the spirit of old England at his cottage at Eynsford in Kent, where he kept open house for a constant stream of visitors. Heseltine lived there with his vast collection of cats of all descriptions, his diminutive girlfriend Barbara Peach, the florid-faced Anglo-Irish composer Jack Moeran, and his faithful retainer Hal Collins, or Te Akau, a New Zealander of Maori descent who did the housekeeping and was himself a talented graphic artist and untrained musician.

Nina spent most of the spring and early summer of 1927 at Eynsford living with Jack Moeran, who was an amusing raconteur and shared Heseltine's enthusiasm for folk songs and drink. Heseltine was a fanatical campaigner for good beer and in 1929 published under the name Rab Noolas (Saloon Bar spelt backwards) an anthology of writing on drink and drunkards entitled *Merry-Go-Down: a gallery of gorgeous drunkards through the ages. Collected for the use, interest, illumination and delectation of serious topers.* And the company at Eynsford were certainly that, spending riotous days and nights drinking and singing. With his bawdy humour, delight in limericks and musical parodies, Heseltine was a convivial, if unpredictable, host who might recklessly light bonfires and perform solo dances to celebrate his high spirits one moment, and lock himself away for days at a time to work the next.

His fellow composer Constant Lambert often appeared on Sundays, a day with special rituals at Eynsford. In the morning a noisy, ribald concert was held to rival the service of the neighbouring church. Heseltine, Moeran and Lambert would join forces to provide a hilarious programme of musical parody, followed by much rowdy singing of sea shanties, to which the scandalized congregation responded with prayers for their souls. Everyone then helped to prepare a large lunch and while it cooked they retired to do some serious drinking in the garden of the Five Bells pub opposite, returning with a large earthenware jug of ale. After lunch they all piled into Moeran's car and went on an expedition to the several pubs in the area where drinks could be had. Nina did not escape entirely unscathed from these mammoth drinking bouts and once fell flat on her face on the stone kitchen floor, knocking herself out and damaging her nose so that she had to be carried to bed by Hal, who bathed her nose in gin to revive her.

On one memorable occasion the extravagant antics of the household were paraded before the bemused gaze of the locals of a nearby village. Heseltine organized a fancy-dress protest against the eviction of a young woman who bred Sealyhams by her rich and religious landlady, whom he detested. Dressed in a tall black hat and a spangled, purple Moroccan robe, his nose painted with red lipstick, Heseltine loudly interrupted the auction of the girl's few meagre possessions with lengthy speeches. He was noisily applauded by Constant Lambert in a false nose and black beard, and Nina, wearing a sheet and a large white death's head mask. Barbara Peach appeared in a child's short, full dress, with a bow on her head and her face coloured bright pink. Their mission completed, the bizarre group beat a hasty retreat before the arrival of a detachment of mounted police sent for by the alarmed villagers.

There was, however, a darker side to life at Eynsford. Heseltine's dual nature was becoming ever more apparent. There seemed an irreconcilable dichotomy between the gentle, sensitive, coolly intellectual, rather melancholy Heseltine and the violent, drunken, often obscene and blasphemous Warlock. His increasingly volatile temper led to frequent arguments with his friends and it was inevitable that Nina and Heseltine would eventually quarrel. She was forced to return to London and sobriety, living for a time in Gertrude Kingston's comfortable house at 73 Marsham Street, Westminster. Loyal friends such as Augustus John made her small loans and exhorted her to 'Keep on the water waggon; it will pay you like anything. Good for your work and your looks.'[15]

Nina's illustrations to *The Silent Queen* formed the focal point of an exhibition of her work at the Claridge Gallery in July 1927, although the novel itself was not published until the autumn. She also showed drawings of The Plough, a pub in Museum Street; statues at the Crystal Palace; and local Norfolk characters met on a visit with Moeran, whose portrait was included in the exhibition. Nina painted him wearing a butcher-blue shirt seated in front of a picture of a fiddler which once hung on the walls of The Windmill, a well-known pub in Norfolk where Moeran learned many of his folk songs.

The show aroused a great deal of interest and was widely and favourably reviewed in the press. The critic of *The Referee* praised her bold, free line and economy of means, adding that: 'Her drawings have a naivete and innocence which speaks of truth, and their humour is the outcome of a wise and sympathetic appreciation of her subject.'[16] *The Times* critic was particularly impressed by the Crystal Palace drawings, which he thought 'express a glad astonishment that such things can be';[17] while the unsuspecting diarist of the *Westminster Gazette* could not have been nearer the truth about Nina's life when he commented that her drawings 'lead me to suppose that this clever young Bloomsbury artist must spend all her life in "pubs". At any rate all her most delightful characters have been found there.'[18]

The opening of the exhibition was a crowded, fashionable event reported in the gossip columns. Augustus John came and Nina was particularly pleased to meet Sickert's friend, the French painter Jacques Emile Blanche, who complimented her on her work. Lady Leconfield bought one of the illustrations from *The Silent Queen* depicting a wedding procession passing under an awning at St Margaret's, Westminster, for seven pounds, and most of the drawings were sold later.

Nina's living arrangements were still very haphazard and she continued to stay with various friends until she came to a curious agreement with Dr Stafford Hatfield, a scientist whom she had known for some time. He lived in an elegantly dilapidated house at 35 Maple Street, off Fitzroy Square, known as Thackeray House because the novelist had once resided there and described the large upstairs studio shared by the scientist and his wife in *The Newcomes*. There were two smaller studios on the ground floor, one of which was occupied by the young painter Adrian Daintrey, and the other was used as an office by Dr Hatfield. He suggested that if Nina would share the fifteen shillings a week rent with him, she could sleep on the sofa in the office at night. Nina was happy to have a roof over her head that she could almost call her own, and before long Dr Hatfield relinquished his share in the studio so that it became her permanent home.

Osbert Sitwell was a great admirer of Nina and her work and once remarked that, 'Of course Nina is the sort of person one couldn't possibly imagine doing a mean thing.'[19] He liked her illustrations to *The Silent Queen* very much and asked her what she intended to do next. Nina was still full of enthusiasm for the statues at the Crystal Palace and declared that she would like to do life-size paintings of the statues of London. The idea immediately appealed to Osbert's sense of humour and he proposed that they should collaborate on a book which he would write and Nina illustrate. The project took concrete shape in the form of some advance royalties from the publisher Duckworth and Nina happily set to work, asking everyone she knew for suggestions.

Osbert was of the opinion that

The queerer the statues, the duller the people the better – that is, apart from Royalty – Your Queen Vic[toria] as Boadicea sounds quite perfect . . . Whiskered and forgotten peers in top-hat and classical togas should be our aim . . . The drawings for the book should be beautiful and wistful, and particularly typical of London .[20]

With her keen eye for the unusual and the comic, Nina's final choice of thirty-two statues represented a mixture of dignified public figures – monarchs, noblemen, politicians, lawyers, soldiers, inventors, poets and churchmen complete with wigs, togas, ceremonial uniforms, robes, plumes and appropriate gestures – and the humble and anonymous statuary which gives London much of its special flavour. In this category she included the fat boy with his jaunty fig leaf at Pie Corner, which used to bear the inscription 'This boy is in memory put up of the late fire of London, occasioned by the sin of gluttony, 1666'; two ship's figureheads which hung on a wall outside a timber-yard in the Waterloo Road; and an exquisitely delicate fountain in Guildford Place. The drawings are among Nina's best work and admirably display her masterly draughtsmanship. She manages to infuse even the most solemn official statue with humour, vitality and movement, wittily capturing these respected dignitaries from unexpected angles. Nina's sense of the ridiculous was well matched by Osbert Sitwell's urbanely amusing commentary, designed to deflate public pomposity.

Nina's renewed friendship with Osbert Sitwell brought her into contact again with Edith, who sat for a drawing to her. She was very interested to learn that Nina knew Mr Joyce, the Keeper of the Ethnographic Department at the British Museum, and one afternoon they went together to see the collection of African masks and artifacts, which made a great impression on her. This visit was the

Left The Fat Boy at Pie Corner   *Right* Achilles, Hyde Park
(Both from *The People's Album of London Statues*)

beginning of Edith's fascination with the habits of the Gold Coast tribes, and she spent most of 1928 working on a long poem called 'Gold Coast Customs'.

Nina finished the illustrations to the book some time before Osbert completed his text and she went to Paris for a short visit. It was disappointing. There was no one she recognized at the Dôme and the Americans were more numerous than ever. She realized fully for the first time that Paris was over for her and she returned to London with fresh enthusiasm and determination to succeed.

All the drawings for *The People's Album of London Statues* were exhibited at Tooth's Gallery in Bond Street during the first two weeks of June 1928. Nina also showed a few additional watercolours of fountains and statues at the Crystal Palace and Alexandra Palace, whose painted plaster-cast figures of the kings and

queens of England she had excitedly discovered on a day's visit with Tommy
Earp. The catalogue contained a highly complimentary notice by Augustus John,
which had appeared in *Vogue* in April:

> Although already distinguished as a painter, it is as a draughtsman, perhaps,
> that Miss Nina Hamnett is best known to her compatriots. Her light, savant
> and malicious touch is well employed in the series of illustrations she has of
> late embarked upon. If she has brought back from a prolonged sojourn abroad
> a slight French accent, it only seems to adorn with a charming oddity her
> perfectly original talent which (in the case of her drawings) falls into line with
> the grand tradition of British humouristics.

The show was well received and a good number of watercolours and drawings
were sold. Later in the year Nina exhibited an oil of an *Apache Bar, Paris* at the
Goupil Gallery Salon; and three of her earlier works were included at the
London Group retrospective at the New Burlington Galleries: the portrait of
Rupert Doone, a still life and a portrait, both of 1917.

It was while delivering the drawings of the London statues to Duckworth that
Nina met the twenty-one-year-old aspiring novelist Anthony Powell, recently
down from Oxford and beginning a career in publishing. Nina, who later
referred to him as her 'little Etonian',[21] took an immediate liking to Powell and
invited him to her studio to draw him. For Powell, who was eager to taste
something more of London life than the conventional round of upper-class deb
dances, Nina held out the promise of adventure into an unknown Bohemian
world. According to Powell's Oxford friend and fellow writer Peter Quennell:
'Nina was Anthony Powell's first grown-up love affair. He was rather pleased
with it at the time. She satisfactorily deprived him of his innocence, which is a
thing people were anxious to get rid of in those days. He built her up as a
romantic *femme de trente ans*, a Bohemian mistress.'[22]

Nina did not altogether disappoint him. During their brief friendship Powell
caught a glimpse of a bizarre Firbankian world, which he reproduced in an early
novel *Agents and Patients* (1936). Nina took him and Constant Lambert to visit the
impoverished, opium-smoking Count de Malleisque and his wife, who were
staying at the legendary Cavendish Hotel in Jermyn Street accompanied by their
Pekinese and a pet monkey who was perpetually trying to defend itself from the
unwelcome sexual attentions of the dog. They had come over from France to try
to raise money and seemed to be always surrounded by an odd collection of
dubious-looking characters. Powell described the scene at the Cavendish, where
the Count 'would play the guitar, or do newspaper puzzles (which were to win
him some enormous prize), while the company drank Pernod, and a clergyman's

Anthony Powell, 1927

voice intoned church services on the radio.'[23] The Count provided the inspiration for the comically eccentric, mercurial Marquis de la Tour d'Espagne in *Agents and Patients*, who raised hell when his supply of opium was scarce.

The Cavendish was ruled by the formidable Cockney Rosa Lewis, a former beauty said to have been Edward VII's mistress when he was Prince of Wales. Her hotel, which had something of the atmosphere of a decayed country house, was a second home for chosen members of Upper Bohemia – particularly Augustus John – and the Brigade of Guards. Nina could stand her own with Rosa Lewis and was one of the few women looked on favourably by her. Champagne flowed freely at all times of the day and night for Rosa's intimates, the most affluent member of the company being expected to foot the bill, often an unsuspecting American guest staying at the hotel. One such American from Dayton, Ohio, who had made his fortune in cash registers, invited Nina and Powell to supper with Rosa at the Savoy, astounding them by tipping the cloakroom attendant £5. However, not all Powell's outings with Nina were so colourful, and Bohemian life did not have quite the same glamour viewed close to as from a distance. In his autobiography, a clear-eyed Powell wrote of Nina's belligerent manner and heavy drinking: 'a condition not affecting her gift, but restricting continuous work to a few months at best; human relationships to equally fragmentary associations.'[24]

Nina did not confine her interests to upper-class young men. She always had some new enthusiasm or discovery that she was eager to impart to anyone who would listen. In the late twenties boxing – and boxers – became something of a passion with her. One evening in the Fitzroy Tavern she met a good-looking young boxer called Vernon Campbell, who worked as a labourer. Nina found him amusing and was attracted to him as much as anything because he was different from the people with whom she usually mixed. She had been a couple of times to the Ring at Blackfriars and had always wanted to know more about boxing. Walking down Windmill Street with Campbell, her attention was caught by a bright red and yellow poster announcing 'Slosh Saunders', the forthcoming star attraction at the Comrade's Hall in Camden Town, and the

The Ring, Blackfriars (From
The Silent Queen)

following Sunday they duly went and paid two shillings and sixpence for ringside seats. The tough crowd of local workpeople and tradesmen screamed out insults and jokes throughout the matches and Nina was delighted with the atmosphere of crude good humour and bawdy repartee.

The promoter Johnny Hughes, an ex-flyweight champion, gave Nina a free pass and she took to going to Camden Town every week to draw, relieved to have found a way of killing the boredom of dreary Sunday afternoons, which always held a special horror for her. Nina quickly got to know the other regulars and when Campbell boxed she joined in the crowd of supporters cheering and shouting 'Come on Vernon!'[25] Sometimes Nina and Campbell went to the big fights at Premierland, Olympia and the Albert Hall. He also took her to Professor Newton's famous Academy of Boxing, off the Edgware Road, where she met the young boxers and drew them while they trained. The Professor took a great liking to Nina and obligingly demonstrated the complexities of right hooks and upper cuts along with the rest of the boxing repertoire so that she became something of an expert on the finer points of the sport. Nina liked to air her knowledge to her friends and took large parties of up to fifteen people, which often included the poet Roy Campbell, to the Comrade's Hall, 'basking in their clamour as if she were the entrepreneur of the event'.[26] After the matches at Camden Town – and later at the Charlton Ring, Euston – Nina and her friends would bring the heroes of the afternoon back to her room, where they drank tea and beer until the pubs opened. Nina did many drawings at the matches, some of which were included in the de luxe edition of *Laughing Torso*, and she also persuaded some of the boxers to pose for her at home.

The hours which Nina spent at the ringside obviously taught her a few things. One evening, at a party given by Augustus John at his studio in Chelsea, Nina discovered Campbell sitting on a high-backed sofa facing away from the company with a rather mild young woman called Miss Cowles. Already the worse for drink, an incensed Nina seized Miss Cowles by the hair and pulled her over the back of the sofa with such violence that she almost scalped her, leaving her victim streaming with blood and in need of a doctor.

Nina was evidently not to be trifled with and timid spirits could find her alarming. Rhys Davies recalled visiting her in the late twenties:

> She was sharing a flat off Fitzroy Square with a handsome young boxer, and it was what is called a 'bohemian' flat. I went to the floor through the seat of the armchair in which, unobservantly, I sat. But this collapse neither Nina nor the boxer found worthy of interest, surprise or remark . . . and I continued my discourse, such as it was, from that position. I can still see Nina's cockle eye on me (it was morning) and the boxer's grave vacancy of demeanour. A few

days after this, I learned that both had been taken by ambulance to Middlesex Hospital; there had been a terrific smash up of things.[27]

In 1931 the novelist Ethel Mannin published *Ragged Banners*, in which she described the scene at the Fitzroy Tavern from the viewpoint of a cynical outsider. There is a harsh and unflattering fictional account of Nina as an ageing, drunken sculptress (Laura) in love with a young boxer. One of the central characters, Starridge, watches her and reflects: 'There was something dreadful about that middle-aged, passée woman who had once been attractive, and her passion for this completely selfish and unscrupulous young man . . . She was dreadful, too, with her glazed eyes, and her tawdry clothes, a ruin of a woman.'[28] Nina was furious when she heard about the book and threatened to give Ethel Mannin a black eye when she next saw her, but the novelist wisely gave the Fitzroy Tavern and its environs a wide berth from then on.

Nina undoubtedly developed a taste for 'rough trade' and many of her numerous anonymous lovers were casually encountered boxers and sailors. Her neighbour Adrian Daintrey observed that

the best of her was to be had in bars or pubs, places to which she gravitated usually twice a day in the company of some 'wonderful man', a 'boxah', or, on one occasion, a champion canoeist pausing for refreshment on an arduous journey round the world in his frail craft. That her catholicity of taste was considerable, I knew, but she surprised me once when she made a rapid switch from the world of Hemingway hunter types to the following 'My deah . . . you've no ideah: last nightah I met an officah with a bowlah and an umbrellah. He gave me some drinks and . . . (with triumph) a fivah. He's coming to luncheon tomorrow. I will introduce you.' I wondered what seedy creature Nina had landed this time and was agreeably surprised when the man with the worthwhile props turned out to be an amiable, eccentric officer on leave from India. Out of touch with Society life in England, he was seeking companionship and enlightenment in Art, in Charlotte Street . . . it may have been a relief to find, while venturing on the unchartered seas of the bohemian world, a companion not too unlike the conventional English lady.[29]

The Australian writer and publisher Jack Lindsay's first impressions of Nina when he met her in the Fitzroy Tavern in 1926 were similar. Knowing nothing of her background, he described her as looking 'rather like the Colonel's Daughter at first glance, perhaps a bit seedily down on her luck, but able to retreat when necessary to a Cheltenham croquet-garden.'[30]

An indomitable spirit, undeterred by her poverty, Nina would mix unselfconsciously in the most exalted social circles. Somehow or other she always managed to turn up trumps, and however odd she might look, her blithe self-confidence would triumph. On one occasion, invited to a grand party, she managed to acquire a cream satin ball-gown, which she fastened to herself with a couple of ill-concealed safety pins, and swept off in a suitably regal manner, announcing to a circle of admiring friends that the dress had once belonged to no less a person than Queen Mary. Nina unashamedly enjoyed luxury and on the rare occasions when she had money, loved to spend it on some mad extravagance. Once, having sold some drawings, she bought a second-hand car and persuaded one of her young men to act as a chauffeur. Her head swathed in an elegant motoring veil, she took her friends on drives round Regent's Park.

Nina discovered an ingenious way of getting round the Sunday licensing laws. As an alternative to watching boxing, she and her friends would take the fully licensed steamer which plied the river from Westminster Pier to Greenwich, spending the whole afternoon drinking. On soberer visits she drew the fine Wren buildings at Greenwich, showing a good eye for architectural detail. She also painted watercolours of the wharves and passing barges from the balcony of the Prospect of Whitby at Wapping, made famous by Whistler, and from the Angel, a mile on from Tower Bridge. Some of these river scenes were included in an exhibition of her drawings and watercolours held in June 1930 at Prince Vladimir Galitzine's small gallery in a basement in Berkeley Street. Several drawings were sold at the private view and Tommy Earp wrote in a review that the show 'will increase her reputation as one of our foremost women artists. Her view of the human comedy is deepening, as there is now a graver finality in the decorative quality of her landscape.'[31] The year before, Nina and Tommy Earp had planned to work together on a book to be called *Under Magog: Sketches of Life in London*. It was duly announced in the press and Nina did twelve drawings, but the book was never finally published as Earp failed to complete the text.

Between 1929 and 1932 Nina exhibited regularly with the London Group, showing mainly portraits, café and pub scenes, and an oil of the British Museum. On one of her daily visits to the Fitzroy Tavern she met up again with Dolores, the famous Epstein model who had sung and danced at the Cabaret Club before the war. As neither of them had any money, Dolores agreed to sit for Nina in the hope that they might then be able to sell some drawings to their mutual benefit. They worked for four or five hours a day, Nina allowing only one of Dolores' numerous admirers into the studio to watch at a time. She did several drawings and a large portrait of Dolores in profile, wearing a black petticoat that highlighted her pale skin and dark hair. It was shown with the London Group in October 1932, when it was bought by the Bradford collector Wyndham T. Wint for £52 10s. Wint's collection was exhibited at the Whitechapel Art

*To Annie with love & best
wishes for her birthday Friday 13th
1936.
Nina Hamnett.*

Docker at Wapping, 1936 (inscribed to Annie Allchild)

Dolores, 1931

Gallery in 1939 and included two earlier portraits by Nina of Ossip Zadkine and Torahiko Khori. Seen together, the portrait of Dolores, which was thinly and loosely painted in muddy tones, conspicuously lacked the stylish distinction and rigorous handling of Nina's earlier work and showed a move towards a more literal representation of appearances.

Through helping a friend write art criticism for a newspaper, Nina gained confidence in her literary ability and decided to try to write the story of her life.

When word of this got round the neighbourhood, she was bemused by the number of people who would anxiously approach her and beg her not to mention certain incidents in which they had been involved. They need not have worried. Nina was not interested in exposing people or scandalmongering. In her own words: 'I thought I owed it to some of my friends who were dead, partly to amuse myself and incidentally to earn an honest penny.'[32] Uncertain of its worth or quite what to do with it, she showed the first few thousand words to Douglas Goldring, who encouraged her to continue. One evening at the Eiffel Tower, Harold Nicolson read part of the typescript. He thought that it was 'very funny and most illiterate'[33] and offered to find her a publisher.

Harold Nicolson had given up his promising career in the diplomatic service at the end of 1929 and was rapidly establishing a reputation as a writer, journalist and broadcaster. With his friend Robert Bruce Lockhart he was employed by the *Evening Standard* to compile 'The Londoner's Diary', a daily column of social, political and literary gossip. In April 1931 Nicolson reviewed H. S. Ede's biography of Gaudier-Brzeska, *Savage Messiah*, in which Ede recounted the story of how Gaudier persuaded a young woman artist to sit for him and after he had done a dozen or so drawings took off his own clothes and posed for her. A few days later, on 4 May, under the heading 'An Art Secret', Nicolson revealed in 'The Londoner's Diary' that the young woman was Nina and reproduced a quick drawing that she had done at the time of Gaudier crouching nude.* Lord Beaverbrook, the newspaper's proprietor, claimed to be shocked and offended by the drawing, which he pronounced 'crude, rude and rather suggestive of a man on the cabinet or presenting his backside as an invitation'.[34] Nicolson, however, thought that it was 'a fine, bold drawing of historic interest'[35] and duly interested Constable in publishing Nina's autobiography.

Laughing Torso, dedicated to both Goldring and Nicolson, was published by Constable in 1932 and launched with a retrospective exhibition of her work at Zwemmer's Gallery in the Charing Cross Road. She showed illustrations from the book, recent portraits, river and London views, figure studies, nudes, pub and café scenes, and seven expressive drawings of birds, chimpanzees, an antelope and a buffalo. Many of her friends came to the opening and the press noted Lord Berners, Constant Lambert, Augustus John, Tommy Earp, Evan Morgan and Harold Nicolson amongst the crowd. The *Daily Herald* commented on the fact that there were four millionaires present, including two Rothschilds.

Both the exhibition and the book received much publicity. Largely conversational in tone, *Laughing Torso* is a blithe gambol through Bohemia, a rapid succession of people, places and events recounted in a somewhat breathless and artlessly witty style. Although reviewers dwelled on the book's directness and candour, and the American edition was advertised as 'the frankest

*See page 55

autobiography ever written by a woman',[36] in many ways *Laughing Torso* is curiously impersonal and reveals little of Nina's inner thoughts or feelings. She shows a marked reticence about the more intimate details of her life. Names are changed, some people are identified only by initials – in some cases deliberately the wrong ones – and many important aspects are glossed over with a veneer of respectability that was far from the real Nina, a self-conscious rebel against convention if ever there was. This was not entirely caused by fear of the libel laws, and Nina offers some justification for her autocensorship when she says: 'I think the fullest details can be told to a select company of sympathetic people, but not written down for everyone to read.'[37]

In view of this, it is all the more surprising that *Laughing Torso* should have been the subject of a sensational libel case, described as 'one of the most extraordinary trials of the twentieth century',[38] which made newspaper headlines for several days.

Nina in 1932

13

```
┌──────────────────────┐
│  The wickedest man   │
│     in the world     │
└──────────────────────┘
```

BEFORE the publication of *Laughing Torso* Nina wrote to her old friend Aleister Crowley: 'I have written quite a lot about you, very nice and appreciative. No libel, no rubbish, simply showing up the *sale bourgeois* attitude to all our behaviour.'[1] Crowley raised no objections and later went to Nina's exhibition at Zwemmer's Gallery where the book was prominently displayed.

For the past twenty years Crowley had been pilloried in the British press as the 'wickedest man in the world' and the 'King of Depravity', and had done nothing to refute his evil reputation. When his novel *The Diary of a Drug Fiend* appeared in 1922 he was virulently attacked by *John Bull* and the *Sunday Express*, which published a series of sensational revelations about life at his Abbey of Thelema in Sicily, accusing him of devil worship and orgies of drug-taking and sexual debauchery. The *Sunday Express* redoubled its ferocity the following year when Betty May alleged that her husband Raoul Loveday had died in Sicily as a result of being forced to drink the blood of a cat after one of the ritual sacrifices at the Abbey. Crowley blamed these articles for his expulsion from Sicily by the Italian authorities and the subsequent decline of his fortunes. He bitterly regretted that he had not sued the Beaverbrook Press for libel, but distance, ill-health and lack of money had prevented him from taking legal action at the time.

As chance would have it, Crowley was walking down Praed Street in January 1933 and happened to see a copy of his novel *Moonchild* on sale in a bookshop window with a notice falsely claiming 'Aleister Crowley's first novel *The Diary of a Drug Fiend* was withdrawn from circulation after an attack in the sensational press.'[2] Crowley seized his opportunity to prosecute the bookseller, Mr Gray, for libel and duly won his case, being awarded £50 damages with costs. Mr Justice Bennet decided that the bookseller wanted the public to believe *Moonchild* was an indecent book, and made the rather surprising statement: 'There is not the smallest ground for suggesting that any book Mr Crowley has written is indecent or improper.'[3]

Crowley was elated by his victory. Convinced that he had discovered an easy way of making money, he cast around in his mind for further potential candidates for the law-courts. Considering the numerous rabid attacks on him in the press and the lurid description of life at the Abbey of Thelema that had appeared in Betty May's ghosted autobiography *Tiger Woman* in 1929, it is all the more remarkable that Crowley should have taken exception to a relatively mild paragraph in *Laughing Torso* which stated that 'Crowley had a temple in Cefalu in Sicily. He was supposed to practise Black Magic there, and one day a baby was said to have disappeared mysteriously. There was also a goat there. This all pointed to Black Magic, so people said, and the inhabitants of the village were frightened of him.'[4]

Crowley decided that the imputation to him of black magic was an infamous character defamation and against all advice from his friends and lawyers instigated proceedings for libel against Nina, Constable and Company, and the printers. The novelist J. D. Beresford, who had commissioned *The Diary of a Drug Fiend* for Collins, warned him: 'I haven't the least doubt that some very extraordinary and damaging charges will be made against you if you come into court, the kind of charges that would spoil any chance you might have with a judge, who is a kind of professional moralist.'[5]

The trial opened at the High Court on 10 April 1934 before Mr Justice Swift and a special jury, the defendants denying that the words complained of were defamatory and further pleading that if they were, they were true in substance and fact. In taking on the large publishing house of Constable, Crowley had overreached himself. Far from vindicating him the trial quickly turned into a moral exposure of Crowley. There was an inescapable element of second-rate melodrama in the scene played out before Mr Justice Swift. Crowley, a flabby, ageing magician in a top hat, took the starring role as arch-villain; while Betty May, the witness for the defence, was effective in the part of a virtuous young wife innocently caught up in the sinister antics at Cefalu. Nina kept a low profile throughout the four days of the trial. She attended court each day very smartly dressed, no doubt in borrowed clothes, and appeared the apogee of conventional respectability. On numerous occasions Crowley's flippant replies to questions reduced the solemn proceedings almost to the level of music-hall comedy and the judge repeatedly threatened to clear the court if there was any more laughter.

Crowley's counsel Mr J. P. Eddy opened the trial by stating that if at times Crowley had shown a want of restraint and a passion for the unconventional, this could be attributed to the fact that he had been brought up in the strict environment of the Plymouth Brethren and had taken the first opportunity of manifesting the spirit of revolt. He painted a flattering picture of Crowley as a man of education, taste and money, dedicated to the arts and sciences, who had been led to metaphysical – or magical – studies as a further branch of learning. An avid traveller and explorer, he had taken part in the first climbing expeditions to Choga Ri (K2) and Kanchenjunga, the highest mountains in the world after Everest; walked across China and the Sahara; and lived in Indian villages. For many years he had studied the religions of the world and had been interested in magic since 1897. Eddy stressed that Crowley was a white magician dedicated to the fight against black magic and that the two should not be confused: 'There is White Magic, which is on the side of the angels, and rests on faith in the order and uniformity of Nature. Black Magic is a degrading thing, associated with the degradation of religion, the invocation of devils, evil in its blackest forms, and even the sacrifice of children.' He asserted that the allegations in *Laughing Torso* were quite inaccurate. Crowley had established his little community at Cefalu in 1920 for the sole purpose of studying white magic, and nothing remotely resembling black magic took place there. No child had disappeared mysteriously and the only goat was kept for milk.

Crowley then stepped into the witness-box to give evidence, stating that the principle of his belief was embodied in the words 'Do what thou wilt shall be the whole of the law. Love is the law; love under will.' He explained that far from being a licence for unbridled self-indulgence, these words meant that no man had a right to waste his time doing things which resulted from mere wishes and desires but ought to devote himself wholly to his true work in the world, which he should discover by self-examination and by seeking the advice of a wise man. There were different forms of magic: 'In boxing you can fight according to Queensberry rules or you can do the other thing.' 'Does that mean', Malcolm Hilbery, KC, counsel for Constable, interposed, 'that his definition of Black Magic is the same as all-in wrestling?' Ignoring the ensuing laughter, Crowley continued:

the basis of all black magic is that utter stupidity of selfishness which cares nothing for the rights of others. People so constituted are naturally quite unscrupulous. In many cases black magic is an attempt to commit crime without incurring the penalties of the law. The almost main instrument of black magic is murder, either for inheritance or for some other purpose . . .

Crowley vigorously denied that black magic had ever been practised at Cefalu.

Hilbery's cross-examination quickly destroyed the picture of Crowley as an altruistic seeker after truth. Crowley admitted that he had practised magic since he had come down from Cambridge and had adopted the titles Frater Perdurabo, The Beast 666 and Master Therium, which, he said, meant 'Great Wild Beast'.

Asked if these titles conveyed a fair expression of his practice and outlook on life, he replied, 'The Beast 666 only means ''sunlight''. You can call me ''Little Sunshine''.'

Hilbery had prepared his case well and was familiar with a wide range of Crowley's writings, many of which had been privately printed and from any conventional viewpoint could only be considered 'erotic in tendency and grossly indecent'. He read passages from several of Crowley's works, including verses from the graphically titled *White Stains*, and asked Crowley if he knew this was an obscene book. Crowley replied:

> 'I don't know. Until it got into your hands it never got into any improper hands at all.'
> 'Have you not built a reputation on books which are indecent?'
> 'It has long been laid down that art has nothing to do with morals.'
> 'We may assume that you have followed that in your practice of writing?'
> 'I have always endeavoured to use the gift of writing which has been vouchsafed to me for the benefit of my readers.'
> 'Decency and indecency have nothing to do with it?'
> 'I do not think they have. You can find indecency in Shakespeare, Sterne, Swift, and every other English writer if you try.'

Hilbery read further examples of his verse from *Clouds Without Water* and enquired:

> 'Isn't that filth?'
> 'You read it as if it were magnificent poetry, I congratulate you.'
> 'You have been well known for years as the author of all these things which I have been putting to you?'
> 'No. I wish I had a far wider reputation. I should like to be hailed as the greatest living poet. Truth will out.'

Hilbery then quoted from an article that Crowley had written for the *Sunday Dispatch* the previous June in which he boasted that: 'They called me ''the worst man in the world.'' They have accused me of doing everything, from murdering women and throwing their bodies in the Seine to drug peddling.' Questioned about his general reputation, Crowley answered:

> 'I hear a canard about me every week. Any man of any distinction has rumours about him.'
> 'Does any man of any distinction necessarily have it said about him that he is

"the worst man in the world"?'

'Not necessarily. He has to be very distinguished.'

'Have you said that Horatio Bottomley branded you as a "dirty degenerate cannibal"?'

'Yes'.

'You have never taken action against any of the people who have said such things about you?'

'No'.

Hilbery continued to read from the same article Crowley's account of his first steps in magic. He described how he had constructed a temple in his flat in Chancery Lane and invoked certain forces which resulted in people being attacked by unseen assailants. He also fed a skeleton with blood and small birds to see if he could make it live and experimented with becoming invisible:

> By invoking the God of Silence I gradually got to the stage where my reflection began to flicker like the images of one of the old-fashioned cinemas. . . . I was able to walk out of the house in a scarlet robe and a crown on my head without attracting any attention. They could not see me.

Crowley affirmed the truth of his published statements and added that he believed in the efficacy of human sacrifice for magical purposes, although he did not approve of it. He admitted that Thelema was a cult of magic and that he had furnished a large room at his Abbey of Thelema as a temple for the performance of magic rites. It contained an altar within a polygon on which stood a book of the laws. Candles and incense were used in the rituals as well as daggers and swords. During the ceremonies, words were intoned and Crowley walked around the floor at a pace which he described as resembling a tiger stalking a deer.

Hilbery returned to the subject of the attacks made on him in the press:

> 'Have you ever been called "the thoroughly exposed and pernicious Aleister Crowley"?'
>
> 'I don't think I know that one. I cannot read everything!'

Mr Justice Swift then asked: 'When you read "It is hard to say with certainty whether Crowley is a man or beast" did you take any action?'

'It was asked of Shelley whether he was a man or someone sent from Hell.'

'I am not trying Shelley. Did you take any steps to clear your character?'

Crowley was forced to admit that he had not, and that he had been friendly with

Nina for some time and had no reason to suppose that she would do anything intentionally to harm him, but had acted in error rather than malice.

Once Hilbery had revealed the nature of Crowley's art and magical practices and successfully indicated to the jury that his reputation was such as to render it almost impossible to libel him, it was left to Martin O'Connor, one of the best known bar personalities, acting on behalf of Nina, to expose him as a fraud. He challenged Crowley to demonstrate his magical powers in the courtroom and suggested that he 'try his magic on Mr Hilbery, to attack him and see if he could do him any harm.' When Crowley declined, O'Connor asked: 'Is that because you are too considerate or because you are an impostor?'

'I have never done any harm to any human being,' Crowley replied. Mr Justice Swift objected: 'We cannot turn this court into a temple,' and O'Connor proposed that as an alternative Crowley might like to become invisible. But Crowley refused and remained stubbornly visible, insisting that he had never at any time practised black magic, which he had always condemned. He claimed, 'My particular branch is the raising of humanity to higher spiritual development.'

Before he concluded his evidence, the judge asked Crowley for a definition of magic.

> 'Magic is the art of causing change to occur in conformity with the will. White Magic if the will is righteous, and Black Magic if the will is perverse.'
> 'Does magic involve the invocation of spirits?'
> 'It may do so. It involves the invocation of the Holy Guardian Angel, who is appointed by Almighty God to watch over each of us.'
> 'Is magic the art of controlling spirits so as to affect the course of events?'
> 'That is one small branch of magic.'
> 'If the object of the control is good then it is White Magic, but if the object of the control is bad it is Black Magic?'
> 'Yes'.
> 'When the object of the control is bad what spirits do you invoke?'
> 'You cannot invoke, or bring down, evil spirits. You must evoke them, or bring them up.'
> 'When the object is bad you evoke evil spirits?'
> 'You put yourself in their power, but it is possible to control evil spirits for a good purpose.'

Out of all Crowley's supporters and acquaintances in the artistic and literary world only one man, Mr Carl Germer, a German merchant living in England, came forward to testify to Crowley's good character and affirm that he had never practised or advocated black magic.

Betty May was called for the defence. She described life at the Abbey of Thelema where the inmates began their day at five-thirty with the adoration of the sun. Crowley slept until tea-time in his room known as the *chambre de cauchemars* because of the indecent paintings on the walls. After the evening meal Crowley, wearing a robe with a cowl, conducted the pentagram ceremony, which lasted for two hours. His 'spiritual wife', known as the Scarlet Woman, also took part, dressed in scarlet with a jewelled snake under her robe. Everyone sat round the circle in the temple while Crowley went before each person making passes with a sword, 'breathing' them in and out of him. A ritual was read and on Fridays there was a special invocation of Pan. On one occasion after an invocation lasting three hours, a cat was killed and Betty May's young husband Raoul Loveday had to drink a cup of its blood. Shortly after he was severely ill with enteritis and died of laudanum poisoning.

Eddy tried to discredit Betty May's evidence by suggesting that before her marriage she had lived 'a very fast life in London' consisting of 'drink, drugs and immorality'. He questioned her reliability as a witness, pointing out the discrepancies of the account she had just given of life at the Abbey of Thelema with the versions that had previously appeared in the *Sunday Express* and in *Tiger Woman*. Betty claimed that the *Sunday Express* had not accurately reported the facts as she had told them and admitted that certain incidents in *Tiger Woman* were untrue. In particular, her supposed adventures with an Apache gang in Paris were fabricated to make the book more exciting. Eddy put it to her that her sole interest in the matter was to make as much money as possible and that she was present in court as a bought witness. In support of this he produced letters written from Betty May to the defendants' solicitors requesting further expenses in connection with the trial on top of the £15 to £20 she had already been paid. Eddy also referred to another letter discussing the trial written to Bumbletoff (Betty's nickname) from her friend Poddlediff. When it transpired that these letters had been stolen from Betty May, the judge ordered them to be retained by the court. Far from helping Crowley's case, they were to be the subject of a further trial thirteen months later at the Old Bailey where Crowley was fined £50 for being in possession of letters which he knew to be stolen.

O'Connor then addressed the jury and said that it was appalling that 'in this enlightened age a Court should be investigating magic which is arch-humbug practised by arch-rogues to rob weak-minded people. I hope this action will end for all time the activities of this hypocritical rascal.' As to his reputation, O'Connor concluded that there was no one in fact or fiction against whom so much iniquity had been alleged. After his speech the jury, without wishing to hear Nina in defence, asked whether they could intervene to stop the trial, but the judge replied that Eddy had the right to address them once more. He did

IN MAGICIAN'

Drank Blood of Cat Sac

SCATHING comments on the writings of Aleister Crowley were made by Mr. Justice Swift after the jury, with a dramatic suddenness, intimated that they desired to stop the libel action he had brought this week against Miss Nina Hamnett and the publishers in connection with a paragraph in her book "The Laughing Torso."

Mr. Crowley alleged that the paragraph associated him with black magic, but after a four days' hearing, during which the whole of the sinister trappings of black magic, with its unholy rites and ceremonies, including the murder of babies and the sacrifice of animals were referred to, the jury, without wishing to hear Miss Nina Hamnett in defence, decided that no damage had been done to Mr. Crowley's character, and awarded the verdict against him with costs.

Mr. Justice Swift, speaking in measured tones, told the jury he thought that during the 40 years with which he had been connected with the courts in one way and another he had heard of every conceivable vice and wickedness, but this case had shown him that there was always something more to learn.

The trial had been replete with sensational revelations, for in addition to

Miss Nina Hamnett (right) with Miss Betty May, authoress of "Tiger Woman."

Crowley admitted he had himself assumed—and stories of drugs accessible to everyone without restriction.

EPSTEIN'S MODEL

Aleister Crowley is a complacent-looking man of comfortable proportions, who speaks in a high pitched voice, slightly querulous in tone. For two-and-a-half days he was in the witness-box under a fire of cross-examination, ruthless beyond description.

And then—in strong contrast to his imposing bulk—came the slight figure of Mrs. Betty Sedgewick—better known in Bohemian circles as Betty May—one-time model of Epstein (who did a

She was the only witness ca the defence, and, like Crowle submitted to a withering fire tions in cross-examination su that she had fabricated the st the temple at Cefalu, had del invented the story about the of the cat, and that she had con court not to assist the jury unravelling of the true facts order to get money.

STOLEN LETTERS

It was put to her that she ha her evidence," a suggestion wh indignantly denied. Certain were produced showing that written to the solicitors acting

Empire News, 15 April 1934

TEMPLE

iced on "Altar"

"I HAVE NEVER HEARD SUCH DREADFUL, HORRIBLE, BLASPHEMOUS, ABOMINABLE STUFF AS THAT WHICH HAS BEEN PRODUCED BY THIS MAN WHO DESCRIBED HIMSELF TO YOU AS THE GREATEST LIVING POET."—Mr. Justice Rigby Swift.

Aleister Crowley.

ificent poetry. I congratulate you," as the smiling reply.

Mr. Justice Swift took a hand when veral extracts from Press articles nouncing Mr. Crowley were read.

"Did you take any steps to clear your aracter?" asked the judge in refer-ice to one phrase: "It is hard to say ether Crowley is man or beast."

"It was asked of Shelley whether he as a man or someone sent from hell," e witness replied.

"I am not trying Shelley—did you ke any action?"

"LITTLE SUNSHINE"

Once Mr. Hilbery asked whether Mr. owley had assumed the designations Beast 666" and "The Master erion."

Mr. Crowley explained that the latter m meant "Great Wild Beast," whilst 666" was the number of the sun.

"You may call me 'Little Sunshine'," suggested, and the court roared, for s massive bulk made the title congruous.

He denied that Black Magic had ever en practised at Cefalu or that he had actised it at any time. He also nied that drugs were free of access the inmates of the Temple at Cefalu that he had ever advised Raoul Love-y to take drugs.

Mr. Martin O'Connor, cross-examining Miss Hamnett, whom Mr. Crowley d described as "a kind of clearing

"The women sat on boxes round the circle," she went on. "Everything was grotesque and rather mad. Crowley wore a robe, sometimes of bright colours, some-times it was black, with a cowl which he used to put over his head.

"Leah, the Scarlet Woman, took part in the ceremony. She was the spiritual wife of Crowley, and wore a scarlet cloak. Sometimes she wore a jewelled serpent round her waist, fastened just over her middle under the cloak. She had a magical name which I do not remember.

"Crowley, Raoul, Shumway, and Leah took part in the ceremony, and Crowley sat on a chair before the brazier. Then with a sword he would approach a person, and breathe the person into him, then he would breathe out. He read the ritual out of the Equinox."

CAT SACRIFICED

Asked whether she had ever seen a sacrifice at the abbey, Mrs. Sedgewick replied:

"Yes, indeed, I saw a terrible sacrifice —the sacrifice of a cat. It was sacrificed on the altar.

"It was a rule that no animal should be allowed in the abbey. But one day a cat got in, and got under the table. Crowley knew it was there, and he reached down. It scratched him ter-ribly, and he got hold of it and made a pass over the cat with his sword.

"'You shall be sacrificed within three days," he said.

"There was great excitement in the abbey, and preparations were made.

"Mr. Crowley had a knife with a long handle. The cat had been put in a bag and was crying piteously. It was taken out of the bag and my husband held it up. He had to kill it.

"The cat was held over the altar, and the Scarlet Woman held a bowl to catch its blood. The knife was blunt except the top, which was very sharp.

"When my husband tried to cut the cat's throat, he cut his finger badly, and became frightened and let the cat fall.

"It dropped out of the circle, and that is very bad for magic.

"Crowley asked me to pick it up, but I wouldn't, and when they did finally kill the cat, the blood fell into the bowl, and my young husband had to drink a cup of that blood."

And on this tense note Mrs. Sedge-wick's examination concluded.

what he could, claiming that no evidence had been brought to support the allegations that a baby had disappeared from the Abbey nor that the local inhabitants were afraid of Crowley. But when he had finished the jury indicated that they were still of the same opinion and Mr Justice Swift accordingly gave his summing up:

> I have been over forty years engaged in the administration of the law in one capacity or another. I thought I knew of every conceivable form of wickedness. I thought that everything which was vicious and bad had been produced at some time or another before me. I have learnt in this case that we can always learn something more if we live long enough. I have never heard such dreadful and horrible, blasphemous and abominable stuff as that which has been produced by a man who describes himself to you as the greatest living poet.

The jury returned a unanimous verdict against Crowley and judgment was awarded for all the defendants with costs. Crowley lost his subsequent appeal, but the defendants had to bear the costs themselves as Crowley declared himself bankrupt.

The trial had had high entertainment value in a pre-television world. The combination of strange occult practices and the vagaries of Bohemia was irresistible to the mass-circulation newspapers, which rivalled each other with lurid headlines. If neither Nina nor Crowley gained materially, the resulting publicity ensured that they both became household names overnight.

Nina was not slow to realize the possible advantages to be gained from legal action, and suing people for libel, or threatening to do so, became a regular feature of her precarious financial existence. Even before Crowley's lawsuit, *Laughing Torso* had been the subject of another legal skirmish, this time settled out of court. Dylan Thomas, who was then working as a young reporter in Swansea, carelessly remarked in an article entitled 'Genius and Madness Akin in World of Art' published in the *South Wales Evening Post* on 7 January 1933 that Nina was the 'author of the banned book *Laughing Torso*'. The following week the paper, obviously acting on legal advice, published a formal apology for suggesting that *Laughing Torso* had been banned and added that 'We are informed by Miss Hamnett it enjoys a very wide circulation.'[6] This episode certainly hastened the end of Dylan's journalistic career and he demonstrated his indifference to facts once again in a letter he wrote to Pamela Hansford Johnson later in the year, making light of the incident: 'I ran the Northcliffe Press into a libel suit by calling Miss Hamnett . . . insane. Apparently she wasn't, that was the trouble.'[7]

On another occasion, Nina was sitting in the Fitzroy Tavern one morning when the young Scots poet Ruthven Todd pointed out to her a photograph of Betty May and an unnamed gentleman in a popular newspaper. It was wrongly captioned 'Miss Nina Hamnett, the artist and author of *Laughing Torso*, takes a walk in the Park with a friend.'[8] Nina suddenly became very business-like, borrowed half-a-crown and the newspaper in question, and promptly went off in a taxi to the offices of the paper in Fleet Street where she complained that she had been libelled. To avoid further trouble the newspaper paid her £25 on the spot and produced a release for her to sign. Three-quarters of an hour later, a triumphant Nina arrived back in the Fitzroy Tavern announcing that all the drinks were on her. When Betty May appeared she was astonished to be handed a double whisky by Nina, but as soon as she discovered the reason for this unwonted largesse she too disappeared in a taxi to Fleet Street and claimed that she had been libelled. Evidently not wanting to tangle with such a notoriously dangerous character as Betty May, the paper dispensed a further £25 without demur. The subsequent celebrations went on all day, the ceiling of the Fitzroy Tavern no doubt also benefiting from Nina and Betty's unexpected windfall.

When all the fuss about the Crowley trial had died down, Nina went to Paris to stay with Princess Violette Murat. She immediately took Nina in hand and set about tidying her up and replenishing her wardrobe before they set off to Vichy, where the Princess was going for a cure. Nina thought the water tasted like the smell of drains, but she dutifully swallowed it for the first few days to keep the Princess company, later discreetly tipping it away when her back was turned. Despite the distinctly depressing effect of the water, Nina was glad to be away from London and declared, 'At last, for the first time for ages I was able to think, there being no men about and no drinks here of any kind.'[9] With no distractions she was also able to paint and did several watercolours at Vichy. Nevertheless, she welcomed the arrival of her old friends François de Gouy and Russell Greeley and after the Princess went to bed they sat up drinking whisky and telling funny stories until the early hours. Nina had hoped that the Princess would send her to stay on her yacht at Toulon, but Violette decided that with so many sailors about and endless opportunities for getting drunk, it was no place for Nina and gave her 1,000 francs to return to Paris. Nina consoled herself by drawing and painting at a fair in the Avenue d'Orléans, where she saw a young man who reminded her of the first 'abominable Pole' with whom she had fallen in love when she went to Paris in 1920. He gave her an enchanting smile, but Nina decided to return to England before she got into mischief.

Back in London Nina's life took on its familiar social rhythm. The success of *Laughing Torso* and the publication in the same year of a short essay by her entitled 'What I wore in the 'Nineties' in *Little Innocents*, a collection of childhood reminiscences edited by Alan Pryce-Jones, encouraged Nina to begin writing a second volume of autobiography. But work became less and less important and her day was increasingly organized around pub opening-hours.

Nina saw a good deal of the wealthy Irish Michael Shawe-Taylor, who divided his time between England, Ireland and the West Indies. Some fifteen years younger than Nina, he had suffered badly from gout since he was twenty-eight but had a large enough private income not to work. Although he hated women he was very fond of Nina. Her warmth and generosity, her indifference to social and sexual categories, gave Nina a special understanding and affinity with homosexuals. In the same way, her openness and interest in people enabled her to reach across the generations and feel at ease with those much younger than herself. She shared with Michael Shawe-Taylor a mutual interest in sailors and drink and they got on extremely well.

He took Nina to spend Easter at his family home, Castle Taylor, in Galway. She had not been to Ireland since she was a girl of fifteen and had the happiest memories of it. She loved everything: the horse-breeders and bookmakers on the boat, the bustling market at Galway, and the fields of wild flowers in County Kerry. They went on excursions to Connemara, Limerick and the Aran Islands, accompanied by the butler who carried baskets of Guinness and Nina's paints and sketch books. The landscape reminded Nina of Brittany and she found the easy-going, fantastical Irish temperament much to her taste. She drew and painted, but as it was often too cold to work outside, she and Michael studied local life in the pubs, where she was invariably the only woman. Nina explained: 'Ladies in Ireland do not, as a rule, use the bar of public houses, the reason being that Irish ladies are of modest and retiring dispositions and do not like it to be known that they ''take a drop''. I, not being Irish and S.[Michael] not being a lady, I drank with him.'[10]

Life with Michael Shawe-Taylor, whether in Ireland or England, was not conducive to work. Indeed his friends and relatives have commented on the fact that he took an almost sadistic pleasure in buying Nina drinks and watching her get progressively drunker while he teased her unmercifully about not having any money, being badly dressed and a failed artist. Unperturbed, Nina would beam happily and down the next glass.

14

Fitzrovia

ONLY beware of Fitzrovia . . . It's a dangerous place, you must be careful
. . . If you get Sohoitis . . . you will stay there always day and night and
get no work done ever. You have been warned.[1]

Tambimuttu, the Ceylonese poet and editor of *Poetry London*, could well have
pointed a melodramatic finger at Nina to illustrate the ghastly truth of his words
to the young and impressionable writer Julian Maclaren-Ross. There she sat on
the inevitable bar-stool, 'erect as though on horseback, turning her head sharply
like a bird, missing nothing: the eyes and ears of the district.'[2]

By the mid-thirties Nina was producing very little work beyond quick
portrait sketches in pencil or chalk. She still had the odd commission – such as
doing line drawings for the *Radio Times* or illustrations to Marcel Boulestin's
cookery articles in *Vogue* and *Harper's Bazaar* – but there were no sustained
projects, no exhibitions. She had not lost the ease and fluency of her earlier
work, but this very facility proved to be counterproductive and her once
masterly draughtsmanship became increasingly slight and superficial. Distracted
by life, Nina had not been able to develop her talent and fulfil the faith that
people had had in her. Spending more and more time in pubs, she worked
erratically. Concentration was difficult and money to buy materials scarce.
Always willing to tell another anecdote in return for the next drink, gradually
Nina Hamnett the personality, the celebrated *reine de bohème*, took over from the
serious artist.

She showed one painting, *The Victorian*, with the London Group in 1936, but
no other work by her was exhibited for the rest of the decade. With no one to
encourage her and no dealer to back her, Nina suffered a definite artistic decline
in the mid-thirties. Although she knew and was friendly with many of the young
artists who frequented the Fitzroy Tavern, and had posed nude in 1930 for a
Surrealist painting by the flamboyant John Banting in which her head and arms

Surrealist portrait of Nina, 1930, by John Banting

sprouted huge leaves, her work had nothing in common with theirs. Nina, who always took a lively interest in what was going on and went to the opening of the International Surrealist Exhibition in 1936, knew that the artistic tide had completely turned against her. Her concerns seemed hopelessly out-of-date and irrelevant to a younger generation of painters busily exploring the possibilities of abstraction and Surrealism. But for all that, Nina never lost her belief in herself as an artist and retained what Anthony Powell recognized as 'an unshakeable confidence in her own myth'.[3]

For a short time in the thirties and forties it is possible to talk about a London Bohemia centred on the area which later came to be known as Fitzrovia. The Fitzroy Tavern, over which Nina presided, gave its name to the district north of Oxford Street and running parallel to Tottenham Court Road based on Fitzroy Street, Charlotte Street and Rathbone Place. It had acquired a cosmopolitan flavour from the many foreigners living there, mainly French, German and Italian, and was the nearest equivalent in London to the Quartier Latin. Studios were plentiful and cheap, and the narrow streets were full of pubs, restaurants and Continental food shops. Since the development of the area in the eighteenth century, it had always been closely associated with artists. John Constable was one of its most famous early inhabitants, and Sickert, Duncan Grant, Vanessa Bell, Matthew Smith and Rex Whistler all lived and worked in Fitzroy Street in the thirties. Fitzrovia acquired a more literary character as it became the favourite meeting-place for a new generation of poets, writers and editors such as Dylan Thomas, Stephen Spender, Louis MacNeice, William Empson, Geoffrey Grigson, Arthur Calder-Marshall and Keidrych Rhys. A whole society of artists and writers congregated there; not so much the fashionable and successful but the young and struggling, the rising stars as well as the hangers-on, the drop-outs and alcoholics, who either lived there or went there every night.

Almost everyone was poor in Fitzrovia and lived from hand to mouth. Borrowing money was an accepted fact of everyday existence and if you could afford to lend someone a few shillings you did – without seriously expecting to get it back. This was one of the unwritten rules of behaviour in Fitzrovia that the newcomer had to learn before he was accepted. You were unpopular if you did not pay your share of the drinks, came only at weekends, as a tourist or patronizingly. You never asked people what they did. If you published a book it was expected that you would bring it in and show your friends to help promote it. A certain amount of talk about art went on, but more at the level of personalities than ideas. One quickly learnt who was respected among artists and who was not. As the poet John Heath-Stubbs said:

> It was a whole community. For many people it was in a real sense their home . . . the only place where they really related to other people. It was a very definite society with its own curious codes, its own hierarchy. Nina stood high in that hierarchy in terms of a kind of respect. She was always there every night and one always treated her with politeness, bought her a drink, listened to her stories.[4]

Until the outbreak of war the Fitzroy Tavern remained the central focus of Fitzrovia. Augustus John compared it to Clapham Junction, saying that sooner or

later everyone had to pass through it. Nina was the acknowledged Queen of the
Fitzroy and in 1936 Lett Haines did a drawing of her and the well-known lesbian
Jane Agate seated at the bar, entitled *Les Fitzreines*. As one regular, the writer
Constantine FitzGibbon, commented: 'To enter Kleinfeld's and not buy Nina a
drink – if one had the price of two – was in those days and in that world a solecism
that amounted to a social stigma.'[5] As before in Montparnasse, Nina acted as the
unofficial hostess and guide to the neighbourhood, and was extraordinarily
generous in introducing her friends to one another and to people she thought
could help or be of use to them. She herself was witty and direct in her approach
to those who caught her attention. Her first words to the young painter and
window dresser Denis Wirth-Miller, who moved to Fitzroy Street in 1938,
were, 'My deah, what's your name? You look evil!' The epithet stuck, and she

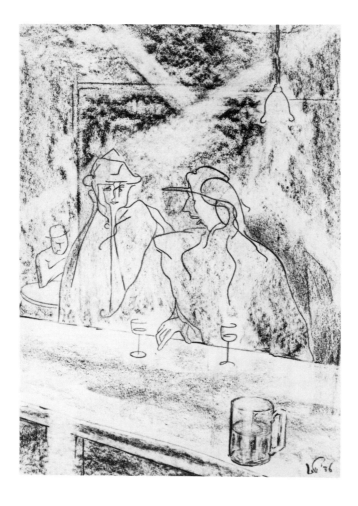

Les Fitzreines, 1936,
by Lett Haines
Jane Agate and Nina
in the Fitzroy Tavern

would always after introduce him to others with 'Here's Denis Wirth-Miller – he's evil my deah, evil!';[6] and she was immensely disappointed when the drawing she later did of him did not make him look evil enough.

When Nina was introduced to Ruthven Todd by Dylan Thomas she exclaimed, 'You know me, m'dear . . I'm in the V & A with me left tit knocked off!'[7] – referring of course to the famous torso of herself by Gaudier-Brzeska of which she was justly proud. Nina knew she was a central figure in the Bohemian world, something of a tourist attraction, and she was not above charging an entrance fee. On meeting someone she would often not wait to be asked but declare, 'I'll have a double gin.' In return she would entertain them with a constant stream of amusing anecdotes about the artistic and literary great as well as the many rich, famous and titled people she had known. Nina was an indefatigable name-dropper, 'a bohemian snob who collected names. Not that it mattered to her whether the significance of your name lay in a title, a boxing championship, a criminal record or skill in training fleas, an abnormal beer capacity or high achievement in art.'[8]

Nina threw herself wholeheartedly into the daily celebration of life that went on in Fitzrovia. Every small event – the arrival of somebody from abroad or out of town, the publication of a book or the selling of a picture – all were wonderful excuses for another drink. She blithely carried on the careless life of the twenties. The political polarization of the thirties and the fervent idealism of many of the younger poets and painters around her meant very little to Nina. Important political events such as the Italian invasion of Abyssinia in 1935 were lightly brushed aside to become merely the subject of an irreverent limerick. She wrote to her friend Robert Pocock, a journalist whom she had first met when he was a policeman at Tottenham Court Road:

> Latest from the front – having a grand time shall be drunk till Friday. Italian prisoners lament – cheerio old cock – and

> There was a young girl of Adowa
> Whose quim was the shape of a flower
> She was so very teeny
> It intrigued Mussolini
> Who put off the War for an hour.

> Much love from the Baroness Von Bergen.[9]

Nina had a seemingly inexhaustible supply of often bawdy jokes, limericks, songs and verses such as

Nina in the Fitzroy, 1939,
by Adrian Ryan

I sometimes wish when I am tight
That I were an hermaphrodite
And then, united to a black
Deep-bosomed nymphomaniac
We'd be wafted up to heaven
In position forty-seven.[10]

Nina delighted in old music-hall songs and sang them with great gusto and enjoyment. She loved the one about Madame Tussaud's:

Now every Saturday afternoon we tries to drown our sorrows,
We always goes to the waxworks shows to see the chamber of horrors.
There's a beautiful picture of mother there what gives me pleasure rather –
With the same old smile on her dear old dial as the night she strangled
father![11]

On a good night, with the right company and a suitable amount of alcohol, Nina was very amusing. She was always on show, always playing to the crowd, and at her best she gave command performances. With a little too much to drink she could be disconcerting – as when she would boast that Modigliani said she had the best tits in Europe and pull up her old jersey to show them off.

Apart from the Fitzroy there was a nucleus of some half a dozen other pubs that formed the hard core of any Fitzrovian pub-crawl. Going up Rathbone Place from Oxford Street a sombre Victorian pub called the Black Horse was the first one on the right, though usually the last to be visited as the patron did not encourage 'arty types'. Further up, taking a right turn down Stephen Mews, was the Bricklayer's Arms in Gresse Street. A quiet pub with a large four-ale bar and a small saloon with a billiard table, it had been christened the Burglar's Rest by Stulik because a gang of burglars had once broken in and slept the night there, leaving a pile of empties as evidence of their occupancy. Nina always liked to joke that she was going to meet a burglar friend there for a drink and would say, 'Well deah, must go off to the Burglar's Rest.'[12]

Serious drinking took place in the Wheatsheaf, the last pub on the right of Rathbone Place, next to a Continental newsagent on the corner of Percy Street, where Nina was living at number 33. As the Fitzroy became increasingly invaded by sightseers anxious to get a glimpse of Bohemia, the Wheatsheaf gradually took over as the main meeting-place. Nina, however, always remained faithful to the Fitzroy, which had the added attraction to her of being something of a London headquarters for sailors on leave. The Wheatsheaf, constructed in mock-Tudor style, was far more salubrious than the Fitzroy. Smaller and quieter, with a long narrow bar, green upholstered tables and chairs, and a red linoleum covered floor, it was cheerful and warm in winter. As it was a Younger's Scotch House the wood-panelled walls were appropriately decorated with squares of various tartans, and there were small booths for intimate conversations. Mrs Stewart, a small elderly woman dressed in black silk, was the doyenne of the Wheatsheaf. Like Nina she had a fund of stories about the artists and writers she had known in Montparnasse such as Pascin, Hemingway and Joyce, but she never divulged what she herself had been doing there. She arrived every day promptly at six when she would order a bottle of Guinness and sit down at a table to do the crossword in two evening papers, timing herself with an alarm clock. Special tact was needed to offer her a drink and the worst possible offence was to try to help with her crosswords. Nina did several drawings and portraits of Mrs Stewart in the forties, and for many years after her death one of them hung above the spot where she used to sit.

Opposite the Wheatsheaf, at the end of Rathbone Place, was the Marquis of Granby, which was rougher and dirtier than the Fitzroy. It was much favoured by bookies and small-time crooks as well as Guardsmen in search of homosexuals to taunt and beat up. Frequent fights broke out there and on one occasion a man was viciously killed in broad daylight, watched by a large crowd of onlookers. Branching off diagonally past the Marquis of Granby on the left was a roofed-in passage containing a pub appropriately called the Beer House as it had no spirit

A Finch's The One Tun
B L'Étoile
C Schmidt's
D The Duke of York
E Bertorelli's
F Plumbing Supplies
G The Fitzroy Tavern
H Pogiolli's
I The Marquis of Granby
J Le Tour Eiffel
K Mrs Buhler's First Café
L The Wheatsheaf
M The Bricklayer's Arms
N Winsor & Newton
O The Black Horse
P W. R. Loftus

Q "The Two-thirty House"
R The Highlander
S The Pillars of Hercules
T The Shanghai
U Bakery
V All Night Café
W The Gargoyle Club
X The Mandrake Club
Y Patisserie Valerie
Z The Swiss
AA Mrs Buhler's Second Café
BB F. Denny, outfitters for
    Chefs and Waiters
CC The York Minster
DD St. Anne's
EE Zwemmer's Bookshop
FF The Colony Club

Map of Fitzrovia and part of Soho drawn by Ruthven Todd

licence and only sold beer. Beyond this passage, continuing up Rathbone Street, was the Duke of York, whose patron hung a large placard on the bar proclaiming himself Major 'Alf' Klein, Prince of Good Fellows.

The Duke of York came into its own on Sundays as customers were served with a bowl of soup and a chunk of cheese. Old Fitzrovian hands would then proceed to the Marquis of Granby, which offered cold spaghetti and various sauces left over from Poggioli's Italian restaurant in Charlotte Street. The special Sunday ritual was rounded off with a visit to the Fitzroy Tavern. Although Kleinfeld had retired in 1934, leaving his daughter Annie and her husband Charles Allchild to run the pub, he made regular appearances behind the bar on Sundays when he presented his favourites with small cigars. At two o'clock, when the pubs north of Oxford Street closed, there was a general scurry to a small pub in Soho Street known as The Half-past Two House, which because of the vagaries of the licensing laws was allowed an extra half-hour of grace on Sundays.

The boundary between the boroughs of Holborn and Marylebone ran along the middle of Charlotte Street. The Fitzroy and the Wheatsheaf were in Holborn and stayed open until ten-thirty, while the Marquis of Granby and the Duke of York came under Marylebone and closed half an hour later, causing a nightly stampede across the street and into Soho proper, just south of Oxford Street. There the first pub to be visited was the Highlander in Dean Street, which became very popular during the war with documentary film makers such as Paul Rotha and Donald Taylor. The next port of call was the Swiss, around the corner in Old Compton Street, 'a vast cavernous place, patinaed with the rich deposits of pea-soupers'.[13] From there the Fitzrovian pub-crawl would end at the York Minster, known as the French Pub after Victor Berlemont, famous for his huge curving mustachios and believed to be the first French licensee in England. Today it is run by his son Gaston and is little changed. The walls are crammed with old photographs of actresses, singers, boxers and cyclists, all dedicated to Victor. Screwed to a corner of the bar is a contraption for slowly dripping water through a lump of sugar placed on a leaf-shaped spoon over a glass of absinthe – or Pernod.

Apart from the pubs there were numerous clubs. The smartest and most fashionable was the Gargoyle in Meard Street – inevitably called Merde Street – which occupied the top three floors of a building above a printing works. The club had been founded in the late twenties by the Hon. David Tennant with Augustus John as president, and aimed to bring together artists and wealthy socialites to the material benefit of the former, although this was all too rarely achieved. Like the Eiffel Tower earlier, the Gargoyle tended to be the preserve of the better-off and more successful. The narrow entrance from the street led through a short passage to a rickety lift which complainingly deposited its load of passengers into the reception-hall hung with drawings of nudes by Matisse. This gave on to a bar and a large room intended for banquets and private parties. At Matisse's suggestion the whole club had been decorated with squares of mirror-glass, including the ceiling and the stairs which descended to the dancing and dining area, where Alexander's Band played in the evenings. The floor beneath housed the club's excellent wine-cellars and David Tennant's private apartment.

A host of other very different small social clubs of varying degrees of seediness sprang up, where one could drink in the afternoon and after closing-time at night away from the prying eyes of the over-inquisitive. To justify their name they would usually have a few pin-ball machines and a coin-operated game called Russian billiards. Other clubs had fruit machines and one-armed bandits. They were all raided continually by the police for serving drinks after hours, gambling, or some other infringement of the law. The premises were then banned as a club for a certain period of time and the owner would either be fined or serve a sentence – and then open up again somewhere else under a different name. All sorts of unexpected, apparently respectable people could be found drinking in the clubs during the afternoon as well as a good mixture of businessmen, artists and crooks. Two of Nina's favourite clubs were the Horseshoe in Wardour Street and the Byron in Greek Street. For many years in exchange for a few drinks in between pub-opening hours she was engaged in painting murals on the walls of the Jubilee, a small club upstairs and next door to the Eiffel Tower.

For more solid sustenance, or a cup of coffee, there was the café on the corner of the Scala Theatre in Charlotte Street run by Madame Buhler, whose son Robert is now a distinguished Royal Academician. The café started when the Swiss Madame Buhler took over an agency for the Librairie Hachette to provide foreign newspapers and books for the sizeable colony of waiters, porters and chefs in the area. Realizing that they had nowhere to read them, she opened the café, which soon became immensely popular with all the local work people, artists, students and teachers from the nearby Slade including William Coldstream, Edward Le Bas, Cedric Morris, Lett Haines, Rodrigo Moynihan, Geoffrey Tibble, Freddie Gore and Adrian Ryan. Madame Buhler did not like drunks and would refuse to serve Dylan Thomas, but she adored Nina because she was very funny and could hold her drink, and enjoyed her very English way of speaking French with a slightly staccato, military accent. Her coffee finished, Nina would briskly tuck a newspaper under her arm and announce, 'Must go back and dash off a drawing, what?'[14] – and continue on her way to the inevitable pub. The café was destroyed by bombs in 1942 but, undaunted, Madame Buhler opened up again in more spacious premises at 4 Old Compton Street. Other eating places in Charlotte Street for those who could afford them were L'Étoile,

Schmidt's, Pogiolli's and Bertorelli's, the last being particularly popular with local artists as a plate of spaghetti with grated cheese and butter could be had very cheaply.

By the mid-thirties the Eiffel Tower had fallen dramatically from favour. Over the years customers had taken advantage of the credit Stulik so good-naturedly offered, with the result that he was owed thousands of pounds. Standards inevitably declined and the socialites ceased to flock there. Things got so bad that when the writer and critic John Davenport ordered an omelette he was asked to pay in advance so that a waiter could be sent out to buy some eggs. Augustus John wrote of Stulik that 'an alarming corpulence, a growing neglect of his person and a progressive deterioration of his mental faculties, began to efface the air of efficiency and charm which had made him for so long the most popular of restaurateurs.'[15] To complete the dismal tale another *habitué*, Peter Quennell, described

> a sad evening at the almost deserted restaurant some time in 1938. Lights were dimmed; the fountain of fresh green foliage that had once sprung beside the staircase had now shrunk into a dusty tangle; and two old waiters stood miserably flicking their napkins and gazing towards a door that never opened. Stulik himself, his pointed moustaches adroop, his fat round face a yellowish grey, paced to and fro, muttering half-audibly about his debtors and creditors, and the wrongs and woes of human life, with his hands behind his back, while his dog Chocolate (who also produced the impression of harbouring dark and anxious thoughts) walked slowly in the opposite direction.[16]

Bankrupt, Stulik sold the restaurant in 1938. His supporters raised a fund to set him up in a coffee or snack bar but by that time he was very ill and died before the plan could be carried out.

The Brasserie at the Café Royal remained a favourite place for ending an evening. One could eat upstairs on the balcony surrounding the large red room or downstairs at one of the tables laid for dinner, but the Fitzrovians usually headed for that half of the room where the marble-topped tables were left bare and as long as you had a sandwich you could order as many drinks as you liked, or just a coffee. Among the regular habitués in the thirties were Nina's friends Evan Morgan, Tommy Earp, Wadsworth, Bomberg, Matthew Smith, Paul Nash, Edwarde Wolfe, Epstein, Constant Lambert, Cyril Connolly and Anna Wickham.

Apart from Betty May – the famous Tiger Woman – who would occasionally go down on all fours in a pub and lap her drink from a saucer as a party trick to amuse visitors, Nina's only serious rival for drink and attention was Sylvia

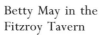
Betty May in the
Fitzroy Tavern

Gough. Over the years they had reached a mutual understanding that they
operated in separate spheres and would not poach on each other's territory. Thin
and frail, with the features and figure of a model, Sylvia still retained traces of her
former beauty and elegance. Like Nina she belonged essentially to the twenties.
She was the daughter of George Cawston, the millionaire diamond king, and had
once been the toast of London Society and a model for Augustus John, Sargent
and Orpen. Twice married – to General Gough's son, Captain Wilfred Gough,
and the American sculptor Wheeler Williams – she had been a film and stage
actress, playing in the Ziegfeld Follies in New York. Augustus John and a
Rothschild had been cited as co-respondents in one of her divorces and her sons,
whom she never saw, went to Eton. Fate had been cruel to Sylvia and by the
thirties she was a near-destitute Fitzrovian drunk, passively sitting out the hours
on a bar-stool or at Madame Buhler's. She was a permanent fixture at the Fitzroy
Tavern, and her small regular allowance rapidly disappeared in immediate
celebration of its arrival. Although she did not hold her drink as well as Nina and
could become a nuisance, she always remained a lady and would spend her last
sixpence on a bath. With few inner or outer resources, she was essentially

vulnerable. All her life she had been over-dependent on men. She had a great weakness for young boys and they took everything she had.

In 1936 the Fitzroy Tavern was at the centre of a notorious murder case involving Sylvia Gough and Betty May. Douglas Burton, a thirty-year-old book reviewer, was passionately in love with Betty May whom he had met at the Fitzroy Tavern. Obviously unbalanced and made self-conscious by a facial disfigurement, he was obsessed by what he called Betty's 'pantherine' movements and eyes, and tormented by her refusal to marry him. Sylvia Gough was then forty-two and had been living for about a year with the twenty-one-year-old Douglas Michael Bose, a writer fascinated by black magic and the occult. Although he was jealous and ill-treated her, Sylvia claimed that Bose's 'hypnotic powers' made her stay with him. But on the night that Burton met Sylvia at the Fitzroy Tavern, Bose had beaten her up and she had a black eye. She told Burton that she could bear no more and he took her home and looked after her for a few days. To take her mind off things they went to dinner at the studio of a mutual artist friend, where by chance Bose appeared during the course of the evening. Without thinking Burton sprang at him with the first object to hand, a sculptor's hammer, and killed him. At the trial the judge found Burton guilty but insane and summed up the case as 'singularly squalid and unpleasant'.[17] The public enjoyed a further glimpse of the lurid details of Bohemian life, and Betty May naturally capitalized on the occasion by selling the characteristically frank and outspoken story of her association with Burton to the popular press.

There were many colourful characters in Fitzrovia with varying degrees of aristocratic pretensions. Perhaps the most conspicuous was the poet Count Geoffrey di Montalk. The son of a New Zealand milkman, he claimed to be the rightful King of Poland and peddled copies of the *Right Review*, written and printed by himself, for a shilling each. He affected the dress of a medieval knight and was a striking sight with his shoulder-length brown hair and peakless velvet cap, striding along in sandalled feet clad in a flowing red cloak over a tunic, with a golden medallion at his breast and a sword sheathed in a green scabbard at his side. Another exiled monarch and poet was John Gawsworth, otherwise known as the King of Redonda, a tiny Caribbean island which he had inherited from the novelist M. P. Shiel, whose literary executor he was. He would don robes and hold ceremonies where he bestowed the various secular and ecclesiastical titles of what he was pleased to call the intellectual aristocracy of his realm on friends such as Victor Gollancz, Henry Miller, Dylan Thomas, John Waller and John Heath-Stubbs. When later the *Daily Mail* falsely reported that Nina had been present at one of these title-giving ceremonies, she gleefully seized the opportunity to threaten them with libel action and was highly pleased with the £150 she received in compensation. Then there was the Zulu Prince Monolulu, an improbable but impressive racing tout known as 'I've-Gotta-Horse', who was over six feet high and dressed as a Zulu chieftain complete with feathered head-dress.

Although not a true Fitzrovian, one of the most poignant figures who would appear from time to time wearing a black coal-scuttle lace hat and fringed leather gloves was the fabulous and extraordinary Marchesa Louisa Casati, whose fantastically opulent palaces in Rome, Paris and Venice had been the settings for lavish and spectacular entertainments. By the thirties she had run through her massive fortune and was living humbly in London supported by faithful friends such as Augustus John, Napier Alington, Evan Morgan and the Duke of Westminster. But she still retained a few treasures from her legendary past and when the young writer and ballet critic Richard Buckle took her and Nina out to lunch one day, she rewarded him with a photograph of Ida Rubenstein as St Sebastian in a frame designed by Count Robert de Montesquiou. Even further down the scale of the aristocratic fallen was the Countess Eileen Duveen, a cured drug addict who was said to live entirely on benzedrine and cream puffs. She scraped together a living rag-picking among the leavings of Mayfair and doing odd stints of washing up at Claridges. The Cockney Iron Foot Jack, so called on account of his six-inch iron foot, had pretensions of another sort. Like Crowley he claimed great occult powers and started a new religion in Charlotte Street whose followers were known as the Children of the Sun. He was always surrounded by a crowd of acolytes, young girls and wealthy old Kensington ladies who paid dearly for the privilege of praying naked.

A constant visitor to all the pubs and clubs in the area, Nina knew everybody's movements and the very latest gossip, 'over long years remaining head of Soho's bush telegraph service'.[18] There was no more familiar sight in Fitzrovia than Nina walking erect and purposefully on her thin legs with her feet turned out at a quarter-to-three angle, her hands clenched and arms held stiffly at her sides, cheerily greeting her friends with a brisk 'Hello ducks!' Nina's highly individual way of walking was peculiarly hers. According to Mark Holloway:

She walked directly forwards . . . . at a steady unvarying pace, faster than slow, slower than fast, in ordinary low-heeled shoes, and there was this slight but strongly defined rhythmic movement involving the whole body swung about the hips . . . The pace was the pace of a marcher and the movement could have been called some kind of modification of a sailor's roll, but was more controlled and elegant . . . What made it a supreme joy to watch . . . was the fact that the intriguing clock-like precision of this very human and unmechanised rhythm was accompanied, balanced, driven perhaps, by a pendulum. The pendulum was her right arm, its hand grasping a rolled-up newspaper and swinging out and back, out and back, out and back in a short arc or curve, a half-circular movement restricted to an area about a foot away from her hip, and twisting the baton of paper back and forth, back and forth, with a turn of the wrist at each swing . . . Her head was up, looking straight ahead . . . it was impossible to watch that walk without thinking of her as filled with confidence and optimism.[19]

Nina never betrayed her real feelings about the kind of life she led. However frustrated she may have been by the little work she was producing, the lack of recognition or encouragement of her talent, she was not letting on. To have appeared vulnerable would have seemed an intolerable weakness to her. She always put on a brave face; a swaggering braggadocio was her style. Nevertheless, by the mid-thirties Nina was desperately hard up and knew what hunger was. Princess Violette Murat, who was always very generous to her, died in 1936 and Nina had little visible means of support. Joan Osiakovski, who ran the Bloomsbury Gallery in the thirties, recalled a very uncharacteristic occasion when Nina came in the gallery while she was having a meal on a tray and Joan invited her to share her lunch. Nina, who must have been in unusually low spirits, was so touched that she burst into tears and confessed that, 'Nobody ever offers me anything to eat. They offer me drinks but nothing to eat.'[20]

In an attempt to raise money Nina would sometimes hawk around a portfolio of tattered drawings, the price always in guineas. When all else failed she went round the pub rattling the tin tobacco-box she kept her money in and asking for contributions towards her next drink. One of Nina's most audacious solutions to the perennial problem of money was to compose a postcard which she got Ruthven Todd to run off on a hand press and then sent to her family and friends. The postcard read: 'WHAT DO YOU DO WITH YOUR OLD CLOTHES? Do you give them to the SALVATION ARMY or the poor? If so, DO NOT, REMEMBER NINA.'[21] Although she received disapproving letters from certain members of her family, her ingenuity was well rewarded on this occasion.

Nina had a distant family connection with Viva King, whose husband Willie was the Keeper of Ceramics at the British Museum. When in 1937 Viva heard that Nina was living in extreme poverty, she started a fund to help her, writing to all Nina's friends asking them to donate half-a-crown a week. Initially there was an enthusiastic response but after a few years the contributors inevitably dropped off, Osbert Sitwell being one of the first to plead war expenses as his excuse. Nonetheless, Viva King continued to pay Nina's rent and made her a small additional allowance.

Nina's outburst to Joan Osiakovski about no one ever offering her anything to eat was more an expression of her mood at that moment than the truth. She always had devoted friends who cared about her welfare. Augustus John appeared from time to time with kind words and the occasional loan or purchase of a picture. He remained a hero-figure to Nina and she would exclaim excitedly, 'I've just seen Augustus!' He sometimes invited her to L'Etoile and Denis Wirth-Miller often used to take her to the Wheatsheaf and make sure that she had a hot meal. On his visits to London Michael Shawe-Taylor entertained Nina royally, regularly taking her and Denis Wirth-Miller to lavish Sunday lunches at L'Escargot in Greek Street, where they usually had a private room upstairs. Lunch frequently went on until four in the afternoon when they would retire to Michael Shawe-Taylor's room at the Hyde Park Hotel. While her two companions drank from decanters of whisky and brandy, Nina would luxuriate in a hot bath, appearing some time later pink and sparkling, without her clothes, to join them. Denis Wirth-Miller sometimes did drawings of her and she wanted to draw him, but he thought it wiser to keep his clothes on.

Nina sometimes went off with Michael Shawe-Taylor on short trips to Brussels and Amsterdam. It was then possible to travel abroad on a weekend ticket without a passport, provided that one was back by Tuesday evening at the latest. After a good lunch one Friday in 1938, Nina and Michael Shawe-Taylor decided to spend the weekend in Paris. There was no time to go home for a change of clothes and they set out at once. Not long after they arrived, Michael Shawe-Taylor went off with a friend and Nina wandered down to Montparnasse to visit some of her old haunts. As she was rounding a corner of the deserted Rue du Vieux Colombier a short, tough little Apache grabbed her round the waist and carried her under one arm up to a room at the top of six flights of stairs. Nina found him quite attractive and commented drily that she could quite well have walked. But when she woke up the next morning she discovered that her handbag had disappeared with her return ticket and money, leaving her with no means of identification. The King and Queen were about to arrive in Paris on a state visit and the strictest security was in force, so that any foreigner without documents was the object of grave official suspicion. Nina went to the British Consul and was told that she would have to remain in Paris until her birth certificate arrived from England. This was a lengthy procedure as it had to come from Tenby and Nina was stranded in Paris for thirteen weeks.

Michael Shawe-Taylor left her some money when he went back to England and he and various other friends sent more from time to time, but her situation was very precarious. She had just the clothes she stood up in and lived from day to day, in debt at her hotel and not knowing for sure where her next meal was coming from nor how long she would have to stay in Paris. Peter Quennell came across her sitting at a café terrace with a large pile of saucers in front of her, waiting for someone she knew to pass to pay them off. But still in high spirits,

Nina gaily recounted her nocturnal adventure with the Apache — '"a perfect fiend m'dear!" And . . . raised her thin jersey to reveal her naked ribs and a large expanse of welts and bruises.'[22] Dick and Simonette Strachey were if anything more shocked when she asked them to give her a mere franc.

Before long Nina found many old friends such as Evan Morgan, Ferdinand Tuohy, Wassilieff, Poulenc, Bill Bird, Brancusi, and Abdul, who did what they could to help her, gave her clothes and fed her. She began seriously to enjoy life in Paris again, particularly the long bar-crawls with Bob McAlmon. Nina took Peggy Guggenheim and a party of friends to Wassilieff's studio to see her very amusing Surrealist hats and animals. Peggy Guggenheim liked them so much that she bought 800 francs' worth there and then and offered her an exhibition at her gallery in London. Wassilieff gave Nina 50 francs in gratitude and painted a life-size nude portrait of her holding a bleeding heart in one hand with a depressed-looking cupid on the floor beside her as the *pièce de résistance* for her show.

The Café des Deux Magots and the Flore in the Boulevard Saint Germain had replaced the Dôme and the Rotonde as the main meeting-places for artists and writers. Nina realized just how much things had changed on 14 July when there was no orchestra outside the Rotonde and the whole quarter was dead. Instead there was dancing at the Bar Martinique in the Boulevard Saint Germain. As Nina met more and more old friends she felt increasingly less inclined to return to London and would have liked to have taken a studio in Paris and worked at the academies again. But when her birth certificate arrived she had no excuse to stay and had to tell the British Consul the date she intended to leave.

A tired and dishevelled Nina arrived back in London, welcoming the chance of a rest after the hectic weeks in Paris, which, she admitted, was beginning to get her down. Nevertheless by eleven o'clock the next morning she was back on her familiar bar-stool at the Fitzroy Tavern with new adventures and anecdotes to recount. But her listeners were increasingly preoccupied with more serious matters.

As the thirties drew to a close, politics loudly and intrusively demanded the centre stage. Moderation had come to an end with the Spanish Civil War, and Left stood sharply divided from Right. The finest and bravest had put their beliefs to the test on the fighting fields of Spain. Many more preferred to continue the ideological struggle from the vantage-point of a Fitzrovian bar-stool. Politics and the latest offerings of the Left Book Club were discussed late into the night. But for all the insistent urgency of world events, there was a strange unreality about such talk. Ruthven Todd commented: 'Even the most fervent of my political friends were, comparatively, amateurs at the game. There was a curious unwillingness to involve the individual, whom one might like personally, with his party, which one might hate with every atom of one's being.'[23] While the poets, painters and intellectuals talked, the countdown in Europe had inexorably begun: Abyssinia, Spain, Munich . . . Suddenly time ran out and not even Nina could avoid politics.

Bob Pocock, who later became a radio scriptwriter and producer for the BBC Features Department, gave Nina, thinly disguised as Cynthia, the closing words in his play about Charlotte Street in the thirties, *It's Long Past the Time*. At the end, war is announced and we hear Chamberlain's speech and an air-raid siren. With the noise of a busy pub in the background, Cynthia declares:

My dear, but did you hear what that man said. What a monster that one is, my dear. And then that air-raid siren. I was just tottering along to the café for some breakfast and off it went. Some silly little bitch ran into me full tilt. 'Ow! we're all going to be killed,' she screamed, 'Nonsense,' I told her. 'You pull yourself together, my girl.' And then there were various gentlemen going very odd colours in the face rushing about trying to hide themselves. I must say I felt rather pec-u-li-ar myself, but I didn't run. Not the thing a lidy should do, don't you agree, my dear? Yes thank you, I'd love a gin, darling.[24]

15

Candlelight

IF the cast changed, the scene remained essentially the same. In many ways the war intensified the unique character of Fitzrovia. The call-up necessarily scattered a lot of the younger faces, but there was still a hard core of Fitzrovian old-timers above military age as well as those variously unfit for active service. Writers and intellectuals found London-based jobs with the Ministry of Information, the BBC, the Army Education Corps and Intelligence. The shadier characters – crooks, black marketeers and prostitutes – proliferated. In the highly charged, noisy and smoke-filled atmosphere of the pubs, there was a grim determination to carry on as usual in defiance of the bombs, the black-out, rationing and countless restrictions. The beer might run out in the course of the evening but word would swiftly pass along the grapevine of where more was to be had – and the merry-go-round continued. Danger and the constant threat of death swept aside peace-time inhibitions and reserve, and life acquired a new urgency.

Many talented young painters such as John Craxton, Lucian Freud, John Minton and the two Roberts Coloquhoun and MacBryde made their first appearance on the Fitzrovian scene during the war. More than the slightly older generation of artists, they were interested in Nina, willingly bought her drinks when they had the money, and listened to her stories. John Craxton thought that she was a kind of mascot for them, a link with the artistic world of Paris from which they were completely cut off by the war. Nina got on well with Dylan Thomas, who was working as a documentary script-writer for Strand Films. He included her in his satirical novel *The Death of the King's Canary*, which he wrote with John Davenport in the summer of 1940. The action takes place at a large country-house party attended by all the leading poets and artists of the day to celebrate their host's appointment as Poet Laureate. Nina was affectionately caricatured as 'Yvonne Bacon, pillar of Charlotte Street, monument of the old

Dôme, artist, collector of celebrities, professional introducer'.[1] Dylan was often to be found drinking at the Wheatsheaf with his fellow script-writers the historical novelist Philip Lindsay and Julian Maclaren-Ross, conspicuous with his yellow waistcoat and silver-topped cane, as well as the scenic artist Gilbert Wood. Tambimuttu made regular appearances accompanied by a bevy of aspiring poetesses and his friend the artist Gerald Wilde. Even those Fitzrovians who had been called up did not lose touch altogether and servicemen on leave, such as the young poet and naval officer Alan Ross, returned there like homing pigeons.

The extent to which life continued its old course in Fitzrovia was graphically evoked by Ruthven Todd, who recalled leaving the Highlander during an air raid one night in 1942:

> In the light of a parachute-flare dropped by a German plane, I saw a most peculiarly flaccid tripod approaching me from the North. The legs wobbled and wove and crumpled and it was clear that it was only possible for the three persons to move as a tripod linked by arms over one another's shoulders. The tripod seemed unaware of the air-raid and of the nasty sharp splinters of ack-ack shrapnel that were pitter-pattering down in the streets. I remained in the shadow of the Highlander waiting for a lull in the gunfire and stayed there as the tripod wobbled past. The three legs were Augustus John, Nina Hamnett and Norman Douglas, all three, to use an expressive Mallorcan phrase, as drunk as sponges, on their way to the Gargoyle for an unneeded drink.[2]

New clubs sprang up all the time. One of the most popular was the Mandrake, which was opened in a basement in Meard Street by the Russian Boris Watson, a keen chess player. The club's chess room provided its *raison d'être* in the eyes of the licensing authorities, and quite good chess players did in fact frequent the club, including the cartoonist Vicky; but inevitably it was not long before the drunks took over. Nina went there often and John Heath-Stubbs remembered her singing the cockney version of a well-known ballad about a girl who had been seduced:

> A maid again I'll never be,
> Till apples grow on the orange tree.
> He told me that he loved me so,
> So he upped me skirts and he had a go.
> A maid again I'll never be,
> Till apples grow on the orange tree . . .[3]

War transformed London into a truly cosmopolitan city. The West End was thronged with foreign uniforms: French, Polish, Dutch, Belgian and a host of other nationalities. America's entrance into the war in December 1941 swelled the crowds even further and boosted the black-market economy. But transient foreigners played little part in Fitzrovia. Tucked away behind Oxford Street, the pubs and clubs were strictly for *cognoscenti*, not places to be stumbled upon accidentally by the average GI, more intent upon bargaining with the prostitutes who lined the streets of Piccadilly. However, one GI, the aspiring writer Julius Horwitz, knew what he was looking for, and in the time-honoured way of all strangers asked a policeman if there was anywhere in London like Greenwich Village in New York. He was directed to the Fitzroy Tavern.

Julius was stationed at the US Eighth Air Force base in Suffolk between the summer of 1943 and 1945. Going into London on leave he would head straight for Fitzrovia, where he met Nina one day in the Highlander. She liked him immediately and took him to the Wheatsheaf, introducing him to everyone as 'Julius Horwitz, my friend the American writer'. Her faith in him encouraged Julius actually to become a writer and in 1964 he published a novel about his experiences in wartime London, *Can I Get There by Candlelight*, in which the central character Nora is closely modelled on Nina. The novel is based largely on a series of lengthy letters recording Julius's experiences, impressions and emotions written to his friend Clement Greenberg, later to become the influential art critic and spokesman for a whole generation of American Abstract Expressionist painters. They give a frank, first-hand account of Fitzrovia in wartime with an outsider's freshness of vision and alertness to details passed over by those more familiar with the scene.

The letters describing Julius's first encounters with Fitzrovia are infused with a breathless enthusiasm. Even its more sordid aspects were imbued with an aura of romantic glamour. He was aware from his first meeting with Nina that she was someone special and eagerly listened to her stories about the famous artists she had known: 'God what warm excitement sitting in Nina's garret and listening to her rushingly talk about her past life.'[4] He knew that he would write about her one day and saw her as the archetypal Queen of Bohemia. Dressed in worn, usually second-hand clothes, with holes in her stockings, she certainly did not look like the queen of anything and less charitable people referred to her as 'Dirty Nina'. But she could still produce striking remnants of her legendary past and would appear from time to time in a dramatic black cape designed by Worth, no doubt given to her by friends in Paris.

Friendship with Nina gave Julius an anchor in an alien world, a destination point when he arrived in London on his thirty-six-hour passes. As the train drew closer to London his excitement and anticipation mounted, made even more

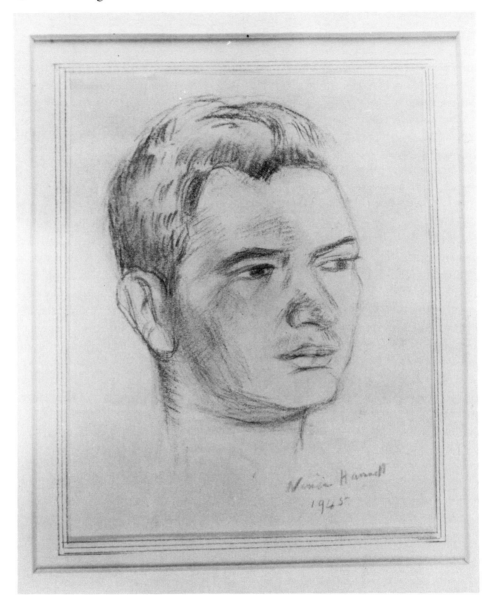

Julius Horwitz, 1945

acute by the element of uncertainty and danger, the question-mark over survival itself:

> Coming into London, the black-out, bombs were falling, the ack-ack guns were out everywhere, those balloons were up with the wires . . . All you could think of was the immediate: how quick can I get to the Fitzroy, get a drink into me, a woman, who was Nina going to introduce me to, who am I going to meet. London became a great theatre.[5]

Nina took Julius to all the pubs in the area, where as her friend he was immediately accepted. He described a scene in the Wheatsheaf:

> Nina saw me through the smoke and talk and shouted, 'Julius – Julius Horwitz come over here to the peasants' . . . Nina was tight, more tight than I'd ever seen her and she grabbed hold of my hand and asked 'Julius, how have you been?' I bought her a rum and there was another woman sitting at the bar and her name was Violet Grant. She lived with Nina in Paris . . . Nina and I talked and Violet told stories . . . Nina had a drunk on and she wanted to go pubbing, so we dashed over to the Bricklayers where it was quiet and then back again to the Wheatsheaf.[6]

Nina would always make sure that Julius was included if anyone offered her a drink: 'Instead of eating we went drinking at the Highlander . . . A kind gent walked in with a bottle of scotch and he poured some out for my friend Nina Hamnett. Nina winked at me and I was invited over for a glass full.'[7]

Julius met many of the crowd of artists and writers around the pubs with Nina:

> They're always drunk or rapidly approaching. They see the comedy; realize their own helplessness and hate their selfish compromise with morals and society. Insanity or drunkenness. Their talk is seldom the intellectual sauerkraut of polite gatherings. Always dirty stories or funny stories; songs and love affairs. Flighty. Their own minds are too damm heavy with unsolved problems to bring them into their fun.[8]

Julius was soon familiar with Fitzrovia's evasions of the licensing laws and afternoons would disappear in the clubs. Nina took him to the Horseshoe:

> I spent the afternoon in a club on Wardour, drinking light ale, laughing and talking, with an English writer, his West Indian wife, and Nina. The radio played sentimental war tunes, a couple of weird characters drifted in, draped

themselves around the bar, and a few active women sat and sipped and waited for generous propositions[9] . . . Nina told stories in four letter words and we all laughed.[10]

Comments scattered throughout the letters draw attention to Nina's colourful language: 'I got tight with a number of Soho parasites. Nina shouting her stories; lovely stories filled with words like shit . . . fuck etc. Good anglo-saxon talk.'[11]

Nina evidently could get spectacularly drunk and Julius's descriptions of her are not without their humour:

> While walking down Regent Street to get to the Café Royal I heard a woman swearing at the people rushing by in the blackout. She hung on to the revolving door of the Café, cursing at everybody and reciting stories to herself. When I reached the door I noticed that it was Nina. But all of London knows Nina and the bobbies certainly wouldn't book her for cursing at civilisation once in a Saturday night. I didn't say anything to her because the party I was taking to dinner didn't want Nina to upset the evening for me.
>
> The Café bar upstairs was crowded with the usual Yankee queers, and of course, or so it seems, their RAF lovers, the pleasant people from the screen world, successful writers and too, successful mistresses. The Café doesn't cater to the crude prostitutes easily located on Piccadilly . . . We had a couple of gins, sodas, and then downstairs to a late supper. Magnificent service but the usual war-time London fare. The menu was printed in French, in fact, all that I saw during the weekend were French menus. Sunday afternoon I had a grand dinner on Old Compton Street. The Soho restaurants are absolutely the most amazing places in the world. From the sidewalk the restaurants have the appearance of an old junk shop, perhaps a rundown café, but once inside, all plush and velvet, silver, spacious rooms. It took us over an hour to eat. The meals are all priced at five shillings, but then cover, special attention, extras etc. and the check usually totals to a pound.[12]

Nina was living on the top floor of 31 Howland Street in two rooms piled with books, papers and drawings. There was no bathroom, only a little wash-basin wedged in a corner on the staircase and frequently misused by her gentlemen friends as the only lavatory was far below on the ground floor. Thanks to Nina, Julius was able to escape the anonymity of GI life. When he had nowhere to sleep for the night or if he needed somewhere to go, Nina always let him use her spare room and she never stood on ceremony. Once, thinking Nina was out, Julius took a girlfriend to her flat and unexpectedly found her there, 'drunk and tired . . . buried under blankets in her outer room'. They lamely said that they had come to share a tin of pineapple with her, to which Nina replied with characteristic brusqueness, 'Pineapple hell, you two go into the other room and go to bed.'[13]

Julius's letters graphically describe just how squalid Nina's flat was:

I left the café and meandered down to Howland Street to find a bed. Earlier in the evening Nina said I could use her other bed. Perhaps she meant her own bed. Mrs McPherson [Nina's landlady] let me in. I had never really spoken to Mrs McPherson. Always she was a woman I saw when I stumbled into Nina's place drunk and tired. Always I slipped a pack of Luckies in her hand and stumbled up the five flights of stairs to Nina's other room. This time Mrs McPherson invited me to her room for a chat. Forty-five minutes, an hour, two hours, for two and a half hours she droned on and on about her life on the stage, her breakdown, the people of Charlotte Street, her roomers, past and present; their loves and mistresses; her own sedate life in the midst of every perversion known to the inhabitants of the Fitzroy Tavern. At three in the morning she freed me and I crawled up the stairs and climbed into Nina's bed with all my clothes on. She was bundled up in the other room. I heard a mouse poking his nose around her drawings. I struck a match and noticed little deposits of rat turds on the bed. The pillow crawled. I started to scratch myself. From the next room I heard the moan of a woman who finds a man too heavy, too pleasurable, or herself delighted. Nina had a man in bed. The bed squeaked. She kept up a running line of chatter. More moans. I decided to leave.[14]

Drunk, Nina might leave the pub and spend the night with some unknown man, or perhaps a woman — at that stage it hardly mattered — whom she would probably never see again. Asked why she liked sailors so much, she replied, 'Because they go away.' On another occasion she remarked, 'I woke up next to a big fat sailor. Nice and warm — we'll have to give coupons for them next winter!'[15] Nina's back room seems to have been used as a convenient doss-house by most of the genial drunks of Fitzrovia and she was always very generous to the young artists she met in the pubs. Bruce Bernard, then a young art student, stayed with her for a few days when he had nowhere to go and she made him a dried-egg omelette for breakfast out of her meagre rations.

Julius rarely found sleeping at Nina's uneventful: 'A war correspondent who's staying at her place and who is a bit queer returned during the night with two tremendous Americans. As Nina said, "I suppose that he thought one would crawl into bed with me and he'd take the other for himself."'[16] The night when 'Rattlesnakes' — a well-known Irish drunk described by Ruthven Todd as 'queer as Dick's hatband' – accepted the offer of Nina's spare room became a Fitzrovian legend. He was seen the next morning shaking with shock and indignation, muttering, 'D'ye hear? D'ye hear? The ould hen seduced me.' Questioned later in the Fitzroy, Nina raised her hands in a gesture of astonishment and exclaimed, 'M'dear, he fucks just like a rattlesnake!'[17]

Perhaps inspired by her trip to Paris just before the war, Nina had begun to work seriously again. She was drawing and, according to Julius, was also writing a book to be called *Arms, Legs and Man*. Painting was more difficult due to the cost and wartime scarcity of materials. The extent to which she valued her painting

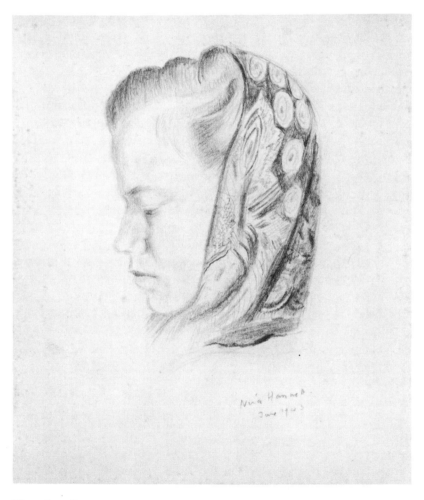

Flora Isserlis, 1943

materials and still considered herself a professional artist is evident in the tone of haughty indignation with which she once wrote rebuking Julius: 'I am far from pleased with you. Miss MacPherson had no business to let you in anyway. I found the floor all trampled over with my most expensive and almost unobtainable cadmium yellow, the egg powder all over the floor.'[18] As Nina could not afford to pay her models she would promise to give them a commission when she sold their portrait – but as often as not the payment failed to materialize.

To say that Nina was working seriously again is not to suggest that she was doing so steadily and consistently every day. She was far too wedded to pub life for that. It was much more haphazard and erratic. One of her models, Flora Isserlis, recalled that Nina might see her in the Fitzroy Tavern and say, 'Can't work today,' or again, depending on her mood, 'Would you like to come back? I feel like working.' She could be on the binge for days at a time and then suddenly take herself in hand and get down to work, discouraging people from interrupting her. Between 1943 and 1945 she exhibited portraits and figure-studies at the London Group, the New English Art Club, and the Leicester Galleries' mixed show of 'Artists of Fame and Promise'. But by this time Nina's art had undoubtedly lost most of its dash and flair, and painters such as Edward Le Bas dismissed it as no better than competent art-school standard.

1944 was particularly fruitful for her. In the summer she exhibited a watercolour of an old lady and her 1916 portrait of Horace Brodzky at the Leicester Galleries. Later in the year she showed three pictures with the London Group: an oil of Flora Isserlis bought by Augustus John for £30, another of a Burmese boy which sold for £26, and a watercolour of Mrs Stewart from the Wheatsheaf. Julius went to the London Group show at the Royal Academy and described Nina sitting on a sofa with Julian Maclaren-Ross, her

legs crossed, ragged stockings hanging limp on her hair[y] legs, watching the people circle the exhibition program in hand . . . Nina asked 'What are you going to do with yourself this afternoon? We can't drink, the Horseshoe Club is closed. Come up to my place, we'll have a cup of tea, you can stretch out on the couch.'

They left in a taxi and Julius stopped off at the Red Cross to pick up a bottle. Back at Nina's he particularly admired another unfinished portrait of Flora Isserlis and asked her to give him an easy way to buy the picture.

'We'll talk about it in the morning; now how about some of your American cigarettes, a glass of stout?'
In the evening we went on a pub crawl . . . Back to the Marquis. The

whores listening to Paul play, pretending with Yanks, raising, lowering prices, home for free, home for love, home for six pounds. Out of the Marquis. Fitzrovia. Hustlers invading the artists. Out to the Duke of York . . . Nina, Violet Grant sitting in the Wheatsheaf waiting for someone to buy them a drink. Bearded men holding papers under arms, talking the Times. Three scotch ales. No gin. I'm running out of money . . . Time, no woman. 'Julius you come home with me.' Nina body warming to a man. 'Julius you come home with me. First we'll eat.' Walk down Charlotte Street with two women totalling 110 years. Laughing, talk of the London Group. Tony's Café is across the Scala Theater . . . White dirty tables. Cigarette smoke. Pansies waiting for the end of night. An unsuccessful whore . . . Food for Nina and Miss Grant. Two cups of stewed coffee for me. More people piling in . . . I pass around cigarettes. A woman is sitting alone. I want to make a pass at her. Nina finishes eating. Violet whispers to me. 'Do you want to sleep with bugs? Don't with Nina. She has bugs in her bed.' I'm tired. I don't have a room for the night . . . 'Come along Julius,' Nina sings out.

Up the stairs again. Kick the door open. 'I don't know what bed you'll want to sleep in but you'll probably be in my bed before the night is over.' I sit alone for a few minutes . . . 'Do you have a match?' Nina cries. I light a match and the candle lights the room. Nina in a one piece shift. The Laughing Torso, Modigliani, the Pole, on and on and on, and now Horwitz. 'Don't forget I'm a museum piece darling.' I drop into bed next [to] Nina.

I dressed in front of Flora's portrait. Slipped into my GI shorts. Nina wore a pair of men's trousers. 'Darling I'll tell what I'll do. You can have the painting for ten pounds. God knows I can get more at an exhibition . . . Give a pound this morning, and you can send me a few shillings every week from your pay. But first I have to finish the painting. Now give me some money to buy milk and stuff.' Nina and I clop clopped down Charlotte Street. Rain again . . .[19]

Nina undoubtedly considered men as potential meal-tickets or at least providers of drink. She could be surprisingly shrewd about money and never undervalued her work. In the Wheatsheaf one lunchtime:

Nina kept shouting that she had been with George Barker and when I asked her sensible questions she started telling me some more of her famous stories. Evidently she was broke and wanted a few gins from me . . . She did a drawing of Flora and sent it to me with a request for £5. Nina said the price had gone up since Augustus John had looked at a few of her drawings rather favourably . . . £5 is a fantastic price . . . With the fine and stupid poker playing I haven't enough money to support Nina for a couple of weeks . . . I shall have to send the drawing back to her.[20]

Nina never underestimated the importance of money, or 'mun', as she called it. When she introduced a girl to a man she would whisper, 'This is so-and-so, he's good for mun.' If she saw that a girl was getting attached to someone, Nina's first question was always, 'Has he got the mun, deah?'[21]

Nina evidently knew when she was on to a good thing and when Julius's staff sergeant Amos Neilson took a liking to her, she was not slow to exploit the situation.

Nina looked fine, lean, well dressed. It was still early and Nina always starts the day out with a glass of lemon which she sips until someone walks in and buys her a gin. The Wheatsheaf looked empty. An old bitch excused herself the minute I started talking to Nina (part of the Code) and left for the Fitzroy. Nina asked about Neilson. Blond Neilson. You'll wet your pants Clem but Nina is more than tremendously interested in Amos. Since the Tuesday afternoon about four weeks ago when Neilson opened a bottle of scotch in her room, and bought gin at the Café Royal and showed more than a tourist interest in her, the crown princess of the Wheatsheaf has been anxiously sweeping her studio and procuring clean white sheets to cover herself and Neilson. Modigliani, the Pole, Sickert, and Neilson. It looks like a decent affair. All of us are going into town this week, after pay call, and four of us are going to have dinner at Wapping down on the Thames in the East End.[22] . . . The love affair is real to the huff and puff and Nina when she dropped her clothes said, 'Here's the old torso, how does it look?'[23]

Nina was always very proud of her body and never lost her instinct for self-display. She surprised Flora Isserlis one day by asking, 'Would you like to see the old torso?' and matter-of-factly stripped off to reveal her remarkably well-preserved body.

Nina was unlikely to maintain a discreet silence if she successfully extracted money or drinks from someone and it was not unknown for her to boast of it in the wrong quarter. On one occasion she was very pleased with herself for getting something out of a sailor. The story did her no credit but she thought it was extremely funny and told everybody about it around the pubs, sooner or later inadvertently telling it to the sailor himself. Julius experienced something of the same nature:

I woke up in the morning on Charlotte Street and walked down the road to have a morning cup of coffee and a couple of rolls at the Scala Café. The place is wonderfully clean and all sorts of modern paintings and reproductions are inside to give charm to London's wartime coffee. While I cooled a cup of coffee Nina walked in and ordered a cup of tea. I overheard her tell a burly looking man that a Julius Horwitz, an American who she knew, was going to give her five pounds ten for a painting. Oh my dear what a fine afternoon that will be. Nina walked over [to] a table and after she was seated I sort of crept up on her and said good morning. We had another cup of tea and then Nina suggested going to the Leicester Galleries to see the Hugh Walpole Collection. 'You won't have to pay to see the exhibition my darling. I'm an artist and you're a friend. No, we'll get in free.' . . . Nina lived and loved and knew quite a few of the artists on exhibition. I've been to three exhibitions with Nina and once in a gallery she loses her beer stained look and becomes the Master. Her eye is sharp and her knowledge isn't questioned by many people. The paintings were great: Degas, Rodin, Steer, Duncan Grant, Nicholson, Gauguin, Augustus John, Picasso, Cézanne, Renoir, Modigliani; and how does the song go – lots more . . . The exhibition was certainly exciting and the noisy air of mid-afternoon London was a bit unnerving after stepping out of another age. The Paris before Verdun and Hitler.[24]

VE day came just eight days after Julius wrote this last letter:

In the morning after V-Day I had a cup of coffee and a roll in the Scala Café on Charlotte. The artists were already up. The intense young men were sitting around cups of tea discussing the night before. The women, hair wind-blown, bodies loose, clothes flightily and politely disarranged were resting their fannys. Nina wandered in with Doc Winters. The Doctor who owns a delightful beard and a magnificently fragile body is a nephew of the late Sir James Barrie. His clothes were ragged and he didn't have a ha'penny in his pocket. Nina told of spending the night in Wapping. Winters wandered through the East End. More tea; Nina dashed off and then we started for a pub . . .

The Fitzroy opened the doors of its famous establishment and we settled down to glasses of ale. Nina told tales of the characters of the neighborhood and a charming story about Augustus John . . . A British soldier started to play some silly tunes on the piano and we all hurried out of the pub. The Wheatsheaf was closed; only the Bricklayers' Arms was open in Soho. Ale, gin; I bought drinks; talked; said hello to a couple of my lesbian friends and then rushed off . . .

Doc Winters and Violet Grant were in Nina's flat. Nina stretched herself out in bed and was busy reading Julian Ross's book about the army. I picked up Flora's portrait. The stains of rat feet and the dirt of the flat were cleaned away . . . Nina had a bit more work to do on the painting . . . I didn't get out of Soho in the evening. V-day and I didn't approach the mobs in Piccadilly Circus. All of the people I ever knew seemed to be drinking in the Bricklayer's Arms. . . .

Nina and I walked down Charlotte and for the first time she asked me about my future. What will you [do]; where are you going; whom do you love? I didn't know any of the answers.[25]

Before Julius was sent back to America in August 1945, Nina did a drawing of him.

I called on Nina. Nina looked terrific in a black turtle neck sweater and pants to match. Nina promised to sketch me and after a cup of tea she washed her hands and posed me for a red chalk drawing. I sat for two hours. Gradually the Horwitz Nina had known for the past two years became more pronounced as she completed the drawing. An almost oriental figure with sad sad eyes . . . It's a fine drawing.[26]

There is a poignant fictionalized account of Julius's final leave-taking of Nina in *Can I Get There by Candlelight*:

I went into London to say good-bye to Nora . . . I took Nora to the Dog and Duck and bought her three double whiskies. Nora walked me to the corner of Tottenham Court Road. She held on to my arm, saying she wasn't drunk, but she was . . . I didn't want to leave Nora drunk on the corner of Tottenham Court Road but she insisted she was all right.

'I got this far,' Nora told me, 'this far and no farther. It's remarkable why anyone bothers to stay alive. But here we are. Good-bye,' Nora said, 'I don't want to talk, I've done that enough. I feel I should say something to you. I like you, and that's enough, and I will think about you, and that's more important, and remember me, and here we are.' Nora kissed me. I watched her go up Tottenham Court Road. She turned once to wave to me. I waved to her, and Nora turned forever into Windmill Street.[27]

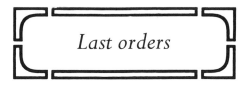

16

Last orders

Vᴇ day came as an enormous relief to the war-weary, exhausted masses. But despite the pealing of bells and dancing in the floodlit streets, public rejoicing was more restrained than it had been after the First World War. There was a new political seriousness and no one any longer expected that the end of the war would solve all problems.

The overwhelming victory of Clement Attlee's Labour Party in the General Election of July 1945 was a vote for radical social change – for full employment, housing, nationalization of industry, and social security. In its first three years of office the new government passed an unprecedented amount of social and economic legislation which effectively set up the whole complex apparatus of the Welfare State. But even before this was completed, the nation's buoyant mood of confidence and optimism had been seriously undermined by the country's severe financial crisis. In a desperate attempt to avert bankruptcy the government was forced to impose a siege economy, a new era of austerity even more stringent than during the war. Food rations were reduced, imports from dollar areas tightly controlled and tourist spending stopped altogether; while new targets were set for British industry. The Marshall plan for economic aid to Europe temporarily alleviated the situation, but the initial visionary momentum could never be recaptured. There was a widespread disillusion and disappointment among the Left wing when confronted with the drab bureaucratic reality of post-war Britain.

Cyril Connolly, writing in 1947, graphically evoked the prevailing mood of dispirited apathy:

Here, the ego is at half pressure; most of us are not men and women but members of a vast, seedy, overworked, over-legislated, neuter class, with our drab clothes, our ration books and murder stories, our envious, strict, old-world apathies and resentments – a care-worn people. And the symbol of this mood is London, now the largest, saddest and dirtiest of great cities, with its miles of unpainted half-inhabited houses, its chopless chop-houses, its beerless pubs, its once vivid quarters losing all personality, its squares bereft of elegance, its dandies in exile, its antiquities in America, its shops full of junk, bunk, and tomorrow, its crowds mooning round the stained green wicker of the cafeterias in their shabby raincoats, under a sky permanently dull and lowering like a metal dish-cover.[1]

The arts too came under the spreading government aegis. The success of the wartime Council for the Encouragement of Music and the Arts led to the formation of the Arts Council, which after May 1946 had power to award grants and interest-free loans to artists. The BBC's Third Programme started broadcasting in September 1946. Artists and intellectuals found jobs in the universities and art schools, in advertising, journalism, television and films, and with the omnivorous Features and Talks Department of the BBC. This nominal official patronage bestowed a new respectability on the artist, who tended to become more bourgeois in dress and behaviour. Bohemianism was no longer relevant in post-war Britain.

The years immediately after the war saw the last flickering of the dying flame of Fitzrovia. The blitz had destroyed many of the old buildings and dispersed for ever its special artistic community. When the council classed the district as industrial, rents became way out of reach of the artists, writers and students who had lived there for generations. Trade names and business-plates rapidly appeared on the doorways, and former studios became tailoring sweat-shops. Later, property speculation and development completed the destruction of Fitzrovia.

More than ever Nina became a monument of a lost Bohemia and was affectionately valued as such by some, considered a boring irrelevance by others. Sitting back on her bar-stool, a little drunk, she would talk straight ahead of her, barking out stories or exclamations before demanding, 'Who's going to buy me a drink?'[2] and launching into some new anecdote about someone from way back she identified only by a Christian name, assuming that everyone knew whom she meant, or perhaps not caring if they did not. The young did not always find her easily approachable; with her pronounced upper-class voice, she could seem haughty and stand-offish. When Mark Holloway once boldly ventured to ask her who the half-named person was, she witheringly replied in comic indignation, 'Where have you been living all these years, ducky?'[3]

Nina was always touchingly pleased to see her friends and greeted them as if they had arrived from the ends of the earth. She would eagerly announce the expected visit of some figure from her past or a sailor on leave, anticipating the fun they were going to have. But somehow, like most of the men who came and went in her life, they were always a bit of a disappointment and were not as hospitable or generous as she had hoped. Viva King was often dismayed by the 'ghastly' men Nina would bring to the regular Sunday tea and drinks parties she started after the war. Another frequent guest at these parties was Janey Ironside, who recalled how Nina would 'sit in a corner eating and drinking as much as she could. She wore a very shabby navy suit, with a rusty black shirt and grubby, wrinkled cotton stockings. She was dirty, smelt of stale bar-rooms, and very pathetic.'[4] When Nina went to the Kings' house in Thurloe Square to collect the small allowance they continued to give her, she always exerted herself to be witty and amusing and would tell funny stories to earn her keep, even if sometimes she did get lost in the middle.

The end of the war brought a marked improvement in Nina's fortunes. She exhibited watercolours of Mrs Stewart, Maclaren-Ross and Judy Hill with the London Group; and early in 1946 Amos Neilson, who had stayed on after the war to work in the American Embassy, commissioned her to paint his portrait. Instead of giving her an agreed fee on completion, he paid her for each sitting. This suited Nina perfectly, but Neilson quickly regretted the arrangement and wrote to Julius Horwitz that 'given the material for doing a binge up every day nearly wrecked the whole affair.'[5] The portrait did, however, turn out to be a good likeness and Nina received several other commissions from friends. She was asked to design the cover of Maclaren-Ross's book of short stories *The Nine Men of Soho* and to do thirteen black and white illustrations and a colour frontispiece for a book by Evan Morgan called *Not Behind Lace Curtains*, although this was never published.

Any money Nina earned was rapidly swallowed up by the solicitor's fees needed to do legal battle with her landlady Miss Macpherson, who was trying to evict her tenants so that she could sell the house in Howland Street with vacant possession. The case was heard in February 1947 and gave rise to much hilarity in the pubs. The story went round that when Miss Macpherson accused Nina of misusing the sink, the magistrate interrupted her with, 'What do you mean, a woman urinating in the sink? It is not possible',[6] and refused to accept her evidence. This caused a good chuckle among the denizens of Fitzrovia who had a clearer idea of life in their quarter than the magistrate. But although Miss Macpherson lost her case, the tenants did not sit tight for long.

In April Nina spent a fortnight in Broadstairs with her sister Helen, who had married the flamboyant Augustine Booth-Clibborn, grandson of the founder of the Salvation Army, General Booth. Augustine was a wild, extrovert character whose frustrated artistic ambitions ensured a highly precarious existence for his family. While he painted in the garden shed Nina's sister did her best to maintain a semblance of gentility within the house. When Nina arrived back at Howland Street she was horrified to discover her house surrounded by fire-engines and gaping crowds. She rushed up the badly burnt staircase to her two rooms where she was immensely relieved to find that although everything was soaking wet, no real damage had been done. However, the fire had proved fatal for one of the house's inhabitants, who in her panic had rushed to the window and fallen out, being impaled on the railings below. In view of later events there was a chilling irony in Nina's comment that, 'She died, I hope, at once. If I had been there this would never have happened. When I got to the "Fitzroy", I heard that "poor Nina had jumped out of the window and was dead". It can perhaps be imagined what I had to say about that.'[7]

As Nina had nowhere else to go she slept that night in the remains of her bed, almost suffocated by the heat and smell of burnt clothes. When she woke in the morning, dirty and wet, she was confronted by a startled fireman who told her that she could not remain in the house as it was unsafe. Nina retired to the Wheatsheaf to consider what she should do. The police's well-intentioned attempts to rehouse her in the Marylebone workhouse met with great indignation from Nina. Her mother, for whom she never expressed the least affection, had recently died in a mental asylum, and Nina was due to inherit £564. She wired to her naval officer brother Bernard to advance her £10 to get her out of trouble. Instead of the workhouse, Nina found two rooms on the second floor of a house at 164 Westbourne Terrace near the Regent's Canal in Paddington, a quiet, picturesque backwater with a small colony of artists and writers. The prospect of soon receiving some money gave Nina a new lease of artistic life and she started drawing at an art class for three or four hours every day and exhibited portraits of Mrs Stewart and Helen at the London Group show in May.

In July Nina finally received her eagerly awaited inheritance and decided to go to Ireland to paint and see Michael Shawe-Taylor, who was being treated for gout in a Dublin nursing home. Carefully made-up and wearing a hat with a veil, Nina enjoyed acting the grand lady and travelled first class from Euston. But she soon reverted back to her old form when she discovered that all the cabins were taken on the boat and unceremoniously lay down on the bare deck outside the third class. As the boat approached Ireland a technicolour dawn lit up the sky and Nina commented drily, 'Everyone is silent – we are in heaven and the bar is not open'[8] – a lamentable oversight which she more than made up for during the next few blissfully drunken months.

Nina spent a few days in Dublin revisiting the scenes of her youth and enjoying Michael Shawe-Taylor's expansive hospitality. She was, however, scathing

Regent's Canal, *c.* 1947

about the art she saw and wrote to Duncan Grant that, 'The galleries are filled with indescribable horrors and bogus Surrealist and what is supposed to be Cubist works.'[9]

Michael Shawe-Taylor kept two race-horses and when he left his nursing home Nina stayed with him at Castle Taylor, happily accompanying him to the races. At Leopardstown she backed his horse The Griffen and was overjoyed when it won at ten to one, excitedly writing to her friends at the Fitzroy Tavern that she was having the time of her life. Amos Neilson saw the postcards she sent to the Wheatsheaf and reported to Julius Horwitz: 'I take it that she has been in a more or less drunken stupor since her arrival there. From all indications she has some of her old buddies around her. Pub-crawls, popping in and out of bed and all the rest!'[10]

Nina was, however, determined to prove to herself that she was not finished as an artist and before long she retired to Carraroe opposite the Aran Islands, where she had rented a room for £3 a week so that she could paint in peace. Needless to say, it was not all solitary contemplation of the countryside and she enjoyed drinking with the locals in the single pub where she was the only woman, and made various excursions along the coast and to the Galway race week with Michael Shawe-Taylor. But away from the distractions of Fitzrovia and stimulated by new places and people, Nina did do a surprising number of paintings and drawings of the landscape and her landlady's children which show a marked renewal of artistic energy.

By the time Nina returned to London in November she had almost no money left. She showed her work to Rex Nan Kivell at the Redfern Gallery in the hope of selling something and was surprised and delighted when he immediately offered to give her an exhibition and to cover the initial costs of framing and mounting. The show opened on 6 April 1948, Nina sharing the gallery with Adrian Ryan and Rowland Suddaby. In her room she exhibited twenty-four mainly small paintings and drawings of Irish scenes, portraits, and studies of the Regent's Canal and Maida Vale.

It was sixteen years since Nina had last had a show and her work was disappointing to those who remembered her at her best. Her paintings seemed slight and her line had lost its distinctive, incisive quality. She also seemed out of place in the unfamiliar surroundings of a smart gallery. Rhys Davies, who had known Nina since the mid-twenties, found that 'the array was depressing. Nina

Connemara Cottage, 1947

sat in the elegant gallery, and her effort to wear a dazzlingly brave mask for the occasion was depressing too.'[11] Nonetheless Nina sold half the show to loyal supporters including Matthew Smith, Edward Le Bas, Philip Lindsay and J. B. Priestley. At the private view a tall man with a large bushy moustache approached her and asked, 'Are you Ham?'[12] It was Arthur Ransome, whom Nina had known since her student days and who had since become famous with his children's book *Swallows and Amazons*. He invited Nina to lunch with his wife and commissioned her to do portrait drawings of them both for thirty guineas. Nina felt rich and confident again. She had work in several mixed exhibitions at the Leicester Galleries in 1948, and showed a drawing of a Connemara boy and a portrait of Subramanian, the Ceylonese writer, lawyer and bookseller, with the London Group in May.

Nina and her work may have deteriorated badly but she was still held in affectionate respect as an esteemed member of the old-guard painting fraternity. She was invited to the lavish dinner given by Edward Le Bas in 1948 to celebrate Charles Ginner's seventieth birthday, at which speeches were made and wine flowed in defiance of austerity. Nina was in fine form, even if she was rather tight and made what seemed to her neighbour Quentin Bell at least thirty visits to the lavatory during the course of the evening. She did, however, sit still long enough to tell him an anecdote which did her no credit and was not even true, saying familiarly, 'Quentin dear, I know you're interested in art history so I'll tell you a thing. The difference between Roger and Sickert, it was this: Sickert always knew I was a bitch, Roger, bless his heart, never guessed.'[13]

Other faces from the past reappeared. She met up again with Winifred Gill, her old friend from the Omega Workshops, who was working at the BBC. When she took her out to lunch and Nina mentioned that she had had all her upper teeth taken out in Ireland but still managed quite well with her remaining few bottom ones, Winifred gently suggested that Nina could get false teeth on the National Health. Nina reacted with characteristically vehement distrust of officialdom: 'God, no . . . once your name gets known to the authorities they are after you for income tax and God knows what . . . Made nearly two hundred with an exhibition and so on. Jolly useful. But I wasn't going to let the income tax people get their hands on it.'[14] After lunch they took a taxi back to Nina's flat, where Winifred was shocked by the bareness of her living-room, which 'contained , beside a useful roll-top desk, a bedstead with only a layer of newspaper on the wire mattress . . . There was no comfortable chair, and her clothes hung on a string which stretched from wall to wall.'[15] In an unusually unguarded moment Nina confided that she wished she could have some comfort before she died. Winifred did what she could to help and bought a drawing of Nina's Irish landlady's son for five guineas and sent her a spare armchair.

Nina's life had changed little since she moved to Paddington. She exhibited with the local art society in 1949 and 1951 but she still spent most of her time in her old haunts. She never abandoned the Fitzroy Tavern and the Wheatsheaf, even though the main social focus for young painters, writers, film and television people had shifted to Soho proper. She was a familiar sight navigating the short distance across Oxford Street to the French Pub in Dean Street and the Swiss House round the corner in Old Compton Street. But sadly, Nina was no longer the centre of attention for a noisy group of admirers. She had lost much of her old vitality and sparkle and easily became boring and repetitive with too much drink. In her beret and shabby brown tweeds, she sometimes looked like a scarecrow, and even when she did make an effort to clean herself up the results could be disastrous. She announced one day, 'I took my grey dress to the dry-cleaners and, my dear, it just shrivelled up because of the gin soaked into it over the years. All they gave me back was a spoonful of dust.'[16] When she was down on her luck she cut a rather pitiful figure scrounging drinks and the loan of a few shillings with her habitual refrain, 'Got any mun, deah?'. She could overdo this even to those who did care about her, such as David Archer, the kind-hearted publisher and bookseller whose shop in Parton Street had been a great meeting-place for artists and intellectuals in the thirties. Exasperated by her repeated demands, he replied, 'No, Nina. Not again,' and hurriedly left, only to return remorsefully a few minutes later with a bunch of flowers and a ten-shilling note for her.[17]

Drinking clubs were very popular after the war and Nina often went to the Mandrake, which had gradually absorbed cellar after cellar under the pavement in Meard Street. A musician friend of Nina's, Cyril Clarke, raised a subscription among the regulars to buy one of her pictures to present to the Tate Gallery, and contributors included Bob Pocock, Gilbert Wood and the writer John Lepper. But although they held a party at the Mandrake and loudly proclaimed their admiration and affection for her, nothing ever came of the plan and the money which had been collected somehow – inevitably – just leaked out of Cyril Clarke's pockets.

Around the corner in Dean Street was the immensely popular Caves de France, described by one habitué as 'a real cultural slum. It was the Mandrake brought up from the basement and revealed.'[18] The Caves was started just after the war by Philippe and his father, and run on the lines of a French wine bar. It was a vast, sleazy, smoke-filled den on two storeys with a long bar at ground level, its floor strewn with cigarette ends and rubbish, the chairs stained with wine and worse. All kinds and ages of people passed the afternoon at the Caves and many old Fitzrovian characters were to be found there. A newcomer to the scene, the young *Picture Post* photographer Daniel Farson, was seduced by the potent charm of the regular Sohoites with their ready intimacy and 'outpouring of dreams and disillusionment'.[19] He remembered how Nina, 'thin and ravaged', would make 'a gallant, though anxious entrance, a beret cocked on the side of her head, and a chuckle that was still resounding as she hauled herself on to a bar stool: ''You couldn't buy me a drink could you love, hah!'' she gasped.'[20]

When the pubs opened at six there was a lull as people went their separate ways. The Caves tried in vain to acquire an incongruous aura of respectability by employing a middle-aged trio in evening dress to play genteel dance numbers. It was even worse when the club-owner's daughter, Mme Hortense, trilled operetta in a refined manner. If nothing else, this was sufficient to drive any self-respecting member of the Soho drinking fraternity two doors along into a dustbin-lined passage next to an Italian restaurant and up the narrow staircase to the Colony Room, a small drinking club with a pianist and atmosphere of

Nina (seated) in the Colony Room, c.1950. Ian Board and Muriel Belcher are behind the bar

constant party. It had been opened in 1948 by the formidable but much-loved Muriel Belcher, who presided over her domain with black beady eyes, her chin tilted sharply upwards and dark hair combed straight back from her face. Perched on a stool beside the door, her hand eloquently waving a cigarette holder, Muriel's first words to new arrivals were invariably 'Members only', followed by a brisk 'Fuck off!' to strangers, or a welcoming 'Hello cunty!' to her favourites, who were well used to her outrageous wit and coolly obscene language. She had a habit of referring to all men as 'she' so that Hitler became 'Miss Hitler' and she remarked on the death of George Bernard Shaw, 'You've got to hand it to her, a clever little woman, that one.'[21]

Predominantly, though not exclusively, homosexual, the club was a skilful mixture of all types and sexual dispositions, only the boring and the mean being made to feel uncomfortable. Muriel's technique with the latter was infallible: ' "Come along everyone," she would cry, "we'll all have a drink with this vision of loveliness beside me." Her chin would tilt even higher after a sharp nod to the barman and the sharper command to the unfortunate man who had been trying to ingratiate himself: "Open your bead bag, Lottie!" '[22] After several such sallies her victim would hurriedly retreat back down the stairs, never to return. Muriel always liked the company of artists and Francis Bacon, Lucian Freud, John Craxton, the Roberts Colquhoun and Macbryde, John Minton, Rodrigo Moynihan and the photographer John Deakin were often to be seen there. Muriel was a warm, mother-figure, sharing in their successes and failures, and she and her club often figured in their work, perhaps most memorably in the triptych of her by her favourite 'daughter', Francis Bacon. Although Muriel's wit could be devastating, she was unfailingly kind and generous. Sympathetic and perceptive, she was never cruel and took care to avoid any real areas of vulnerability. The sensitive and insecure could leave with their fragile egos and dreams intact. Nina was not a permanent fixture in the Colony Room, but she made regular appearances, carrying her money in an Oxo tin. Showing unexpected foresight, she used to request an envelope in which she would place a ten-shilling note and post it to herself so that she had enough money to start the next day before settling down to some serious drinking. Muriel always liked Nina and was very compassionate towards her, even if she did inevitably say bitchy things about her when she left or, as often as not, was carried out.

Nina's habits with money could prove disconcerting to the more convention-ally minded outside the confines of Soho. She was always an avid reader throughout her life and after she moved to Paddington she regularly visited Peter Eaton's second-hand bookshop at the top of Kensington Church Street to buy cheap books. When she had selected her purchases she would unceremoniously lift up her skirt and pull her money out of the top of her stockings. She had by this time acquired other habits which were considered anti-social even by her not over-fastidious Soho friends. The whole of the clientele of the Gargoyle Club as well as the entire membership of the Colony Room attended the three-night wedding-party to celebrate the marriage of the young painters Michael Wishart and Anne Dunn in July 1950. It was held in Francis Bacon's studio, where Nina distinguished herself by peeing on the sofa. This frequently repeated party trick ensured that her habitual seat behind the door at the French pub was indelibly hers: it was as if permanently reserved for her eventual occupation, so assiduously did others avoid the sagging Rexine. At the end of an evening it was not unknown for her to be quietly sick into her handbag before making her drunken way home.

By this time Nina would sometimes sit completely alone, bolt upright and silent, sunk in her own thoughts. Wearing an extraordinary twenties coat with a ginger fur collar, she seemed completely unapproachable, as if she were just not there. Those who had known Nina in better days noticed a great change in her. Somehow, before the war her friends and admirers always believed in her as Nina Hamnett the painter, not just the painter she had been, but the painter she still could be if she drank a little less and ordered her life a little more, as from time to time she did in fact attempt to do. But now all that seemed firmly in the past. She continued to exhibit regularly with the London Group and in the Leicester Galleries 'Artists of Fame and Promise' shows, but the works – almost invariably quick portraits of children or old people and the occasional still life – displayed little of her former talent. Nina could, however, still surprise with the occasional departure from her usual style and in 1950 she produced a startlingly confident, boldly simplified still life of a tropical plant and a snake. With its brightly coloured arabesques, the painting is highly decorative and has points in common with the work produced by her friend Gladys Hynes.

Nina had enough self-knowledge to recognize that her artistic gifts, which had promised so much, remained sadly unfulfilled. She blamed no one but herself. Ultimately, life had beckoned too enticingly for her to shut the studio door firmly behind her and concentrate on her work. But she knew the price she had paid and could be surprisingly harsh on those of the younger generation who seemed to be following in her footsteps. Rhys Davies commented

Her bracing 'Yes' to life included, of course, many 'Noes'. In her later years she would lament if younger people of talent went beyond the bounds, more especially in the domain of sex. I called on her one day, found her topping and tailing gooseberries into an old straw hat, and this severity was much in ascendency. She questioned whether several acquaintances had the stamina, moral and physical, for the hard London round. . . . She protested, too,

Jungle Still Life, 1950

against the frivolity of thought and philosophy that, slowly, can destroy the solidity of talent. She knew that the 'bohemian' life had lost the creative zest of her heyday, with its marvellous crop of talents. It had become despairing.[23]

If no one took Nina seriously as an artist any more, people still remained loyally faithful to her as a person. She often saw her old friend E. J. Moeran, whose music had received considerable public attention during the war. Unstable and volatile, with an underlying deep-seated melancholy, Moeran alternated spells of intense gregariousness around the pubs and clubs of Soho with retreats to the rural solitude of Kenmare in Ireland. One night in May 1953, after a heavy drinking session at the Fitzroy Tavern, Nina was sent home drunk in a taxi. She must have fallen because when she woke up the next morning she was unable to move and lay in bed all day until half-past six, when Moeran and another Irish friend, O'Kelly, came to visit her with two bottles of wine. Horrified at her plight, which did not, however, diminish her appetite for alcohol, they drank the wine and then called an ambulance to take her to Paddington General Hospital where she was operated on for a fractured thigh bone. Nina treated the whole thing as a holiday and much enjoyed the unaccustomed comfort and food. She graciously received visitors, listened to the wireless on her headphones, read Chateaubriand's *Memoires de l'autres temps*, and drew the other occupants of the ward. Nina declared herself delighted with everything and announced that she felt younger every day.

When she came out of hospital she was in optimistic mood and started working seriously on the second volume of her autobiography, *Is She a Lady?*, which brought her story up to date. She was often seen intently writing in the Fitzroy Tavern, where she haughtily discouraged casual interruption. Bob Pocock was amused to witness her technique when a bluff Yorkshireman came in and heartily greeted her:

> 'Hello Nina old girl, good to see you. What are you doing then?'
> 'I'm all right thank you.'
> 'I see you're writing.'
> 'If you're talking to me I'll have a gin.'
> 'You're writing another book are you? What are you going to call it?'
> 'Kiss My Arse!'[24]

Nina's liking for boxers and sailors remained undiminished and she avidly followed the *Sunday Express* astrologer, R. N. Naylor, exclaiming 'May God and Mr Naylor send me soon a buxom sailor!'[25] She was living on and off with Claude Mounsey, a very good-looking Oxford-educated merchant seaman much younger than herself who had run his own prop hire business for films before the war. He stayed with her when he was on leave, Nina anxiously concealing all evidence of him from the Assistance Board. Nina and Mounsey were oddly devoted to each other. He made no concessions to her age and they would go on great drinking binges and have terrific rows before making it up again.

In August 1954 Nina had to return to hospital to have the pin removed from her leg, which had not set properly after her operation. It was the beginning of the end. She came out of hospital to greatly restricted movement, continuous pain and poverty. Her leg had been badly treated and when it healed it was four inches shorter than the other, so that she had to wear a built-up invalid shoe and hobble about on a stick. She still gamely battled on and managed to get down to the Fitzroy Tavern and Soho, but her presence could no longer be relied upon as before. She determinedly carried on working and continued to do quick portrait sketches for small sums of money. A beautiful young boy could still excite her aesthetic interest and she exhibited a watercolour of a boy reading comics with the London Group at the end of 1954, and a drawing of a boy's head at the New English Art Club the following year. Rhys Davies was impressed and moved by her business-like manner when she arranged to draw him:

> prompt to the minute, she rang my bell at nine a.m., her choice of hour. I had forgotten about my stairs, and to see Nina valiantly clumping up about fifty of them with her game leg was a lesson in discipline. The drawings – she attempted two – were failures. Her hand was as shaky as her leg. But she wouldn't touch a drop of anything. Some form of cure was undoing her.[26]

Nina had to make constant visits to her doctor and to the hospital about her leg and was generally in a very poor physical state due to her chronic alcoholism, which had by now affected her nervous system. She went less and less to Soho and spent more time in her local pubs on the canal, the Warwick Arms and the Bridgehouse. Many artists and writers lived in the area. Lucian Freud had a studio there and the poet John Gawsworth, the eccentric King of Redonda, was often seen parading around in a variety of costumes. Charles Wrey Gardiner, the quiet and introspective editor of *Poetry Quarterly* and owner of Grey Walls Press, would always lend Nina a few shillings and buy her a drink. Sometimes she would be her old self but at other times she seemed despondent and did not want to talk to anyone. It was in one of these moods that she gave her GP Dr Precope a scrap of paper with a summary sketch of Gaudier-Brzeska's torso of her. Beneath it she had scrawled the word 'Hell' – a clear enough indication of her state of mind and attitude towards her present condition.

When Nina could not make it to her local pubs, friends would visit her in her squalid rooms where she had put up a passage in French on the walls: '*Il vaut mieux le travail que la rêverie.*'[27] Not that Nina was ever given to dreaming. But she undoubtedly suffered a great deal from her leg and did have moments of deep depression. Lucian Freud, who was very fond of Nina, remembered her at home crying from pain and then pulling herself together with a great effort of the will. Once, when he took a publisher to visit her, they found her in bed. She greeted them cheerily, saying that she had been keeping the tea warm for them, and lifted

Nina and Charles Wrey Gardiner in her room at Westbourne Terrace, *c.*1954

back the bedcovers to reveal herself curled round the teapot – no doubt to keep her warm. Nina could still muster enough of her old spirit to laugh at her situation and declared in her inimitably forthright manner to one visitor: 'I've got boils on my arse my deah, and I can't walk!'[28] Old Soho friends took the trouble to come and see her and the better-off invariably slipped a ten-shilling note or a pound under her pillow before they left.

It was not all gloom. There were some bright spots which gave rise to moods of high elation. When the news got round that Nina was writing another book, several publishers were interested. She wrote gleefully in February 1955 to Annie Allchild, her old friend from the Fitzroy Tavern,

Publishers *rushing* for my book. Victor Gollancz just too late alas. I have sold it to Alan Wingate for £100 and royalties and they hope serial rights. Wild excitement all round . .. . They think I will make £1000 this time. Serve them all right doesn't it again after twenty years. I think this one is much better ha! ha!²⁹

In the event, when *Is She a Lady?* appeared in October 1955, it had none of the breathless charm of *Laughing Torso* but was rather rambling, disjointed and inconsequential, a sad reflection of Nina's own state. There were other reasons for optimism. The BBC paid her a small fee for an interview included in a radio programme on the Café Royal which was broadcast in December; and a Swiss publisher was interested in bringing out a German translation of *Laughing Torso*. The end of the year brought further cause for congratulation when the Arts Council bought a recent watercolour of apples in a basket from the London Group for twenty-five guineas. The show was widely reviewed and Nina must have been heartened by the words of the *Manchester Guardian*'s critic, who wrote that 'it is pleasant to see again work by Nina Hamnett – a small, still-life drawing that is sensitive and intelligent.'³⁰ It was to be the last picture by her exhibited during her lifetime.

The pain from her leg gradually became so bad that Nina had to go back again for a further operation and five-month stay in Paddington General Hospital. Nevertheless, a letter she wrote to her old friend Bob Pocock shows her in good spirits and taking a lively interest in what was going on around her:

I have earphones here thank god but no Third programme. I managed to hear Dylan last night because as a rule at 10.15 the wireless is either turned off or all the bloody patients including myself are asleep! My leg was getting worse and worse and I knew I should crash again but thank god the sadistic Jewish bastard doctor who is responsible for all this has left and now I have a large Scotsman who if I had had before this would not have happened. He said that I was made to walk too soon as I suspected and was horrified when he found that one leg was shorter than the other. You see if one has an accident one is taken to the nearest hospital and delivered into the hands of the nearest doctor and [if] he is a hopeless ass one has had it as I have had, nothing on earth can be done about it. This doctor prescribed 8 ozs of brandy, anyway I don't see what else they can do and its up to him to repair the damage done by the last bastard. I shall be here for weeks anyway. I get about £100 royalties so I shall be all right when I come out. Claude I am thankful to say is on his way to Australia so won't be back yet but ought to have a decent sum when he does. What about Soho? Very funny things go on here. I am continuing my illustrated hospital diary. A deputation of idiots turned up to know if *I* could do anything about getting Ezra Pound out of his loony bin! they are not sure if he is quite all right mentally? Anyway if he is he won't remain so for long if he does get out. I wonder if this is very old, it amuses me. Changing sexes. Women turning into men. Knickers into nackers or why be a cunt all your life! . . . I have told hardly anyone I am here. Was annoyed as I was selling drawings before.[31]

Augustus John attempted to help Nina by recommending her for a place in a home for aged artists, but she indignantly rejected the idea. Other friends did what they could for her. Before she came out of hospital at the end of October, Gladys Hynes cleaned her room, stocked up her food cupboard and left ten shillings in the gas meter. She and Adrian Allinson, another old friend from the Café Royal days, raised a small fund for Nina which was given to her each week by the cheerful Austrian Countess Edith von Ullman, known simply as the Countess, who lived on a barge on the canal and bred Siamese cats.

Nina was now virtually marooned in Little Venice. She could only get around with the greatest difficulty and complained that few people came to see her. In her depressed state of mind she became convinced that she was developing mental and physical symptoms of venereal disease, which she had had when she was younger. Her doctor tried to reassure her but she insisted on going to St Thomas's Hospital for blood tests. There, contrary to all medical practice, the doctor apparently informed her that from what she had told him he thought it possible that she might have the disease, but instead of giving her the results immediately she had to wait for them to be sent to her local GP, Dr Precope. After two weeks the results had still not arrived and she feared that something was being concealed from her. The whole episode upset Nina a great deal and she was in a very agitated state of mind when Bob Pocock visited her. She was expecting Claude Mounsey, who was due back on leave, and she had washed and hung up her sheets to dry in the room. But this time Mounsey did not come to see her.

A few days later, on Wednesday 5 December, Bob Pocock's radio play *It's Long Past the Time*, about life in Charlotte Street in the thirties, was broadcast. Nina featured prominently as the fictional character Cynthia, and Pocock had managed to get her a fee of £10. Cynthia was played by the doyenne of radio, Gladys Young, whom Pocock had coached to good effect in Nina's distinctive voice, complete with the indispensable 'my deahs' and the odd 'ducky'. Those who knew Nina thought the impersonation was magnificent.

It was too good. Nina felt that the programme was a cruel caricature and parody. She was upset and furious and thought her friends had betrayed her. In her vulnerable state, anxious about the results of her hospital tests and the fact that Mounsey had not appeared, it must have seemed to Nina that she was being written off as a figure of the past, an artistic has-been who was merely an object of

Nina in the York Minster, c.1954

amusement to others. Unfortunately, Pocock was suffering from 'flu and could not go to see Nina himself immediately after the programme. An old friend of hers, James Norbury, 'the television knitter', who was PR to Pattons Knitting and taught knitting on television, had written to her to invite her out to lunch on the Saturday after the broadcast. He had no reply, but the following Monday received an uncharacteristic letter from Nina, roundly abusing Pocock and accusing all her old friends of deserting her. Norbury, who visited Nina regularly, thought this was very odd and wrote back to say that he would like to see her the next Saturday. But before this, on Thursday lunchtime, Nina fell the forty feet from her window and was impaled on the railings below. Very seriously injured, she was taken to Paddington General Hospital three-quarters of an hour later and given a blood transfusion, but she did not improve.

James Norbury was one of the first to be informed of what had happened. He wrote a very full account of the events that followed to Charles and Annie Allchild of the Fitzroy Tavern.

> I . . . rushed to the phone to find it was Paddington Police Station to tell me that Nina had had an accident, had fallen out of a window and was in a very serious condition in Paddington Hospital. A few minutes later Eileen Coyle, very much the worse for whisky, rang and said 'You must meet me at once, Nina has committed suicide.' I rang the hospital, spoke to the sister and she told me Nina was in a coma but in no immediate danger and I arranged to go round later that evening. I then rushed down to town to meet Eileen, drunker than ever this time and telling all and sundry that Nina had committed suicide and that she had tried to gas herself twice and cut her throat once before throwing herself out of the window. Luckily at that moment Bob Pocock, who I had phoned and asked to meet me, turned up and off we went to the hospital. I saw the sister who asked me if I knew the address of Nina's relatives. The only one I knew was Viva King in Thurloe Square so I contacted her and she said she would let the relatives know that Nina was in a very dangerous condition. . . . On the Friday morning they operated for internal injuries and on the Friday evening they let me see Nina for a few minutes, but she looked terrible. I had a quiet word with the doctor who told me there was no hope at all but she might linger for a week or two.[32]

The news of Nina's fall spread quickly and quite a few of her friends and relatives went to her bedside. Her supposed last words, as recalled by overfond memories, are as conflicting as the views on her death. But one phrase rings true. As Nina lay there in her wrecked state, a cruelly torn and broken body only kept alive by machines, she cried out in her moments of regained consciousness, 'Why don't they let me die?'[33]

Nina died on Sunday afternoon, 16 December 1956.

Her friends quickly closed ranks and James Norbury reported:

> On Monday I received a phone call from the coroner's officer asking me if I would go to the inquest on Tuesday morning to give evidence of what I thought from my long knowledge of her, of Nina's state of mind. He then mentioned Eileen Coyle and all the rumours. I saw the danger light as we

didn't want a suicide verdict and told the officer that Coyle was a typical Soho type, more often drunk than sober and always full of idle and malicious gossip, so you don't think she could help us if we call her? I told him I didn't and she wasn't called. In the meantime Nina's local doctor had been in touch with the police and told them that he thought that she was a very unstable character, so they decided to call him to the inquest. Then the fun really started. The hospital doctors were charming. One mentioned to me the gash in the throat but said that she died as a direct result of the fall and they did not intend to mention this at all.[34]

At the inquest the coroner, Mr Bentley Purchase, heard from a neighbour of Nina's that she used to look out of her window to see who was at the front door and then throw the keys down for her visitors to let themselves in. On the day of her death, Nina's neighbour heard a thud in the street and looked out to see Nina lying on the pavement. Her window was open but she had not heard anyone knock. Police Sergeant Horne then told the coroner that when he visited Nina's room shortly after the accident he found a stool in front of the open window. Dr Angus Buchanan, the house surgeon at Paddington Hospital, said that he had asked Nina if she had thrown herself out of the window and she had said she had, but he was not certain if she had understood his question. The hospital pathologist then affirmed that the direct cause of her death was shock and cerebral-fat embolism. All seemed to be going smoothly until Dr Precope stepped into the witness-box and told the coroner of Nina's worries about going to St Thomas's Hospital for a blood test. He added that, 'She was very eccentric. At times she was lucid, but at other times her mind seemed to work in a strange way. She had the kind of mind which went with the artistic make up.' The coroner then inquired: 'Although she was somewhat strange at times she did not appear suicidal?' Dr Precope replied that he would not say so. At this point the inquest was adjourned until the following day so that the coroner could make a routine inquiry about the results of the blood tests to see if Nina was in a condition which was worrying her.

Recording the verdict on Wednesday, the coroner said: 'I now have the medical report before me and it is negative. I am satisfied that this was an accident. I think this person was looking out of the window, as she was in the habit of doing sometimes, and over balanced. In the circumstances I shall record a verdict of "Accidental death".'[35]

In the event, with no concrete evidence to the contrary, the coroner quite rightly gave Nina the benefit of the doubt. Nina, with her balance upset by her leg injury, perhaps drunk or taken giddy, certainly could have fallen when looking out of the window. But it was a cold winter and there was no indication that anyone had knocked at the door so that she might have been standing at an open window with a stool before it. Under normal circumstances no one was less likely to commit suicide than Nina. She was robust and tenacious, an embattled survivor, gamely surmounting all the hardships and disappointments that life had brought her. Totally unselfpitying, she lived very firmly in the present and could be relied upon to give a pep-talk to those with suicidal tendencies. As she said in *Is She a Lady?*, published only a year before her death: 'The inhabitants of the quarter in which I live are fond of talking about suicide. They generally come to me and ask my advice. That is why they are still alive.'[36]

Notwithstanding her brave words, there is no doubt that the great majority of Nina's friends – though understandably not her family – did consider that she had committed suicide. Rumours and gossip were rife. It was said that Crowley had put a spell on her after the libel action over *Laughing Torso*; that she had had a fight with a drunken lover who had pushed her out of the window; and, even more scurrilously improbable, that she had been peeing out of the window and overbalanced. The variations were endless and took on elements of baroque fantasy.

Whether or not Nina did commit suicide will always remain an open question, but all the indications are that she did do so. She was in continuous pain, no longer able to get around to her old haunts, anxious about the results of her hospital tests and Mounsey's non-appearance, and the radio programme acted as a fateful catalyst. In moments of solitary depression Nina must have felt that she was finished. She was never one to shirk the truth. She knew that her life was inexorably shrinking into the confines of the four walls of her room. Faced with the undoubted grimness of her reality, even Nina's heroic powers of optimism would have had difficulty in imagining any future in which she wanted a part. In those circumstances suicide, a refusal to continue a life which was more and more a betrayal of everything she had been, was the ultimate courageous action. It would have been quite in character with Nina, indestructible spirit that she was, to choose death rather than pain, indignity and humiliation.

A lengthy obituary appeared in *The Times* on 17 December:

It is an open question whether the world gained or lost by the partial sacrifice of Nina Hamnett the painter of portraits and landscapes and illustrator, to Nina Hamnett, the Bohemian, but readers of her book of reminiscences: *Laughing Torso* will have no doubt that in the latter role she contributed to the gaiety of nations. Her friends will know something more: that whatever she might have done ultimately in painting if she had stuck to it more closely, Miss Hamnett was a complete success as a person; generous, good humoured, loyal, and witty.

Nina's faithful friends and loyal supporters, such as Viva King, made the journey
to Golders Green Cemetery where Nina was cremated two days before
Christmas. James Norbury commented wryly that 'Nina would have laughed her
head off had she been there. Her relatives decided that if in life she had been a
Bohemian of the first order, in death she must be a respectable Christian and they
had the lot.'[37] On a bitterly cold December day, the funeral was a very subdued
affair. Nina's mauve coffin looked a very frail craft for such a long journey. Few
of the mourners who stood and looked at the flowers on the terrace seemed to
know each other and they dispersed in silence. David Wright commemorated
the occasion with his 'Verses at a Bohemian Funeral' in memory of Nina.

I

So by the muddled wreaths the old men stand,
    Former companions,
Among exhalations of an afternoon
    Fog in December;

And the women without figures or tears
    Read what's inscribed on
Their funeral offering of flowers. Where
    All the short paths end

Fire from a caricature of laughter
    Burns away the unreal
And the ignominy of the human.
    Be memorial,

Vanished unwasted hours of being
    (Being not doing)
In the religion of alcohol:
    Be a memorial.

II

Almost the shortest day of the whole year
    Fast close your eyes on
The ash indomitably settled here.

Let the unforgivably lost and gay
    Forget her going
On the longest evening of this short day.

Civilization, leering from its gin,
    – A proper bad hat –
Has left a high stool for the short way home.[38]

Some forty of Nina's friends gathered at the Fitzroy Tavern and raised their glasses to cheer her on her way to the long bar in the sky. Even after she died Nina managed to keep everyone guessing and the question 'Did she jump or was she pushed?'[39] was a favourite topic of conversation in her old haunts for some time. One thing seems certain. In Winifred Gill's words: 'Nina will have been astonished at the shout of welcome greeting her arrival in the Elysian Fields.'[40]

Notes

Nina Hamnett's two volumes of autobiography *Laughing Torso* (Constable, London, 1932) and *Is She a Lady?* (Allan Wingate, London, 1955) provided important source material for this book.

1 — The rebel

This chapter is based on Nina Hamnett's *Laughing Torso* and her essay 'What I Wore in the Nineties', *Little Innocents (a collection of childhood reminiscences)*, edited by Alan Pryce-Jones, Cobden Sanderson, London, 1932

2 — The art student

1. Ashley Gibson, *Postscript to Adventure*, Dent, London, 1930, p 197.
2. Henry Savage, *Nothing is Here For Tears, Reminiscences*, unpublished autobiography, p 73. Courtesy of Guy Savage.
3. Nina Hamnett, *Laughing Torso*, op cit. p 30.

3 — The gateway to life

1. George Dangerfield, *The Strange Death of Liberal England*, Constable, London, 1936, p 297.
2. Ibid., p 194.
3. Roger Fry, Introduction to catalogue of Second Post-Impressionist Exhibition, Grafton Galleries, London, 1912.

4. Wilfrid Scawen Blunt, *My Diaries*, Part two, Knopf, New York, 1921, pp 329–330. Quoted by Samuel Hynes, *The Edwardian Turn of Mind*, Oxford University Press, London, 1968, pp 328–29.

5. Jacob Tonson (pseudonym of Arnold Bennett), *New Age*, 8 December 1910.

6. Walter Sickert, *Fortnightly Review*, January 1911.

7. Letter from Edward Marsh to Rupert Brooke quoted by Christopher Hassall, *Edward Marsh*, Longmans, London, 1959, pp 231–32.

8. Walter Sickert quoted by Denys Sutton, *Walter Sickert*, Michael Joseph, London, 1976, p 145.

9. Enid Bagnold, *Autobiography*, Heinemann, London, 1969, p 75.

10. Wendela Boreel quoted by Michael Parkin, *The Sickert Women and the Sickert Girls*, Parkin Gallery, London, 1974.

11. Marjorie Lilly, *Sickert, The Painter and His Circle*, Elek, London 1971, p 44.

12. Julian Symonds, *The Great Beast, The Life and Magick of Aleister Crowley*, Macdonald, London, 1971, p 124.

13. Report in *Chelsea Mail and Middlesex Advertiser*, 'Chelsea Studio Tragedy', 9 August 1912.

14. Quoted by Robert McAlmon and Kay Boyle, *Being Geniuses Together*, Michael Joseph, London, 1970, p 199.

15. Nina Hamnett, *Laughing Torso*, op. cit. p 44.

4 – The Café Royal

1. Max Beerbohm, quoted in *The Café Royal Story*, edited by Leslie Frewin, Hutchinson Benham, London, 1963, p 27.

2. Wyndham Lewis interviewed in a BBC radio programme on the Café Royal arranged by Guy Deghy, edited by Sacha Morsom, and broadcast 16 December 1955.

3. Walter Sickert quoted by Bernard Denvir, *The Café Royalists*, Parkin Gallery, London, 1972.

4. Wyndham Lewis, *Blasting and Bombardiering*, Calder and Boyars, London 1967, p 227.

5. Evan Morgan quoted by Miriam Benkovitz, *Ronald Firbank*, Weidenfeld and Nicolson, London, 1970, p 125.

6. Ibid., p 182.

7. Betty May, *Tiger Woman*, Duckworth, London, 1929, p 45.

8. Quoted by Guy Deghy and Keith Waterhouse, *Café Royal, Ninety Years of Bohemia*, Hutchinson, London, 1955, p 20.

9. Ibid.

10. From 'Aims and Programme of the Cabaret Theatre Club', May 1912, quoted by Richard Cork, 'The Cave of the Golden Calf', *Artforum*, December 1982, p 57.
11. Quoted by Noel Stock, *The Life of Ezra Pound*, Routledge & Kegan Paul, London, 1970, p 145.
12. Brochure of the 'Cabaret Theatre Club: The Cave of the Golden Calf', quoted by Richard Cork, *Artforum*, op. cit. p 66.
13. Richard Cork, *Vorticism and Abstract Art in the First Machine Age, Volume One: 'Origins and Developments'*, Gordon Fraser, London, 1976, p 34.
14. Osbert Sitwell, *Great Morning*, Macmillan, London, 1948, p 208.
15. Letter from Mark Gertler to Carrington, 6 April 1914, quoted by John Woodeson, *Mark Gertler*, Sidgwick & Jackson, London 1972, p 140.
16. Letter from Paul Nash to Albert Rutherston, quoted by Michael Holroyd, *Augustus John, Volume Two: 'The Years of Experience'*, Heinemann, London, 1975, p 55.

5 – La Fillette

1. Walter Sickert quoted by Wendy Baron, *The Camden Town Group*, Scolar Press, London, 1979, p 23.
2. Horace Brodzky, *Henri Gaudier-Brzeska*, Faber, London, 1933, p 55.
3. Sophie Brzeska's unpublished diary (author's translation), Kettle's Yard, University of Cambridge.
4. Ibid.
5. Nina Hamnett, *Laughing Torso*, op. cit. p 39.
6. Horace Brodzky, *Henri Gaudier-Brzeska*, op. cit. p 66.
7. Sophie Brzeska's diary, op. cit.
8. Ibid.
9. Ibid.
10. Ibid.
11. Ibid.
12. Ibid.

6 – The Omega Workshops

1. Roger Fry quoted by Virginia Woolf, *Roger Fry, A Biography*, The Hogarth Press, London, 1940, p 194.
2. Wyndham Lewis quoted by Virginia Woolf, ibid., p 192.

3. Wyndham Lewis, *Rude Assignment*, Hutchinson, London, 1950, p 124.
4. Omega Workshops Catalogue, undated. Copy in the Victoria and Albert Museum Library.
5. Ibid.
6. Unpublished letter from Winifred Gill to Duncan Grant, 4 July 1966, Victoria and Albert Museum Library.
7. Ibid., 18 August 1966.
8. Ibid.
9. Ibid.
10. Ibid., 28 September 1967.
11. T. E. Hulme, 'Modern Art', *The New Age*, 15 January 1914.
12. Letter from Lytton Strachey to Duncan Grant, 6 February 1914, quoted by Michael Holroyd, *Lytton Strachey: The Years of Achievement 1910–1932*, Heinemann, London, 1968, pp 105–6.
13. Letter from Roger Fry to Charles Vildrac, 1 January 1914, *Letters of Roger Fry*, edited by Denys Sutton, Chatto & Windus, London, 1972, p 377.

7 – Montparnasse

1. Wyndham Lewis, *Rude Assignment*, op. cit. p 115.
2. Quoted by Charles Douglas (pseudonym Douglas Goldring), *Artist Quarter*, Faber, London, 1941, p 147.
3. Ibid., p 213.
4. The *Egoist*, 15 June 1914.
5. Nina Hamnett, *Laughing Torso*, op. cit. p 58.

8 – Marriage

1. Now in the Archives of King's College, Cambridge.
2. Story recounted by Winifred Gill and quoted by Richard Shone, *Bloomsbury Portraits*, Phaidon, London, 1976, p 123, note 11.
3. Walter Sickert, preface to *Paintings and Drawings by Nina Hamnett*, Eldar Gallery, London, June–July 1918.
4. Dolores Courtney quoted by Judith Collins, *The Omega Workshops*, Secker & Warburg, London, 1984, pp 133–4.
5. Mrs L. Gordon-Stables, 'On Painting and Decorative Painting', *Colour*, June 1916, pp 187–188.
6. Judith Collins, *The Omega Workshops*, op. cit. p 134.

7. Nina Hamnett, *Laughing Torso*, op. cit. p 83.
8. Ibid., p 82.
9. Ibid., p 83.
10. Unpublished letter from Winifred Gill to Duncan Grant, 18 August 1966, Victoria and Albert Museum Library.
11. Miss Sheelah Hynes in conversation with the author, 1982.
12. Letter from Roger Fry to Helen Anrep, May 1925. *Letters of Roger Fry*, op. cit. p 570.
13. *Letters of Roger Fry*, op. cit. p 398.
14. Ibid., p 400.
15. Unpublished, undated letter from Roger Fry to Nina Hamnett, Harry Ransom Humanities Research Center, the University of Texas at Austin.
16. Unpublished letter from Winifred Gill to Duncan Grant, 23 June 1967, Victoria and Albert Museum Library.
17. Virginia Woolf, *Roger Fry, A Biography*, op. cit. p 201.
18. Mrs L. Gordon-Stables, 'Nina Hamnett's Psychological Portraiture', *Artwork*, October 1924, pp 112–5.
19. Letter from Roger Fry to William Rothenstein, 6 June 1909, quoted by Frances Spalding, *Portraits of Roger Fry*, Courtauld Institute Galleries, London 1976, p 6.
20. Mrs Pamela Diamond in conversation with the author, 1982.
21. Quoted by Michael Holroyd in the appendix to *Augustus John, Volume Two: The Years of Experience*, Heinemann, London 1975, p 210.
22. Unpublished letter from Roger Fry to Vanessa Bell, 23 March 1917, Tate Gallery Archives.
23. Unpublished letter from Winifred Gill to Duncan Grant, 27 November 1966, Victoria and Albert Museum Library.
24. Nina Hamnett, *Laughing Torso*, op. cit. p 84.

9 – Friends and mentors

1. John Salis, *New Witness*, 3 May 1917.
2. Richard Aldington, *Life for Life's Sake – A Book of Reminiscences*, Cassell, London, 1968, pp 150–1.
3. Unpublished letter from Roger Fry to Nina Hamnett, 10 August 1917, Harry Ransom Humanities Research Center, the University of Texas at Austin.
4. Ibid., 15 August 1917.
5. Carrington to Lytton Strachey, 25 July 1917, *Carrington Letters & Extracts*

from her Diaries, chosen with an introduction by David Garnett, Jonathan Cape, London, 1970, pp 73–6.

6. Unpublished letter from Roger Fry to Nina Hamnett, 25 July 1918, Harry Ransom Humanities Research Center, the University of Texas at Austin.

7. Quoted by Richard Shone, *Bloomsbury Portraits*, op. cit. p 168.

8. Marjorie Lilly, *Sickert, The Painter and His Circle*, op. cit. p 78.

9. Quoted by Marjorie Lilly, ibid., p 84.

10. Osbert Sitwell, *Noble Essences*, Macmillan, London, 1950, p 207.

11. Quoted by Marjorie Lilly, *Sickert, The Painter and His Circle*, op. cit. p 83.

12. Marjorie Lilly, ibid., p 84.

13. Quoted by Marjorie Lilly, ibid., p 110.

14. Nina Hamnett, *Laughing Torso*, op. cit. p 98.

15. Quoted by Richard J. Stonesifer, *W. H. Davies – A Critical Biography*, Jonathan Cape, London, 1963, p 126.

16. Quoted by Osbert Sitwell, *Noble Essences*, op. cit. p 214.

17. Roger Fry to Vanessa Bell, 20 July 1917, *Letters of Roger Fry*, op. cit. p 414.

18. Ibid., 6 October 1917, p 417.

19. Roger Fry, 'The Artist as Decorator', *Colour*, April 1917, pp 92–3.

20. *Globe*, 12 November 1917.

21. *New Witness*, 15 November 1917.

22. Ibid., 7 February 1918.

23. Virginia Woolf, *The Diary of Virginia Woolf, Vol I: 1915–19*, introduced by Quentin Bell, edited by Anne Olivier Bell, The Hogarth Press, London, 1977, p 59.

24. Roger Fry to Vanessa Bell, 12 December 1917, *Letters of Roger Fry*, op. cit. p 423.

25. Unpublished letter from Roger Fry to Vanessa Bell, 10 February 1918, Tate Gallery Archives.

26. Ibid.

27. Unpublished letter from Winifred Gill to Duncan Grant, 16 August 1966, Victoria and Albert Museum Library.

28. Ibid.

29. Roger Fry to Vanessa Bell, 4 May 1918, *Letters of Roger Fry*, op. cit. p 428.

30. Unpublished letter from Roger Fry to Nina Hamnett, 19 June 1918, Harry Ransom Humanities Research Center, the University of Texas at Austin.

31. Ibid., 17 July 1918.

32. Ibid., 21 July 1918.

33. Walter Sickert to Nina Hamnett, 1918. Courtesy of Dr Wendy Baron. Partly quoted by Marjorie Lilly, *Sickert, The Painter and His Circle*, op. cit. p 83.

34. The *Observer*, 12 May 1918.

35. Quoted by Wendy Baron, *Sickert*, Oxford, Phaidon, 1973, p 369.

36. Walter Sickert, 'Nina Hamnett', *Cambridge Magazine*, 8 June 1918, pp 770–1.

37. Ibid.

38. Unpublished telegram from Sickert to Nina Hamnett, 31 May 1918. Courtesy of Dr Wendy Baron.

39. Unpublished, undated letter from Sickert to Nina Hamnett. Courtesy of Dr Wendy Baron.

40. Enid Bagnold, *Autobiography*, op. cit. p 75.

41. Letter from Sickert to Nina Hamnett, 17 July 1918. Quoted by Marjorie Lilly, *Sickert, The Painter and His Circle*, op. cit. p 88.

42. Unpublished, undated letter from Sickert to Nina Hamnett. Courtesy of Dr Wendy Baron.

43. Undated letter from Sickert to Nina Hamnett. Courtesy of Dr Wendy Baron. Partly quoted by Marjorie Lilly, *Sickert, The Painter and His Circle*, op. cit. p 85.

44. Undated letter from Sickert to Nina Hamnett. Courtesy of Dr Wendy Baron. Partly quoted by Marjorie Lilly, ibid., p 86.

45. Unpublished letter from Roger Fry to Nina Hamnett, 24 July 1918, Harry Ransom Humanities Research Center, the University of Texas at Austin.

46. Ibid., 26 July 1918.

47. Undated letter from Nina Hamnett to Roger Fry, quoted by Denys Sutton, *Walter Sickert*, Michael Joseph, London, 1976, p 90.

48. Ibid., pp 90–1.

49. Ibid., p 91.

50. Undated, unpublished letter from Roger Fry to Nina Hamnett, Harry Ransom Humanities Research Center, the University of Texas at Austin.

51. Reproduced in Frances Spalding, *Roger Fry, Art and Life*, Paul Elek/Granada, London, 1980, p 208.

52. *The Times*, 2 February 1918.

53. *New Witness*, 8 November 1918.

54. Unpublished, undated letter from Sickert to Nina Hamnett. Courtesy of Dr Wendy Baron.

55. Undated letter from Sickert to Nina Hamnett. Quoted by Marjorie Lilly, *Sickert, The Painter and His Circle*, op. cit. p 87.

56. Roger Fry to Vanessa Bell, 26 December 1918, *Letters of Roger Fry*, op. cit. p 437.

57. *New Witness*, 8 November 1918.

58. Virginia Woolf to Vanessa Bell, 26 November 1918. *The Question of Things*

Happening: The Letters of Virginia Woolf 1912–1922, edited by Nigel Nicolson, The Hogarth Press, London, 1976, p 300.

10 – Paris regained

1. Ashley Gibson, *Postscript to Adventure*, op. cit. p 197.
2. Frederick Etchells, 'Paintings and Drawings at the Eldar Gallery', *Cambridge Magazine*, 8 November 1919.
3. Quoted by Nina Hamnett, *Laughing Torso*, op. cit. p 105.
4. Ibid.
5. James Wood, *Cambridge Magazine*, 21 June 1919.
6. Osbert Sitwell, *Laughter in the Next Room*, Macmillan, London, 1949, p 149.
7. Letter from Greville MacDonald to the Editor of the *Nation*, 23 August 1919. Quoted by Osbert Sitwell, *Laughter in the Next Room*, op. cit. p 336.
8. Osbert Sitwell, ibid., p 159.
9. *Burlington Magazine*, November 1919.
10. Frederick Etchells, 'Paintings and Drawings at the Eldar Gallery', op. cit.
11. Douglas Goldring, *The Nineteen Twenties*, Nicholson and Watson, London, 1945, p 177.
12. Unpublished, undated letter from Nina Hamnett to C. K. Ogden. Courtesy of Michael Parkin.
13. *Atheneum*, 14 May 1920.
14. Mark Gertler, *Selected Letters*, edited by Noel Carrington, Rupert Hart-Davis, London, 1965, pp 178–9.
15. Nina Hamnett, *Laughing Torso*, op. cit. p 126.
16. Edward Holroyd, *New Statesman*, 4 June 1921.
17. *The Nation and The Atheneum*, 4 June 1921.
18. Unpublished, undated letter from Nina Hamnett to C. K. Ogden. Courtesy of Michael Parkin.
19. Quoted by Julian Symonds, *The Great Beast*, op. cit. p 272.
20. Viva King, *The Weeping and the Laughter*, Macdonald and Jane, London, 1976, p 102.
21. Jean Cocteau quoted by Francis Steegmuller, *Cocteau*, Macmillan, London, 1970, p 281.
22. Jean Hugo, *Avant d'Oublier*, Fayard, Paris, 1976, p 133.
23. Jean Hugo in conversation with the author, 1983.
24. Marcel Proust quoted by Janet Flanner, *Paris Was Yesterday*, London, 1972, p xiv.
25. Augustus John, *Chiaroscuro*, Jonathan Cape, London, 1952, p 570.

26. Douglas Goldring, *The Nineteen Twenties*, op. cit. p 197.
27. Nina Hamnett quoted by Mrs Louise Gordon-Stables, 'Nina Hamnett's Psychological Portraiture', op. cit.
28. Quoted by Nina Hamnett, *Laughing Torso*, op. cit. p 215.
29. Beppo, widow of Abdul-Wahab, quoted by William Fifield, *Modigliani, The Biography*, W. H. Allen, London 1968, p 289.
30. Ibid., p 178.
31. Unpublished, undated letter from Nina Hamnett to C. K. Ogden. Courtesy of Michael Parkin.

11 – Café society

1. Michel Georges-Michel, *Les Montparnos*, Livre du Poche, Paris, 1976, p 97.
2. Douglas Goldring, *The Nineteen Twenties*, op. cit. p 193.
3. Charles Douglas, *Artist Quarter*, op. cit. p 210.
4. Robert McAlmon, *Being Geniuses Together*, Secker & Warburg, London, 1938, p 82.
5. Quoted by Andrew Field, *The Formidable Miss Barnes: The Life of Djuna Barnes*, Secker & Warburg, London, 1983, p 136.
6. James Charters, *This Must Be The Place*, Herbert Joseph, London, 1934, p 112.
7. Quoted by James Harding, *The Ox on the Roof*, Macdonald, London, 1972, p 81.
8. Quoted by James Charters, *This Must Be The Place*, op. cit. p 95.
9. Unpublished, undated letter from Nina Hamnett to C. K. Ogden. Courtesy of Michael Parkin.
10. Ibid.
11. Quoted by Robert McAlmon, *Being Geniuses Together*, op. cit. p 171.
12. Nina Hamnett, *Laughing Torso*, op. cit. p 242.
13. Ernest Hemingway, Introduction to *The Memoirs of Kiki: The Education of a French Model*, translated by Samuel Putnam, Tandem Books, London, 1964, p 9.
14. Quoted by Nina Hamnett, *Laughing Torso*, op.cit. p 275.
15. Roger Fry to Helen Anrep, May 1925, *Letters of Roger Fry*, op. cit. p 570.
16. Unpublished letter from Jean Hugo to the author, 13 June 1982.
17. Francis Rose, *Saying Life*, Cassell, London, 1961, p 109.

12 — *London Bohemia*

1. Roger Fry, *The Nation & The Atheneum*, 11 May 1926.
2. Augustus John, *Autobiography*, Jonathan Cape, London, 1975, p 398–99.
3. Ibid., p 399.
4. Nancy Cunard quoted by Anne Chisholm, *Nancy Cunard*, Penguin, London, 1981, p 96.
5. Augustus John, *Chiaroscuro*, op. cit. p 136.
6. Viva King, *The Weeping and the Laughter*, op. cit. p 89.
7. Tristram Hillier, *Leda and the Goose*, Longman, London, 1954, p 72.
8. Nina Hamnett, unpublished memoir of Ronald Firbank. Courtesy of Richard Buckle.
9. Robert McAlmon and Kay Boyle, *Being Geniuses Together*, op. cit. pp 80–81.
10. Rhys Davies, *Print of a Hare's Foot*, Heinemann, London, 1969, p 108.
11. W. Seymour Leslie, *The Silent Queen*, Jonathan Cape, London, 1927, p 150.
12. Unpublished, undated letter from Nina Hamnett to C. K. Ogden. Courtesy of Michael Parkin.
13. Ibid.
14. Cecil Gray, *Peter Warlock — A Memoir of Philip Heseltine*, Jonathan Cape, London, 1934, p 228.
15. Unpublished, undated letter from Augustus John to Nina Hamnett, Harry Ransom Humanities Research Center, the University of Texas at Austin.
16. *The Referee*, 10 July 1927.
17. *The Times*, 6 July 1927.
18. Town Talker, *Westminster Gazette*, 6 July 1927.
19. Quoted by Anthony Powell, *Messengers of Day*, Heinemann, London, 1978, p 42.
20. Unpublished, undated letter from Osbert Sitwell to Nina Hamnett, Harry Ransom Humanities Research Center, the University of Texas at Austin.
21. Sheelah Hynes in conversation with the author, 1982.
22. Peter Quennell in conversation with the author, 1982.
23. Anthony Powell, *Messengers of Day*, op. cit. p 54.
24. Ibid., p 54.
25. James Hepburn in conversation with the author, 1985.
26. Jack Lindsay, *Fanfrolico and After*, Bodley Head, London, 1962, p 84.
27. Rhys Davies, 'Nina Hamnett, Bohemian', *Wales Magazine*, September 1959, p 30.
28. Ethel Mannin, *Ragged Banners*, Jarrolds, London, 1931, p 80.
29. Adrian Daintrey, *I Must Say*, Chatto & Windus, London, 1963, pp 95–6.
30. Jack Lindsay, *Fanfrolico and After*, op. cit. p 33.

31. Tommy Earp, *Creative Art*, September 1930.
32. Nina Hamnett, *Is She A Lady?*, Allan Wingate, London, 1955, p 87.
33. Ibid., p 90.
34. Quoted by James Lees-Milne, *Harold Nicolson, A Biography*, Chatto & Windus, London, 1981, p 15.
35. Unpublished letter from Harold Nicolson to Nina Hamnett, 6 May 1931, Harry Ransom Humanities Research Center, the University of Texas at Austin.
36. Quoted by Edward Booth-Clibborn, introduction to *Laughing Torso*, Virago, London, 1984, p vi.
37. Nina Hamnett, *Laughing Torso*, op. cit. p 268.
38. John Symonds, *The Great Beast*, op. cit. p 381.

13 — The wickedest man in the world

All quotations from the trial are taken from the law reports published in *The Times* and the *Daily Telegraph* 10–13 April 1934.

1. Quoted by John Symonds, *The Great Beast*, op. cit. p 381.
2. Ibid., p 380.
3. Ibid.
4. Nina Hamnett, *Laughing Torso*, op. cit. pp 173–74.
5. Quoted by John Symonds, *The Great Beast*, op. cit. p 381.
6. Quoted by Paul Ferris, *Dylan Thomas*, Hodder & Stoughton, London, 1977, p 83.
7. Quoted by Constantine FitzGibbon, *The Life of Dylan Thomas*, Dent, London, 1965, p 71.
8. Ruthven Todd, *Fitzrovia and the Road to the York Minster*, Parkin Gallery, London, 1973.
9. Nina Hamnett, *Is She A Lady?*, op. cit. p 100.
10. Ibid., p 106.

14 — Fitzrovia

1. Quoted by J. Maclaren-Ross, *Memoirs of the Forties*, Alan Ross, London, 1965, p 138.
2. Robert Pocock, unpublished radio play *It's Long Past The Time — a recollection of Charlotte Street in the 1930s*. First broadcast by the BBC Third Programme

5.12.56. Courtesy of the late Robert Pocock.

3. Anthony Powell, *Messengers of Day*, op. cit. p 42.
4. John Heath-Stubbs in conversation with the author, 1982.
5. Constantine FitzGibbon, *The Life of Dylan Thomas*, op. cit. pp 171–72.
6. Denis Wirth-Miller in conversation with the author, 1985.
7. Quoted by Ruthven Todd, *Fitzrovia and the Road to the York Minster*, op. cit.
8. Jack Lindsay, *Fanfrolico and After*, op. cit. p 33.
9. Unpublished, undated letter from Nina Hamnett to Robert Pocock. Courtesy of the late Robert Pocock.
10. Quoted by Ruthven Todd, *Fitzrovia and the Road to the York Minster*, op. cit.
11. John Heath-Stubbs in conversation with the author, 1982.
12. Robert Buhler in conversation with the author, 1982.
13. Ruthven Todd, *Fitzrovia and the Road to the York Minster*, op. cit.
14. Robert Buhler in conversation with the author, 1982.
15. Augustus John, *Chiaroscuro*, op. cit. p 136.
16. Peter Quennell, *The Wanton Chase*, Collins, London, 1980, p 122.
17. Report of trial in *Daily Mirror*, 1.5.36.
18. Rhys Davies, 'Nina Hamnett, Bohemian,' op. cit. p 27.
19. Mark Holloway, unpublished *Memories of Sylvia Gough and Nina Hamnett*. Courtesy of Mark Holloway.
20. Joan Osiakovski in conversation with the author, 1982.
21. Quoted by Ruthven Todd, *Dead and Other Friends and Places*, unpublished autobiography, p 174.
22. Peter Quennell, *The Wanton Chase*, op. cit. p 122.
23. Ruthven Todd, *Dead and Other Friends and Places*, op. cit. p 187.
24. Robert Pocock, *It's Long Past The Time*, op. cit.

15 – Candlelight

This chapter is based largely on conversations with Julius Horwitz and Flora and John Isserlis, and on unpublished letters written by Julius Horwitz to Clement Greenberg and various members of his family and friends now in the Special Collections department of the Mugar Memorial Library, Boston University, U.S.A.

JH – Julius Horwitz
CG – Clement Greenberg

1. Dylan Thomas and John Davenport, *The Death of the King's Canary*, Penguin, London, 1978, p 69.
2. Ruthven Todd, *Fitzrovia and the Road to the York Minster*, op. cit.

3. John Heath-Stubbs in conversation with the author, 1982.
4. JH to family 23.12.43.
5. JH in conversation with the author, 1982.
6. JH to CG 13.3.44.
7. JH to CG 27.1.45.
8. JH to Virginia Brown 30.4.45.
9. JH to Joe 13.8.44.
10. JH to CG n.d.
11. JH to Virginia Brown n.d.
12. Ibid., 22.12.44.
13. JH to Joe 22.5.44.
14. JH to CG 1.1.45.
15. Flora Isserlis in conversation with the author, 1982.
16. JH to Virginia Brown n.d.
17. Ruthven Todd, op. cit.
18. NH to JH n.d.
19. JH to CG n.d.
20. JH 22.1.45.
21. Flora Isserlis in conversation with the author, 1982.
22. JH to CG 31.1.45.
23. JH to CG n.d.
24. JH to Virginia Brown 30.4.45.
25. JH to CG n.d.
26. JH to CG n.d.
27. JH, *Can I Get There by Candlelight*, Atheneum, New York, 1964, p 238.

16 − Last orders

1. Cyril Connolly, *Horizon* editorial, April, 1947.
2. Quoted by Mark Holloway, unpublished *Memories of Sylvia Gough and Nina Hamnett*.
3. Ibid.
4. Janey Ironside, *Janey*, Michael Joseph, London, 1973, p 56.
5. Unpublished letter from Amos Neilson to Julius Horwitz, 5 February 1946, Mugar Memorial Library, Boston University, USA.
6. Robert Pocock in conversation with the author, 1982.
7. Nina Hamnett, *Is She A Lady?*, op. cit. p 146.
8. Ibid., p 148.
9. Unpublished letter from Nina Hamnett to Duncan Grant, 14 November 1947. Courtesy of Richard Shone.

10. Unpublished letter from Amos Neilson to Julius Horwitz, 5 September 1947, Mugar Memorial Library, Boston University, USA.
11. Rhys Davies, 'Nina Hamnett, Bohemian', op. cit. p 32.
12. Nina Hamnett, *Is She A Lady?*, op. cit. p 155.
13. Unpublished letter from Quentin Bell to the author, 26 July 1982.
14. Unpublished letter from Winifred Gill to Duncan Grant, 18 August 1966, Victoria and Albert Museum Library.
15. Ibid.
16. Quoted by Rhys Davies, 'Nina Hamnett, Bohemian', op. cit. p 28.
17. Gaston Berlemont in conversation with the author, 1982.
18. Michael Law in conversation with the author, 1982.
19. Daniel Farson, *Out of Step*, Michael Joseph, London, 1974, p 62.
20. Ibid., p 61.
21. Quoted by Daniel Farson, ibid., p 65.
22. Daniel Farson, 'Muriel Belcher – Queen of Clubs', *Artists of the Colony Room Club – A Tribute to Muriel Belcher*, Parkin Gallery, London, 1982.
23. Rhys Davies, 'Nina Hamnett, Bohemian', op. cit. p 31.
24. Robert Pocock in conversation with the author, 1982.
25. Ibid.
26. Rhys Davies, 'Nina Hamnett, Bohemian', op. cit. p 32.
27. Dr Precope in conversation with the author, 1984.
28. Mrs Karin Jonzen in conversation with the author, 1985.
29. Unpublished letter from Nina Hamnett to Annie Allchild, 17 February 1955. Courtesy of Mr and Mrs Charles Allchild.
30. Stephen Bon, *Manchester Guardian*, 11 November 1955.
31. Unpublished letter from Nina Hamnett to Robert Pocock, 9 July 1956. Courtesy of the late Robert Pocock.
32. Unpublished letter from James Norbury to Charles and Annie Allchild, December 1956. Courtesy of Mr and Mrs Charles Allchild.
33. Quoted by Rhys Davies, 'Nina Hamnett, Bohemian', op. cit. p 33.
34. James Norbury to Charles and Annie Allchild, op. cit.
35. All quotations from the inquest are from the report which appeared in the *Marylebone Chronicle*, 21 December 1956, p 1.
36. Nina Hamnett, *Is She A Lady?*, op. cit. p 98.
37. James Norbury, op. cit.
38. David Wright, 'Verses At A Bohemian Funeral', *New Poems*, A P. E. N. anthology, Michael Joseph, London, 1957.
39. Gaston Berlemont in conversation with the author, 1982.
40. Unpublished letter from Winifred Gill to Duncan Grant, 25 August 1966, Victoria and Albert Museum Library.

Bibliography

ALDINGTON, RICHARD, *Life For Life's Sake — A Book of Reminiscences*, London, Cassell, 1968.

ALLINSON, ADRIAN, *Painter's Pilgrimage*, unpublished autobiography.

ANSCOMBE, ISABELLE, *Bloomsbury and the Decorative Arts*, London, Thames and Hudson, 1981.

AURIC, GEORGES, *Quand j'étais là*, Paris, Grasset, 1979.

BAGNOLD, ENID, *Autobiography*, London, Heinemann, 1969.

BARON, WENDY, *Sickert*, Oxford, Phaidon, 1973.

— *Miss Ethel Sands and Her Circle*, London, Peter Owen, 1977.

— *The Camden Town Group*, London, Scolar Press, 1979.

BENKOVITZ, MIRIAM J., *Ronald Firbank: A Biography*, London, Weidenfeld and Nicolson, 1970.

BOWEN, STELLA, *Drawn from Life*, London, Collins, 1941.

BRODZKY, HORACE, *Henri Gaudier-Brzeska*, London, Faber, 1933.

BROGAN, HUGH, *The Life of Arthur Ransome*, London, Cape, 1984.

CALDER-MARSHALL, ARTHUR, *The Magic of My Youth*, London, Rupert Hart-Davis, 1951.

CAMPBELL, IVAR, *Poems*, with a memoir by Guy Ridley, London, A. L. Humphreys, 1917.

CARCO, FRANCIS, *From Montmartre to the Latin Quarter*, translated by Madeleine Boyd, London, Cayme Press, 1929.

CARRINGTON, *Letters & Extracts from her Diaries*, chosen and with an introduction by David Garnett, London, Cape, 1970.

CARRINGTON, NOEL (ed.), *Mark Gertler. Selected Letters*, introduction by Quentin Bell, London, Rupert Hart-Davis, 1965.

CHARTERS, JAMES, *This Must Be The Place. Memoirs of Montparnasse*, ed. by Morrill Cody, London, Herbert Joseph, 1934.

CHISHOLM, ANNE, *Nancy Cunard*, London, Penguin, 1981.

COLE, ROGER, *Burning to Speak: The Life and Art of Henri Gaudier-Brzeska*, Oxford, Phaidon, 1978.

COLLINS, JUDITH, *The Omega Workshops*, London, Secker & Warburg, 1984.

CORK, RICHARD, *Vorticism and Abstract Art in the First Machine Age*,
— *Volume 1: Origins and Development*, London, Gordon Fraser, 1975.
— *Volume 2: Synthesis and Decline*, London, Gordon Fraser, 1976.
— *Art Beyond The Gallery in Early Twentieth Century England*, New Haven and London, Yale University Press, 1985.

CRESPELLE, JEAN-PAUL, *Montparnasse Vivant*, Paris, Hachette, 1962.
— *La Vie Quotidienne à Montparnasse à la Grande Epoque*, Paris, Hachette, 1976.
— *La Folle Epoque*, Paris, Hachette, 1968.

DAINTREY, ADRIAN, *I Must Say*, London, Chatto and Windus, 1963.

DANGERFIELD, GEORGE, *The Strange Death of Liberal England*, London, Constable, 1936.

DAVIES, RHYS, *Print of a Hare's Foot*, London, Heinemann, 1969.
— 'Nina Hamnett, Bohemian', *Wales Magazine*, September 1959.

DAVIES, W.H., *Later Days*, London, Cape, 1925.

DAVIN, DAN, *Closing Times*, London, Oxford University Press, 1975.

DEAN, JOSEPH, *Hatred, Ridicule and Contempt, A Book of Libel Cases*, London, Constable, 1953.

DEGHY, GUY and WATERHOUSE, KEITH, *Café Royal — Ninety Years of Bohemia*, London, Hutchinson, 1955.

DESNOS, YOUKI, *Les Confidences de Youki*, Paris, Arthème Fayard, 1957.

DOUGLAS, CHARLES, *Artist Quarter*, London, Faber 1941.

EDE, H.S., *Savage Messiah*, London, Heinemann, 1931.

ELLBORN, GEOFFREY, *Edith Sitwell: A Biography*, London, Sheldon Press, 1981.

EMMONS, ROBERT, *The Life and Opinions of Walter Richard Sickert*, London, Faber, 1941.

EPSTEIN, JACOB, *An Autobiography*, with an introduction by Richard Buckle, London, Vista Books, 1963.

FARSON, DANIEL, *Out of Step*, London, Michael Joseph, 1974.

FERRIS, PAUL, *Dylan Thomas*, London, Hodder and Stoughton, 1977.

FIELD, ANDREW, *The Formidable Miss Barnes: The Life of Djuna Barnes*, London, Secker and Warburg, 1983.

FIFIELD, WILLIAM, *Modigliani. The Biography*, London, W. H. Allen, 1978.

FITCH, NOEL RILEY, *Sylvia Beach and the Lost Generation, A History of Literary Paris in the Twenties and Thirties*, London, Souvenir Press, 1984.

FITZGIBBON, CONSTANTINE, *The Life of Dylan Thomas*, London, Dent, 1965.

FLANNER, JANET, *Paris Was Yesterday 1925–1939*, ed. by Irving Drutman,

London, Angus and Robertson, 1973.

FREWIN, LESLIE (ed.), *The Café Royal Story. A Living Legend*, foreword by Graham Greene, London, Hutchinson Benham, 1963.

FULLER, JEAN OVERTON, *The Magical Dilemma of Victor Neuberg*, London, W. H. Allen, 1965.

GARNETT, DAVID, *The Golden Echo*, London, Chatto and Windus, 1953.

— *The Flowers of the Forest*, London, Chatto and Windus, 1955.

GATHORNE-HARDY, ROBERT (ed.), *Ottoline — The Early Memoirs of Lady Ottoline Morrell*, London, Faber, 1963.

— *Ottoline at Garsington, Memoirs of Lady Ottoline Morrell*, London, Faber, 1974.

GEORGES-MICHEL, MICHEL, *Les Montparnos*, Paris, Livre du Poche, 1976.

GIBSON, ASHLEY, *Postscript to Adventure*, London, Dent, 1930.

GLENAVY, BEATRICE LADY, *Today We Will Only Gossip*, London, Constable, 1964.

GOLDRING, DOUGLAS, *The Nineteen Twenties*, London, Nicholson and Watson, 1945.

— *Odd Man Out, the autobiography of a 'propaganda novelist'*, London, Chapman and Hall, 1935.

GORDON-STABLES, L., MRS, 'On Painting and Decorative Painting', *Colour*, June 1916, pp 187–188.

— 'Nina Hamnett's Psychological Portraiture', *Artwork*, October 1924.

GREY, CECIL, *Peter Warlock — A Memoir of Philip Heseltine*, with a foreword by Augustus John, London, Cape, 1934.

GRIGSON, GEOFFREY, *Recollections — Mainly of Artists and Writers*, London, Chatto and Windus, 1984.

HAMNETT, NINA, *Laughing Torso*, London, Constable, 1932 (reissued by Virago, 1984).

— *Is She A Lady? A Problem in Autobiography*, London, Allan Wingate, 1955.

HARDING, JAMES, *The Ox on the Roof, scenes from musical life in Paris in the twenties*, London, Macdonald and Co., 1972.

HEMINGWAY, ERNEST, *A Moveable Feast*, London, Granada, 1977.

HEWISON, ROBERT, *Under Siege: Literary Life in London 1939–45*, London, Weidenfeld and Nicolson, 1977.

— *In Anger, Culture in the Cold War 1945–60*, London, Weidenfeld and Nicolson, 1981.

HILLIER, TRISTRAM, *Leda and the Goose*, London, Longman, 1954.

HOLMAN-HUNT, DIANA, *Latin Among Lions: Alvaro Guevara*, London, Michael Joseph, 1974.

HOLROYD, MICHAEL, *Augustus John, Volume 1: The Years of Innocence*, London, Heinemann, 1974.

— *Volume 2: The Years of Experience*, London, Heinemann, 1975.

— *Lytton Strachey, A Biography*, London, Heinemann, 1973.

HORWITZ, JULIUS, *Can I Get There by Candlelight*, New York, Atheneum, 1964.

HUGO, JEAN, *Avant d'Oublier*, Paris, Fayard, 1970.

HYNES, SAMUEL, *The Edwardian Turn of Mind*, London, Oxford University Press, 1968.

IRONSIDE, JANEY, *Janey*, London, Michael Joseph, 1973.

JEPSOM, E., *Memoirs of an Edwardian and Neo-Georgian*, London, Richards, 1937.

JOHN, AUGUSTUS, *Chiaroscuro*, London, Cape, 1952.

— *Autobiography*, London, Cape, 1975.

KIKI, *Memoirs of Kiki: The Education of a French Model*, introduction by Ernest Hemingway, translated by Samuel Putnam, London, Tandem Books, 1964.

KING, VIVA, *The Weeping and the Laughter*, London, Macdonald and Jane, 1976.

KOPS, BERNARD, *The World is a Wedding*, London, Macgibbon & Kee, 1963.

LEES-MILNE, JAMES, *Harold Nicolson, A Biography 1930–1968*, London, Chatto and Windus, 1981.

LESLIE, LIONEL, *One Man's World, A Story of Strange Places and Strange People*, London, Pall Mall Press, 1961.

LESLIE, W. SEYMOUR, *The Silent Queen*, with illustrations by Nina Hamnett, London, Cape, 1927.

LEWIS, WYNDHAM, *Rude Assignment*, London, Hutchinson, 1950.

— *Blasting and Bombardiering*, London, Calder and Boyars, 1967.

LILLY, MARJORIE, *Sickert, The Painter and His Circle*, London, Elek, 1971.

LINDSAY, JACK, *Fanfrolico and After*, London, Bodley Head, 1962.

MANNIN, ETHEL, *Young in the Twenties*, London, Hutchinson, 1971.

— *Ragged Banners*, London, Penguin, 1938.

MAY, BETTY, *Tiger Woman*, London, Duckworth, 1929.

MACLAREN-ROSS, JULIAN, *Memoirs of the Forties*, London, Alan Ross, 1965.

McALMON, ROBERT, *Being Geniuses Together*, London, Secker and Warburg, 1938; reissued with supplementary chapters by Kay Boyle, London, Michael Joseph, 1970.

MEDLEY, ROBERT, *Drawn From The Life: A Memoir*, London, Faber, 1983.

NEVINSON, C.R.W., *Paint and Prejudice*, London, Methuen, 1937.

NICHOLSON, HUBERT, *Half My Days and Nights*, London, Heinemann, 1941.

O'CONNOR, PHILIP, *Memoirs of a Public Baby*, London, Faber, 1958.

OWEN, RODERIC, with DE VERE COLE, TRISTAN, *Beautiful and Beloved — The Life of Mavis de Vere Cole*, London, Hutchinson, 1974.

PEARSON, JOHN, *Façades, Edith, Osbert and Sacheverell Sitwell*, London, Macmillan, 1978.

PINCHER, CHAPMAN, *The Private World of St. John Terrapin, A Novel of the Café Royal*, London, Sidgwick and Jackson, 1982.

PLOMER, WILLIAM, *At Home*, London, Cape, 1958.

POWELL, ANTHONY, *Messengers of Day*, London, Heinemann, 1978.

PRYCE-JONES, ALAN (ed.), *Little Innocents (a collection of childhood reminiscences)*, London, Cobden Sanderson, 1932.

PUTNAM, SAMUEL, *Paris Was Our Mistress*, New York, Viking Press, 1947.

QUENNELL, PETER, *The Wanton Chase*, London, Collins, 1980.

RANSOME, ARTHUR, *The Autobiography of Arthur Ransome*, ed. with prologue and epilogue by Rupert Hart-Davis, London, Cape, 1976.

ROSE, SIR FRANCIS, *Saying Life*: *The Memoirs of Sir Francis Rose*, London, Cassell, 1961.

ROSE, PROF. W.K. (ed.), *The Letters of Wyndham Lewis*, London, Methuen, 1963.

ROSS, ALAN, *The Forties*, London, Weidenfeld and Nicolson, 1960.

SACHS, MAURICE, *Au Temps du Boeuf sur le Toit*, Paris, Editions de la Nouvelle Revue Critique, 1939.

– *La Décade de l'Illusion*, Paris, Gallimard, 1950.

SALMON, ANDRÉ, *Montparnasse*, Paris, 1950.

SAVAGE, HENRY, *The Receding Shore: Leaves from the Somewhat Unconventional Life of Henry Savage*, London, Grayson and Grayson, 1933.

– *Nothing is Here For Tears, Reminiscences*, unpublished autobiography.

SÉCRETAIN, ROGER, *Un sculpteur 'maudit': Gaudier-Brzeska*, Paris, Le Temps, 1979.

SHONE, RICHARD, *Bloomsbury Portraits*, Oxford, Phaidon, 1976.

SICHEL, PIERRE, *Modigliani*, London, W. H. Allen, 1967.

SICKERT, WALTER, 'Nina Hamnett', *Cambridge Magazine*, 8 June 1918.

SITWELL, EDITH, *Taken Care Of*, London, Hutchinson, 1965.

SITWELL, OSBERT, *The People's Album of London Statues*, illustrated by Nina Hamnett, London, Duckworth, 1928.

– *Great Morning*, London, Macmillan, 1948.

– *Laughter in the Next Room*, London, Macmillan, 1949.

– *Noble Essences*, London, Macmillan, 1950.

SMITH, R.D. (ed.), *The Writings of Anna Wickham, Free Woman and Poet*, London, Virago, 1984.

SPALDING, FRANCES, *Roger Fry, Art and Life*, London, Paul Elek/Granada, 1980.

STANFORD, DEREK, *Inside the Forties*, literary memoirs 1937–1957, London, Sidgwick and Jackson, 1977.

STEEGMULLER, FRANCIS, *Cocteau*, London, Macmillan, 1970.

STONESIFER, RICHARD J., *W. H. Davies – A Critical Biography*, London, Cape, 1963.

SUTTON, DENYS, *Letters of Roger Fry*, 2 volumes, London, Chatto and Windus, 1972.

— *Walter Sickert*, London, Michael Joseph, 1976.

SYMONDS, JOHN, *The Great Beast*; *The Life and Magick of Aleister Crowley*, London, Macdonald, 1971.

SYMONS, JULIAN, *The Thirties*, London, Cresset Press, 1960.

THOMAS, DYLAN and DAVENPORT, JOHN, *The Death of the King's Canary*, London, Penguin, 1978.

THOMSON, VIRGIL, *Virgil Thomson*, London, Weidenfeld and Nicolson, 1967.

TODD, RUTHVEN, *Dead and Other Friends and Places*, unpublished autobiography.

TOMKINS, CALVIN, *Living Well is the Best Revenge, two Americans in Paris 1921–1933*, London, Deutsch, 1972.

VOROBËV, MAREVNA, *Life in Two Worlds*, translated by Benet Nash, London, Abelard-Schuman, 1962.

— *Life with the Painters of La Ruche*, London, Constable, 1972.

WARNOD, ANDRÉ, *Les Berceaux de la Jeune Peinture*, Paris, Albin Michel, 1925.

WARNOD, JEANNINE, *La Ruche et Montparnasse*, Paris and Geneva, Weber, 1978.

WILSON, ROBERT FORREST, *Paris on Parade*, Indianapolis, Bobbs-Merrill Co., 1925.

WISER, WILLIAM, *The Crazy Years*, London, Thames and Hudson, 1983.

WISHART, MICHAEL, *High Diver*, London, Blond and Briggs, 1977.

WOOD, CHRISTOPHER, *Letters to My Mother*, 3 volumes arranged and bound by Rex de C. Nan Kivell, unpublished.

WOOLF, VIRGINIA, *Roger Fry: A Biography*, London, The Hogarth Press, 1940.

— *The Question of Things Happening, The Letters of Virginia Woolf 1912–1922*, ed. by Nigel Nicolson, London, The Hogarth Press, 1976.

— *The Diary of Virginia Woolf, Volume 1: 1915–1919*, introduced by Quentin Bell, edited by Anne Olivier Bell, London, The Hogarth Press, 1977.

WREY GARDINER, CHARLES, *The Dark Thorn*, London, Grey Walls Press, 1946.

— *The Answer to Life is No*, London, Rupert Hart-Davis, 1960.

ZADKINE, OSSIP, *Le Maillet et le Ciseau, Souvenirs de ma vie*, Paris, Albert Michel, 1968.

Selected exhibition catalogues

ANTHONY D'OFFAY GALLERY, *The Omega Workshops: Alliance and Enmity in English Art 1911–1920*, with introductory 'Recollections of the Omega', by Pamela Diamond, London, 1984.

ARTCURIAL, *Au Temps du Boeuf sur le Toit*, with an introduction by Georges Bernier and a memoir by Henri Sauguet, Paris, 1981.

COURTAULD INSTITUTE GALLERIES, *Portraits of Roger Fry*, introductory essay by Frances Spalding, London 1976. Subsequently toured to Mappin Art Gallery, Sheffield.

CRAFTS COUNCIL GALLERY, *The Omega Workshops 1913–19. Decorative Arts of Bloomsbury*, with an essay by Fiona MacCarthy, London, 1984.

ELDAR GALLERY, *Paintings and Drawings by Nina Hamnett*, with a preface by W. Sickert, London, 1918.

KETTLE'S YARD, *Henri Gaudier-Brzeska, sculptor 1891–1915*, with essays by Serge Faucherau, Sarah Shalgosky, Rod Brookes, Jane Beckett and Jeremy Lewison, Cambridge, 1983.

PARKIN GALLERY, *The Sickert Women and the Sickert Girls*, with texts by Wendy Baron, Charlotte Haenlein and Michael Parkin, London, 1974.

– *The Café Royalists*, with an introduction by Bernard Denvir and foreword by Michael Parkin, London, 1972.

– *Fitzrovia and the Road to the York Minster*, with a memoir by Ruthven Todd and foreword by Michael Parkin, London, 1973.

– *Artists of the Colony Room Club, A Tribute to Muriel Belcher*, with texts by Dan Farson, George Melly and Molly Parkin, London, 1982.

– *Nina Hamnett and Her Circle*, with an introduction by Denise Hooker, London, 1986.

TOOTH GALLERY, *Drawings and Watercolours of London Statues by Nina Hamnett*, with a preface by Augustus John, London, 1928.

Main unpublished sources

Sophie Brzeska's diary, Kettle's Yard, University of Cambridge.

University of Essex Library.

Roger Fry, letters to Vanessa Bell, Tate Gallery Archives.

Winifred Gill, letters to Duncan Grant, copies in the Victoria and Albert Museum Library.

Nina Hamnett, letters to C. K. Ogden, Collection Michael Parkin; to T. I. F. Armstrong, Jocelyn Brooke, Aleister Crowley and others, Harry Ransom Humanities Research Center, the University of Texas at Austin.

Julius Horwitz, letters to Clement Greenberg and others, Mugar Memorial Library, Boston University.

Walter Sickert, letters to Nina Hamnett, copies courtesy of Dr Wendy Baron.

Letters to Nina Hamnett from Roger Fry, Augustus John, Sir Osbert Sitwell, Sir Harold Nicolson and others, Harry Ransom Humanities Research Center, the University of Texas at Austin.

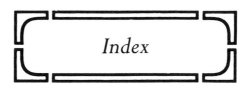

Index

Numbers in *italics* refer to illustrations